W9-BJV-348

LANGUAGE, MIND, AND BRAIN

LANGUAGE, MIND, AND BRAIN

Edited by:

Thomas W. Simon
Robert J. Scholes
University of Florida

LAWRENCE ERLBAUM ASSOCIATES, PUBLISHERS
1982   Hillsdale, New Jersey   London

Lawrence Erlbaum Associates, Inc., Publishers
365 Broadway
Hillsdale, New Jersey 07642

Library of Congress Cataloging in Publication Data
Main entry under title:

Language, mind, and brain.

  Based on material first presented at the
National Interdisciplinary Symposium on
Language, Mind, and Brain, held April 6-9,
1978, in Gainesville, Fla.
  Includes indexes.
  1. Psycholinguistics—Congresses.
2. Languages—Philosophy—Congresses.
3. Thought and thinking—Congresses. I. Simon,
Thomas W. II. Scholes, Robert J. III. National
Interdisciplinary Symposium on Language, Mind,
and Brain (1978: Gainesville, Fla.)
P37.L36   401'.9   81-12537
ISBN 0-89859-153-8   AACR2

Printed in the United States of America

We would like to dedicate this volume
to the loving memory of
Professor Richard Rudner

Contents

Preface and Orientation

The chapters in this volume are extended versions of material first presented at the National Interdisciplinary Symposium on Language, Mind, and Brain held April 6-9, 1978, in Gainesville, Florida. The Symposium was sponsored by The Society for the Interdisciplinary Study of the Mind (SISTM) and the University of Florida through the financial assistance of the Sloan Foundation. Professor Simon was the organizer and director of the Symposium.

The aim of the Symposium was to provide a context in which philosophers, computer scientists, linguists, and psychologists could focus attention on language in order to generate a truly interdisciplinary (as opposed to multi-disciplinary) approach to problem solving within the cognitive sciences. The commonality of concerns among the scholars represented here—in particular, the concerns with "representation" and "context"—provides overt evidence of the potential for an interdisciplinary study of language.

Importantly for interdisciplinary goals, the papers contained in this volume are quite "available"; that is, papers by philosophers can easily be read and understood by linguists and psychologists; the ideas of the linguists are readily comprehensible to any educated reader; the psychologists and neurologically-oriented writers are clear and understandable. It is, then, a volume that cuts, not so much across disciplines, but through them. For this, we are grateful and proud.

The very same source of our pride also provided an editorial headache. Since we could not group the contributions according to disciplines, a motivated ordering principle had to be found elsewhere. The best we could do was a somewhat shaky line between those whose orientation is more toward the theoretical and abstract and those whose concern is more concrete. At the abstract pole are the presentations of Harman, Suppes, and McCawley. Ringle, Schank, Boden, Oppacher and Partee provide bridges to the more empirically-oriented group of Lakoff, Scholes, Valian, Harnad, Pribram, and Griffin. Pearson and Rudner offer important propaedeutics.

Even this classification is doomed to disintegration and will no doubt soon be a relic. Many of the authors here show a concern with common human linguistic behavior and argue that the most elegant of theories should, ultimately, explain what people do. Boden and Lakoff provide excellent examples of how theoretical notions of abstract ideals can and should be applied to directly observable phenomena. Among philosophers Vendler has always been a leading advocate of a more pragmatic or contextualist approach. Artificial intelligence might seem the last area to look for these pragmatic predilections. Yet, not only are contextual concepts such as *frame* and *script* pivotal for the AI researcher (Schank, Boden), but they are also key pragmatic terms.

Conversely, not only are the more autonomous views becoming more pragmatically-oriented, the experimental approaches to language study are becoming increasingly concerned with theory. Griffin's call for greater theoretical orientation on the part of researchers is more than a monovocal appeal. Questions of intentionality, to take just one example, are no longer at the periphery of primate language studies but are at their very core.

Few phrases, except possibly "philosophy of mind," sound as abstruse as "theory of mind." Long thought to be the sole province of the philosophically- and speculatively-included, theory of mind has now become juxtaposed, however loosely, to the nascent "cognitive science itself. This interrelationship between a theory of mind and cognitive science is not as tenuous as it might first seem. If a theory of mind is the establishment and clarification of mentalistic concepts and their interrelationships, then the relevance for a cognitive science should be obvious.

At this stage of development two of the most critical mentalistic notions are intentionality and representation (Pribram). Intentionality is dealt with in a number of articles (e.g., Oppacher, Boden). Representation, a powerful and relatively unelusive mentalistic term, remains at the heart of many central controversies in cognitive (e.g., Pribram). Once the behavioristic yoke is shed, penetrating but difficult issues abound: the identity conditions of mental representations, referential functions of mental representations, the neural substrate for these representations, the sufficiency of natural language as mental representation.

The return to mentalism has not, contrary to some, served to obfuscate issues or to impede scientific progress. As is well-evidenced by this volume, although a caution must be exercised at all junctures, mentalistic/cognitive questions have helped develop sophisticated empirical research programs.

ACKNOWLEDGEMENTS

The Editors would like to express their gratitude first and foremost to the scholars who took the time to organize and write their thoughts on the issues addressed in this volume. We have had, in addition, the benefit of the skills of Lawrence Erlbaum, who dealt patiently with our naivite and who, at the bottom line, is really responsible for the existence of this work. Bonnie Flassig served admirably as our editorial assistant, providing just the right amounts of criticism, support, and nudge. Pamela Zimpfer of the Division of Continuing Education was largely responsible for making the symposium and hence this anthology a reality. Special thanks also go to Martin Ringle, Mary Lou Sena, Scott Olsen, and the Center for the Study of Values at the University of Delaware through the Exxon Foundation.

We must, of course, pay tribute to the Sloan Foundation for funding the Symposium out of which this all came.

Thomas W. Simon
Robert J. Scholes

For the Sloan Foundation

Robert Q. Marston, President
University of Florida

In reviewing the papers of this conference one is reminded of Gene Burdick's description of the Pacific,

> The Pacific is enormous, plural, contradictory. One aches for limitations, for boundaries that reduce the sensation of awe. For each person the limits are different. For some people, the Pacific is no longer than a tiny village. A strip of white sand, a reef. For a tiny group, that inquisitive body of oceanographers, the Pacific is illimitable. So great is their curiosity that their Pacific runs from the Bering strait to the glittering ice cliffs of Antarctica.

Consideration of mind or brain or cognitive sciences or language can be as limitless as Burdick's ocean or as specific as his tiny atoll. However, it was not size or complexity that moved the Sloan Foundation Board on Cognitive Sciences to urge investment in this or rather these fields. Rather it was the importance of the question asked and the sense of potential progress that led to our action.

Herb Simon, gracefully keeping his appointment even after notification of his Nobel Prize, placed the matter in this context at one of our small after dinner discussions. He stated there are three profound questions which we can hope realistically to find answers to in the next few decades:

- The nature of the universe through progress in particle physics
- The nature of life through molecular biology and
- The nature of the mind through the cognitive sciences

I asked Herb for his fourth on the list—he could not think of a fourth.

Invitational conferences in New York and San Francisco confirmed the sense of great opportunity, of the need to blend more effectively efforts in relatively isolated fields and to use language, or more specifically, internal representation, as a focal point of the Sloan Program. Conferences, including this one, were designed along with other activities to display substantive progress in the various fields related to cognition and to bring together expertise in these fields for formal and informal discussion.

I am pleased, both as Chairman of the Sloan Foundation Board on Cognitive Sciences and as the President of the host institution, to thank the contributors to this volume and to express the hope and belief that it will contribute to progress in the Cognitive Sciences.

LANGUAGE, MIND, AND BRAIN

Neoconstructivism:
A Unifying Theme
for the Cognitive Sciences

Stevan Harnad
Behavioral & Brain Sciences, Princeton, New Jersey

My original introductory address to the conference out of which the present volume has grown[1] was entitled *Interdisciplinary projects: Cross-fertilization or miscegenation?* In that talk I expressed certain misgivings about ventures launched on high hopes of interdisciplinary bonhomie (U.S. Committee on Science and Astronautics, 1970; Apostel, Berger, Briggs, & Michaud, 1972), citing such celebrated hybrid misadventures as "cybernetics" and "general systems theory,"[2] movements that have tended to become somewhat cultish, and to attract to their meetings and even into their published literature an unsettling proportion of delusionaries, with their partiality for "holistic" and "organismic" approaches and their penchant for grandiose pseudoscientific jargon. (As a paradigmatic sample of this sort of thinking and writing—which I have dubbed "cybernonsense" or "Marshall McLunacy"—I recommended Stulman, 1969, e.g. pp. 7-9, and *passim.*)

But, gratified as I was at that chance to castigate practitioners of transdisciplinary mediatization, and emboldened by J. H. Hexter's (1979) salutary observation that

> in an academic generation a little overaddicted to *politesse,* it may be worth saying that violent destruction is not necessarily of itself worthless and futile. Even though it leaves doubt about the right road for London, it helps if someone rips up,

---

[1]The national interdisciplinary conference on language, mind and brain; Gainesville, Florida, 1978.

[2]And barely resisting the temptation to list many more, such as general semantics, organismic biology, holistic medicine, and perhaps even some factions of contemporary semiotics and hermeneutics.

1

however violently, a "To London" sign on the Dover cliffs pointing south (p. 138),

I nonetheless felt that some more constructive suggestions would be in order. I accordingly offer here a positive proposal that may help head the cognitive sciences Londonward, rather than off in all disciplinary directions.

CONSTRUCTIVISM IN MATHEMATICS

There is in mathematics a movement (or rather a turn of mind) that is variously referred to as "finitism," "intuitionism," and "constructivism." There are shades of meaning distinguishing the three versions of the movement (which I will call, generically, constructivism) but, for the purposes of the analogy I am about to make, the relevant features are those that all three have in common. Constructivists are not fully satisfied with proofs by contradiction. For example, for them, in order to demonstrate that a certain mathematical object exists, it is not sufficient to show that, if it did not exist, this would give rise to a contradiction (this is called "apagogic proof"). They demand an *instance* of the object in question ("ostensive proof"), or else the explicit rules for constructing one. Constructivists have similarly exacting standards for what constitutes a function or procedure: a constructive procedure is one that comes up with a definite outcome after a finite number of explicit steps (Heyting, 1971; Fraenkel & Bar-Hillel, 1973).

An often-used example of a function that is *not* constructively defined, and hence not acceptable to a constructivist, is the function that equals 1 if, somewhere in the decimal expansion of π, there occurs the string (say)... 123456789..., and it equals 0 if that string never occurs. The trouble with this is that we currently have no way of knowing whether or not this (or any other arbitrary) string does in fact occur in the decimal expansion of π, and hence we don't know whether a search for it will ever halt. An outcome based on a search that may never halt is indeterminate, and hence the function in question is not a constructive one.

There is a deep link between constructibility and computability, via the theory of Turing machines and recursive functions (which I am not competent to discuss beyond pointing out that the link exists—see Davis, 1958; Kleene, 1969). Computability will be mentioned again later, but for now, the only feature of mathematical constructivism that I would like to carry over in the analogy I will make is that of *being answerable to an explicit test as to whether something exists or whether a procedure is well-defined.* What cannot be carried over in my analogy is the unique role of the constraint of consistency (or noncontradiction) in mathematics. For although a constructivist may profess agnosticism with respect to unconstructed objects whose claim to existence rests only on noncontradiction (and the law of the excluded middle), he recognizes that the dictates of apagogic proof are certainly not arbitrary, and that the formal activities of non-constructive mathematicians can hardly be said to be empty ones.

UNDERDETERMINATION AND UNIFICATION IN SCIENCE

Science, too, must be consistent, not only in the formal sense, but also in the sense of not contradicting data. But, unfortunately, the universe of things we can say that are self-consistent and consistent with existing data is still so large that, unlike the truths of mathematics,[3] the truths of science are said to be "underdetermined." Hence, extra constraints, such as parsimony and generality, have had to be brought in to narrow the options. Parsimony prefers the theory, all else being equal, that posits the smaller number of parameters. Generality prefers the theory, all else being equal, that accounts for the larger or more diverse body of data. Parsimony and the size of a data-set can, in principal, be quantified,[4] but questions as to what constitute the *boundaries* of the data domain of a theory—in other words, how diverse the theory should aspire to be—are not so easily settled. There is a definite unificationist trend in science, toward accounting for as much data as possible by one unified theory, even if it cuts across existing specialty or disciplinary boundaries. Hence, it is risky to try to legislate boundaries in advance, in defining a theoretical program. However, it is clear that some unifying theme is necessary, if only so that theorists can come to agree that they are working on the same kind of problem.

Rumor has it that logical positivism is dead, and that one of the principal causes of its demise was the impossibility of fully separating theory from data. Somehow, *what* one defines as data, and *how,* are already infected with one's theoretical preconceptions. It is not clear to what extent, if any, this problem actually affects ordinary day-to-day scientific practice;[5] but, in any case, it suggests yet another reason why it may not be a good idea to be too apodictic about disciplinary boundaries (in terms of the kinds of data one is prepared to count as "native" to a discipline). The only remaining candidates for unifying a scientific endeavor are hence internal ones—internal to the theory, that is, as opposed to the data (to the extent that such a distinction is still workable).

---

[3]With the possible exception of the celebrated "undecidability" results (see Davis, 1965).

[4]Modern complexity theory (Chaitin, 1975; Rabin, 1977) has proposed informational and computational principles for quantifying parsimony.

[5]A computer-science analogue of this problem (in some people's minds) is the "impossibility" of fully separating a computational model from its specific computer implementation. In both cases (theory/data, model/implementation) the apparent absence of pragmatic consequences ought, in my view, to alert the worriers that they may be tilting at a trivium. (See also footnote 11.)

THEORY IN PSYCHOLOGY

Now, until rather recently, one of the peculiarities of research psychologists (and to some extent biologists) has been a decided ambivalence, sometimes verging on an avowed hostility, toward theory. Somehow, the unwritten agreement has been that "hard" data speak for themselves, and all else is mere speculation. Given that it is diminishing in prevalence, this odd attitude would be only a matter of sociohistorical interest were it not for the fact that we are now necessarily being left, in these disciplines, with a legacy of "home-made" theorists, freshly matriculated from a period in which such activities were frowned upon, and in which one had to turn to other activities—mainly experimentation—to sharpen one's wits. Well, perhaps it was to be expected that home-made theorists would generate home-made theories; and indeed, now that the resistence to theory is eroding, one appears to have the license to proffer as "theory" just about any variety of half-baked conjecturing as to what might underlie a data-set (just as long as one does not appear to be wandering too far away from the data in so doing). (See footnote 7.)

So with "theory" no longer a bad word in biopsychology, and virtually any quasicoherent body of discourse eligible to lay claim to being one, it is hardly surprising that the entity in question is no longer recognizable as bearing even a family resemblance to its counterpart in the physical sciences. (The abuse of the word "model" is too flagrant even to broach!) This state of affairs is crying out for more discipline (not more discipline*s*!)—a unifying constraint that will (1) narrow the universe of theoretical possibilities to a tractable size, (2) give an indication as to what sort of science a peculiarly "psychological" one might be, and, most importantly, (3) determine objectively what does and does not count as theory in this field.

NEOCONSTRUCTIVISM IN COGNITIVE SCIENCE

Sometimes a change in terminology will clear the air for a substantive change to follow. "Psychology" seemed a perfectly good name for a scientific discipline, but it clearly came to mean too many things to too many people. For laymen, it was something you "used," and yours could be "good" or "bad." For clinicians, it was associated chiefly with psychopathology. For philosophers, it was what was left over when you subtracted ontology, epistemology, ethics and logic from philosophy. For many linguists, it was what provided the fine tuning for a basically inborn language faculty (see Harnad, 1976). And for generations of undergraduates, it became "the science of behavior," with associations of rats in mazes and taboos about thinking and emotion. So I suppose that it is time to introduce a new name, free of this motley of connotations. But, of course, a name alone won't do it, because all that other stuff is just waiting to spill over and fill any conceptual void—witness, already menacingly materializing, the current spate of "cognitive" therapies, and "cognitive" approaches to everything from business administration to right hemisphere education. But perhaps "cognitive science" is still new enough to assert an identity all its own. And it is a candidate for that unique identity that I would now like to propose.

Something going by the name of "constructivism" already exists as a movement, of sorts, in psychology. Constructivists (Rock, 1980; Ullman, 1980) are those perceptual theorists who define themselves by way of contrast with the Gibsonian view that perception occurs "directly" (Gibson, 1979). Gibsonians believe that since stimulation must contain all the information that is *necessary* to govern adaptive perceptuomotor performance, the information must also be *sufficient* for performance, being merely "picked up" passively by the nervous system. The constructivists simply deny this (in various ways), claiming that the nervous system must do some active processing ("construction") in order to generate adaptive performance. Where the truth lies, in this particular disagreement, is not so much my present concern; rather, I want to point out that neither the Gibsonians nor the constructivists are being particularly "constructive" here, if this word is taken to be in any respect analogous to its mathematical counterpart. In mathematics, construction is a kind of put-up-or-shut-up activity. One cannot be left disputing over whether there is or is not a particular string of digits in the decimal expansion of π. One either comes up with it—or with a finite method for coming up with it—or one moves on to a problem that one *can* say something constructive about!

"But what can possibly perform the function of this put-up-or-shut-up test in cognitive science," you ask? Fortunately, we have at our disposal a "construction kit" of rather recent vintage that can do just that: the digital computer. "Oh, go on," you reply, "why should I hitch my wagon to some here today-gone-tomorrow technology? Look at the seventeenth century, which said that man was like a clock. Surely the laws of 'cognitive science,' whatever that might be, should aspire to be taken *sub specie aeternitatis,* rather than being yoked to today's fly-away fads?" Well, I agree that computers may come and go; but the theory of computation (Kleene, 1969) and the theory of information (Shannon & Weaver, 1949) are here to stay, as eternal as the other platonic verities, and it is the computer as the implementation of an abstract computing device (a Turing machine) that I propose as the construction kit. Moreover, I'm not suggesting anything as simplistic (and obviously wrong) as that man is like an IBM 370. What I'm suggesting is that if you have any clear *constructive* ideas as to what man is like, the way to test them is to formalize them and try them out on a computer.

Not only all psychological theory, but all scientific theory in general can be seen as modeling input/output relations. The boundary conditions and experimental preparation are the input, and the theory is supposed to predict the outcome: the experimental observations. In principle, all physical theories are computer-testable. When a set of differential equations is solved by hand, and actual values are put in, the theorist is performing the role of the computer. Indeed, in certain complex problems of astrophysics and statistical mechanics, a real computer is in fact used to determine what outcomes the theory predicts, given actual data as input.

If we call this restriction to computer-testable theories "neoconstructivism"[6] (to distinguish it from the mathematical and the perceptual kinds of constructivism), then there is no question but that *all* the physical sciences are neoconstructive. (These days, physics' problems seem to lie rather in the area of parsimony, generality and unification—and possibly consistency.) But for the cognitive sciences it still remains to settle on what counts as theory (or explanation) in the first place![7] And if, as I urge, neoconstructivism is taken as the criterion, then it is clear that much of what poses as theory and explanation in psychology is nonconstructive, and hence, I suggest, cognitively (and explanatorily) vacuous, no matter what it calls itself.

In proposing neoconstructivism as the unifying theme for the cognitive sciences I am obviously not claiming any arbitrary uniqueness for these disciplines, since I've already suggested that all of physical science is neoconstructive (usually trivially so, in the sense that one need not have recourse to a real computer to demonstrate neoconstructivity in physics; rather, as in mathematics, a paper and pencil will do). The cognitive sciences are characterized uniquely enough by their data-domain (pace the worriers of footnote 5); this can be very liberally described as all human and animal and human-like and animal-like performance (see footnote 9). But evidently the cognitive sciences do resemble astrophysics and statistical physics more than they do other domains of physics, because the performance of organisms, unlike the mechanics of a billiard game, doesn't seem to be explainable without the aid of the computer.

RIVAL VIEWS OF COGNITIVE SCIENCE

I would like to close by comparing my characterization of what counts as cognitive with some other current candidates. First, mine is clearly only very minimally an *extensional* characterization; in other words, I have not tried to list all

---

[6]I chose the prefix neo-, although neocontructivism does not really constitute the resurrection of some earlier form of constructivism. The prefix can also refer to something that is new, recent or young; an early form of something. All these connotations are welcome, as far as I am concerned; the alternative candidates—para-, quasi-, and pseudo- —all have much less desirable ones.

[7]One has the impression that, for some people, all it takes for something to qualify as an "explanation" is that it give (someone) the soothing feeling of having had something explained!

the examples of what is cognitive.[8] Even my delineation of the data domain as organismic and organism-like performance[9] is potentially so general as to include, if necessary, billiard-ball interactions or cream dispersing in a cup of coffee. I just suggest that real organisms' performance, and things that resemble it, are probably what we should be looking at. Someone will surely object that bipedal locomotion does not strike him as particularly cognitive, even though it's clearly organismic performance. I reply: Fine; proceeding bottom-up or top-down (in one's theorizing!) is a methodological choice, and one is free to take the lowest levels for granted, if one feels safe. But for the Gibsonians (to take only one example) it happens to have turned out to be rather difficult to leave locomotion out of the equation, even when accounting for the kinds of complex visual pattern recognition that no one would want to deny were cognitive (Gyr, Willey, & Henry, 1979). Moreover, I would feel much less comfortable in restricting cognition's phenomenal field to, say, language or language-like performance, particularly before I have any (neoconstructive) idea as to what language and language-like performance really are, and where they stop and lower-order performance begins. Some of the current perplexities about the linguistic capacities of apes (Griffin, this volume; Savage-Rumbaugh et al., this volume) illustrate

---

[8]Needless to say, I reject out of hand the most unabashedly extensional candidate definition, which is that the cognitive sciences are the sum (or is it more than the sum?) of the motley of disciplines deemed to comprise them (psychology, artificial intelligence, linguistics, philosophy, neuroscience, etc.).

[9]I suppose that, in a sense, cognitivists can still be characterized as "behaviorists," in that they recognize that the organism's input and output are all that they will ever get by way of actual data-points. (Perhaps all scientists are "behaviorists" in this sense.) But cognitivists are really "reconstructed" behaviorists, in the following respects:

a. Cognitivists aspire to a neoconstructive theory to account for the (performance) data.

b. Cognitivists are more than willing to use information from introspection, from neuroscience, or from any other source, as long as it makes a constructive contribution to their mission. Moreover, in holding themselves accountable for all performance, cognitivists have no reason to balk at attempting to model its underlying subjective phenomenology—as inferred from, say, verbal report—particularly as successfully simulating the phenomenology would have a high presumptive likelihood of advancing their mission (see Harnad, 1981).

c. Cognitivists are not constrained to the push-pull dynamics of raw performance: higher-order regularities of performance (competence) are perfectly respectable data.

d. Cognitivists recognize the neoconstructive vacuity of the behaviorist's conventional arsenal of concepts (reinforcement, association). Indeed, others have pointed out an affinity between the Gibsonians and the behaviorists, in that, although it is clear that stimuli, rewards, and punishments must carry the necessary information for adaptive performance, this fact alone (and its immediate parameters) are not sufficient to *generate* the performance. Cognitivism attempts to provide the missing nonconstructive link whose absence prevents these other approaches from boot-strapping to a self-sufficient account of performance.

Perhaps it is the neoconstructive variety that he had presciently in mind when Wittgenstein (1967) likened the behaviorists to the intuitionists in mathematics.

some of the problems involved in attempting to draw extensional border-lines between performances of which one has no neoconstructive understanding.[10]

There are also rival *intensional* definitions of "cognitive," that is, definitions in terms of distinctive properties. Some have to do with vague, vogue buzz-words such as "representation" and "intentionality." "Representation" is something on whose meaning philosophers and psychologists have yet to settle. We know that it has something to do with concepts such as reference and description, and their relation to their respective objects. It may even have something (if only negatively) to do with representation as it is used in art and literature. But it is certainly something that these learned folk have not yet pinned down to anyone's satisfaction. Must cognitive science wait? Or can we just bumble along with our more noncommittal concept of "encoding," and wait to see how far that will get us? In any case, equating "cognitive" with "representational" at this point would, it seems to me, amount to the blind leading the blind.

"Intentionality" is another favorite rival candidate. It means, variously, what it is that "think," "want," "expect," "know," etc., have in common with one another and fail to share with such words as "walk," "sit" and "eat." Intentionality is also said to have something to do with the fact that the words in the first category seem to have some sort of built-in object: One wants something, thinks something, etc. In the parlance of some enthusiasts, the word "intentional" has even blithely replaced the word "mental" (and this with some sort of sense of having made progress!). And lastly, intentionality seems to be something that one can *assign* by way of an interpretation (Haugeland, 1978): "That person (dog, machine) behaves *as if* he (it) thinks, wants, etc." — Needless to say, I don't find any of these mysteries particularly helpful, or constructive.

Finally, there is the frank declaration that what is cognitive is computational (Pylyshyn, 1980). Some readers may assume—based on what I've said so far— that I would find this last proposal congenial: It too is a methodological distinction, with minimal extensional commitments, and in fact it is even neoconstructive! However, I find it much too restrictive, and overly biased toward one specific theoretical approach to cognition: a propositional/procedural approach, which is not the only neoconstructive possibility.

Let us make it perfectly explicit: neoconstructivism dictates that all cognitive theories must be *computable,* but not necessarily *computational.* The former requires that a theory be sufficiently specific and explicit to be formalized into a

---

[10]As in the Episcopal Church, there may emerge a "high" and "low" school of cognitivism, with the practitioners of the high protesting that the low is only modeling the "vegetative" aspects of performance, and not the cognitive ones at all. It remains a practical, methodological question whether such schisms are worth encouraging, and whether there are any logical as opposed to merely ideological bases for them. (Indeed, even the distinction between organismic and neural "performance" may not turn out to be a productive one for cognitive science to insist on too strongly.)

computer program that tests whether, given the kinds of inputs that characterize the phenomenon being modeled, the program succeeds in generating the kinds of outputs predicted, using the kinds of principles posited in the theory. The additional constraint of computationality would count as cognitive only those successful programs that have used certain quasilinguistic procedures to generate their performance. I, on the other hand, would admit as cognitive *any* successful neoconstructive generation of performance, even if it involves (the simulation[11] of) analog devices, pre-wired special-purpose modules, statistical filtering, servomechanisms, or any other trick[12] that works.

The computationalists have, I think, been overly taken with such suggestive properties of natural language as that every "state of affairs" seems to be *potentially* describable (to any desired degree of approximation—see Steklis & Harnad, 1976); or properties of computation, such as that every "process" seems to be *potentially* simulable computationally (to an approximation). As a consequence, whenever anyone proposes that an analog or prewired process is going on, computationalists tend to rejoin that "then it's not cognitive" (or, more revealingly, that it's not "yet" or not "fully" cognitive[13]). This seems quite arbitrary to me. After all, computationality is a concept that post-dates such pretheoretic ideas as "perceiving" and "thinking." Why should the question of whether these activities are "really" cognitive now turn out to depend on whether the brain happens to have decided to implement them by the "right" means, by computationalists' lights?

---

[11]I agree completely with Pylyshyn (1978) that the distinction between *computer simulation* of cognition (which tries to model our performance "the way we really do it") and *artificial intelligence* (which is a kind of computational "l'art pour l'art") is a totally artificial one, based on such temporary and arbitrary factors as the lack of generality of our current models ("toy problems") and the low degree of rigor of the performance constraints we currently choose to adopt. There is at this point (largely for want of a coherent rival to computation as the model for mechanism in cognition) no reason to doubt that all approaches will ultimately *converge* as we approach a complete model for the whole organism's performance. In any case, underdetermination is as much a fact of inductive life in cognitive science as it is in physical science. So much naive and parochial criticism of computational modeling can be traced to (1) misunderstandings concerning underdetermination and generality—there may be many ways to compute a factorial, but are there many (equiparametric) ways to design a universe? or even a whole organism (see Dennett, 1978)?—and to (2) handwaving concerning mechanism and explanation. Even sophisticated critics (e.g. Searle, 1980) have inadvertently built their negative cases on the transitory degeneracy of the current state of the art in this new science, taking for granted the restricted horizons of today's toy-problem perspectives. I propose neoconstructivism as the relevant generalization to contend with.

[12]I take it that one can hardly persist in calling something a "trick" once it becomes sufficiently general and convergent (in the sense of footnote 11).

[13]In my own chapter (Harnad, this volume), I sketch a dual-mode representational system to account for lateralized differences in cognition. What I call the "bounded system" therein is clearly more computational, while the "unbounded system" is more analog. But I see no reason why the entire dual system should not be called cognitive. (My sketch is not a formal one, and hence not yet (sic) neoconstructive; but it was clearly motivated by the goal of eventual computer-testability.)

But, in the end, any debate between neconstructivists and computationalists, can, like the debate between the constructivists and the Gibsonians, really only be settled one way: neoconstructively.[14]

REFERENCES

Apostel, L., Berger, G., Briggs, A., & Michaud, G. 1972. *Interdisciplinarity: Problems of teaching and research in universities*. Paris: OECD.

Chaitin, G. 1975. Randomness and mathematical proof. *Scientific American* 232:47-52.

Davis, M. 1958. *Computability and unsolvability*. Manchester: McGraw-Hill.

Davis, M. 1965. *The undecidable*. New York: Raven.

Dennett, D. C. 1978. Why not the whole iguana? *The Behavioral and Brain Sciences* 1:103-104.

Fraenkel, A. A., & Bar-Hillel, Y. 1973. *Foundations of set theory*. New York: Elsevier.

Gibson, J. J. 1979. *The ecological approach to visual perception*. Boston: Houghton Mifflin.

Gyr, J. Willey, R., & Henry, A. 1979. Motor-sensory feedback and geometry of visual space: a replication. *The Behavioral and Brain Sciences* 2:59-94.

Harnad, S. 1976. Induction, evolution, and accountability. *Annals of the New York Academy of Sciences* 280:58-60.

Harnad, S. 1981. Consciousness: An Afterthought. (Submitted for publication)

Haugeland, J. 1978. The nature and plausibility of cognitivism. *The Behavioral and Brain Sciences* 1:215-260.

Hexter, J. H. 1979. *Reappraisals in History*. Chicago: University of Chicago Press.

Heyting, A. 1971. *Intuitionism: An introduction*. New Jersey: Humanities.

Kleene, S. C. 1969. *Formalized recursive functionals and formalized realizability*. Providence R.I.: American Mathematical Society.

Pylyshyn, Z. 1978. Computational models and empirical constraints. *The Behavioral and Brain Sciences* 1:93-127.

Pylyshyn, Z. 1980. Computation and cognition: Issues in the foundations of cognitive science. *The Behavioral and Brain Sciences* 3:111-169.

Rabin, M. O. 1977. Complexity of computations. *Communications of the Association of Computer Machinery* 20:625-633.

Rock, I. 1980. Difficulties with a direct theory of perception. *The Behavioral and Brain Sciences* 3:398-399.

Searle, J. R. 1980. Minds, brains and programs. *The Behavioral and Brain Sciences* 3:417-457.

Shannon, L. E., & Weaver, W. 1949. *The mathematical theory of communication*. Urbana: University of Illinois Press.

Steklis, H. D., & Harnad, S. R. 1976. From hand to mouth: Some critical stages in the evolution of language. *Annals of the New York Academy of Sciences* 280:445-455.

Stulman, J. 1969. The methodology of pattern. *Fields Within Fields* 1:7-9.

Ullman, S. 1980. Against direct perception. *The Behavioral and Brain Sciences* 3:373-415.U.S.

---

[14]Was this paper neoconstructive? No, it was clearly methodological and foundational. Although what psychology certainly needs most at this time—aside from significant data—is neoconstructive theory, this does not mean that there are grounds to stop worrying about what we are doing altogether. There is still plenty of room for foundational and pretheoretical soul-searching. For example (assuming that we are all committed to an eventual mechanistic account of organismic function), do there exist any coherent mechanistic alternatives to neoconstructivism?

Committee on Science and Astronautics. 1970. *Interdisciplinary research: an exploration of public policy issues*. Science Policy Research Division, Legislative Reference, Library of Congress, Serial T.

Wittgenstein, L. 1967. *Remarks on the Foundations of Mathematics*. Cambridge, Mass.: M.I.T. Press.

1 Logic, Reasoning, and Logical Form

Gilbert Harman
Princeton University

I want to discuss two related issues. (1) Does logic play any role in the actual reasoning people do? (2) Do sentences of a natural language like English have logical forms?

In order to address these questions, we must, to begin with, distinguish inference or reasoning, on the one hand, from proof or argument, on the other. Inference or reasoning is a process of trying to improve one's overall view by adding some things and subtracting others. A proof or argument consists in one or more premises and a sequence of steps, each of which is supposed to follow from premises or previous steps in accordance with certain rules of logic, the last step being the conclusion. Reasoning and argument may well be closely related enterprises, although as I will explain in a moment this is not obvious. In any event, it is very important not to confuse reasoning and argument so that, for example, one wrongly comes to think of reasoning as involving premises, intermediate steps and a final conclusion reached by applying so-called "rules of inference" or one wrongly comes to think there is such a thing as "deductive reasoning" or "inductive argument" or "practical syllogisms." These are just confusions.

Reasoning is a process of trying to improve one's overall view. If it made sense to speak of premises and conclusions of reasoning, the premises would be everything one accepts at the start and the conclusion would be everything one accepts at the end. But it is misleading to speak of premises and conclusion since some of one's "premises" might be abandoned in the course of reasoning and since one's "conclusion" will contain primarily what one has believed all along.

Reasoning is a *holistic* process in the following sense. One seeks to make minimal changes that will improve one's overall view, for example one attempts

13

to make one's view more explanatorily coherent by adding explanations of things previously unexplained and by rejecting things that do not fit in well with other things one accepts (also discussed in Harman, 1973, chaps. 7-10; 1975-76, pp. 431-63).

Rules of argument or proof are *local* rules of logical implication, applying to particular propositions, saying that this sort of proposition follows from those. "Whenever propositions of those sorts are true, then a corresponding proposition of this sort is always true." For example, whenever a disjunctive proposition *P or Q* is true and so is the negation of one of the disjuncts *not P*, then the other disjunct *Q* is always true. Such a principle is sometimes called a "rule of inference," but that is misleading. Rules of inference tell one to improve one's overall view in various ways, but inferring a logical consequence of one's beliefs is not always an improvement. There is the problem of unnecessary clutter. And there is the problem of inconsistency. Inconsistent propositions logically imply everything; but, when one discovers an inconsistency in one's beliefs, one should not infer everything. Indeed, in that case it may not be clear what to do, especially if the inconsistency results from a paradox of some sort. Perhaps one should just ignore it and try to stay away from it, in the way that some mathematicians try to stay away from the set theoretical paradoxes. This shows that the rule that *P or Q* and *not P* always imply *Q* does not mean that, if one believes both *P and Q* and *not P*, one may infer *Q*. Perhaps one should not bother to clutter up one's mind with that information. Perhaps one already believes *not Q* and should stop believing *P or Q* or *not P* or should sit tight and hope this inconsistency in one's beliefs will not lead to trouble.

Now, it is not immediately obvious that logic is more relevant to reasoning than is arithmetic or geometry or physics or chemistry. Perhaps logic is simply the study of certain features of the world, differing from other subjects only in being more general and abstract.[1] For, if logic is specially relevant to reasoning, it is not immediately obvious in what way it could be specially relevant.

It might be said that arithmetic, geometry, physics, chemistry, and so on merely provide premises, whereas logic provides rules of inference that allow us to derive specific conclusions from those premises (cf. Carroll, 1895). There may be something to this idea, but it cannot be completely correct, since principles of logic are rules or laws of implication and not, strictly speaking, rules of inference. It might be said that logic is needed in order to get from our finite statements of theory to their infinite consequences, from our finite number of explicitly represented beliefs to the infinitely many things we believe implicitly (cf. Quine, 1966, pp. 77-106). This is suggestive but probably cricular if "getting" one thing from another is the same as inferring one thing from another, for then to say we need to use logic in order to "get" to the consequences of our

---

[1] I am surprised not to be able to find an explicit statement anywhere of this seemingly sensible idea.

explicit beliefs would seem to amount to saying that logic plays a special role in reasoning.

Let us suppose that logic does play a special role in reasoning. What could that role be? Recall that reasoning is a process of trying to make minimal changes that will improve one's overall view, including changes that will increase the explanatory coherence of one's view. This suggests that, if logic plays a special role in reasoning, that might be because logic has something special to do with explanatory coherence. And that does seem plausible. Logical inconsistency in one's beliefs would seem to be a kind of incoherence. And certain explanations seem to take the form of deductive arguments or argument sketches, a point stressed by proponents of the deductive nomological or covering law model of explanation (see Hempel, 1965, pt. 4, pp. 229–496).

An argument consists in premises and a sequence of steps each of which is derived from premises and earlier steps in accordance with certain rules of logical implication. If the argument is to be usefully explanatory, each step will itself have to be immediately intelligible, needing no further explanation. This suggests that, if logic plays a special role in reasoning, it may do so in part because certain rules of logical implication express immediately intelligible connections that can be understood without further explanation. Some psychological investigation of the psychology of reasoning might be interpreted as attempting to discover which rules of logical implication expresses such immediately intelligible connections (e.g., Wason & Johnson-Laird, 1972).

In working this out in detail, we would have to distinguish explaining why something happened from explaining why it is true that it happened. For suppose one knows that, either John's car is in his garage, or he is out driving; one looks in the garage and sees the car is not there; and one concludes that John is out driving. Then one's reasoning involves an argument that does not explain why John is out driving; at best it explains why it is true that John is out driving but does not give a reason why John is out driving.

The suggestion, then, is that logic is specially relevant to reasoning because logic is specially relevant to explanatory coherence and because reasoning involves (among other things) trying to improve the explanatory coherence of one's view. Deductive arguments are specially relevant to reasoning because explanations can take the form of deductive arguments—in reasoning one comes to accept not just the conclusion of the argument but the whole argument; one accepts it as expressing an explanatory connection between its premises and its conclusion.

The last part of this suggestion, about deductive arguments, can be broken down into two parts. First, there is the idea that arguments of some sort play a special role in reasoning by serving as explanations. Second, there is the further suggestion that the rules people follow in constructing such arguments are rules of logic. (Of course we must allow that people sometimes make mistakes and argue fallaciously). To see the force of this second idea, notice that any general proposition could conceivably be used as a rule of implication that could connect steps of argument. For example, the proposition that all metals conduct electricity could be treated as the rule that *X is a metal* implies *X conducts electricity*. Such a rule would authorize the following simple argument:

> Copper is a metal.
> So, copper conducts electricity.

What is being suggested is that people do not construct arguments like this that appeal to nonlogical rules but always treat the nonlogical principles as premises in arguments that proceed in accordance with rules of logic, as in this argument:

> Copper is a metal.
> All metals conduct electricity.
> So, copper conducts electricity.

This is obviously a highly speculative suggestion.

In order to evaluate this suggestion, we must at least ask why it should be true. What is it about principles of logic as compared with other principles that could give them this special function? What distinguishes principles of logic from nonlogical principles?

It is often said that logical principles are formal in a way that nonlogical principles are not. The principle that *P or Q* and *not P* always imply *Q* refers only to the forms of the propositions involved. The principle that *X is a metal* implies *X conducts electricity* refers not only to the forms of the propositions involved but also their content. This idea might be useful to us if there should be a nonarbitrary way to distinguish elements of nonlogical content, like *metal* and *electricity*. If, on the other hand, the distinction between elements of logical form and elements of content should turn out to be an arbitrary one, then the distinction between logical and nonlogical principles would be arbitrary and it would not make sense to suppose that logical rules play a special psychological role in the construction of arguments. And, of course, even if there is a nonarbitrary distinction between logical and nonlogical elements, not every such distinction would give logical rules a special function in argument construction.

Presumably, any useful nonarbitrary distinction will have something to do with grammar. Elements of logical form must be grammatically distinctive in some significant way. Now, reflection on a number of examples suggests this: Elements of logical form are members of small closed classes and elements of nonlogical content are members of large open classes, where the relevant classes are classes of atomic elements of the same logical category. Logical categories include predicates, sentential connectives, quantifiers, etc. For example, *or* is an atomic sentential connective. The class of atomic sentential connectives is small and closed in that new atomic sentential connectives are not easily added to the language. So, *or* is an element of logical form by this criterion. On the other hand, *metal* is an atomic predicate. Atomic predicates form a large open class to which new members are added all the time. So *metal* is an element of nonlogical content by this criterion (see Harman, 1979).

There is, then, some reason to think that the distinction between logical principles and others has a syntactic or grammatical basis, if it is based on a distinction between elements of logical form and elements of nonlogical content that has such a basis. Another possible indication of the role of syntax is the surprising fact that general logical principles cannot be stated in ordinary language as ordinary generalizations but must be stated one level up as generalizations about the truth of propositions. We can generalize from "Copper conducts electricity," "Silver conducts electricity," and so on, to "All metals conduct electricity"; but we cannot in ordinary English generalize from "Copper does not both conduct electricity and not conduct electricity," "Snow is not both white and not white," "It is not the case that both all men are moral and not all men are mortal," and so on without making use of what Quine calls semantic ascent (see Quine, 1972, pp. 11–12). We have to say, "Every proposition of the form *not both P and not P* is true. It would not be good English to try to express this directly as, for example, "Nothing is both it and not it." We *can* perhaps say, "Nothing is both so and not so" (?), if "nothing" means "no proposition" and "so" means "true" or "the case," but this clearly does involve semantic ascent.

These grammatical considerations indicate that logic has a different function from other aspects of one's view of the world. Logic is built into one's language and is relatively fixed. One's view of the world is not built into the same extent and changes constantly over time. One's view of the world is finitely represented. Logical principles are not normally represented as part of one's view, except as a relatively late and sophisticated development using semantic ascent. Logical principles must therefore be manifested as rules of argument. These rules enable a finite representation of one's view to express infinitely many implications. Rules of logic are therefore part of a relatively fixed system of representation in which one's changing view of the world is expressed.

Now, linguists and philosophers of language do put forward hypotheses about the connection between grammatical structure and logical form in sentences of a natural language like English. Such hypotheses presuppose that there is a nonarbitrary psychologically real distinction between aspects of logical form and aspects of nonlogical content. This presupposition would seem to make sense only within a framework like the extremely speculative one that I have been sketching.

This may explain why those who put forward hypotheses about logical form feel compelled to provide a finite truth conditional "semantics" for sentences analyzed in the way they propose to analyze them. It is generally agreed that any such proposal should permit a statement of truth conditions for the sentences being analyzed. Sometimes all that is required is an account of truth conditions in relation to one or another model or interpretation. Sometimes the stronger requirement is imposed that the account of truth conditions imply all appropriate instances of the schema "*x* is true if and only if *p,*" where what replaces "*x*" names or designates a sentence under analysis and what replaces "*p*" is that very sentence or a translation of it. The stronger requirement makes sense given that logic requires semantic ascent. For then, logical principles cannot directly explain their instances in the way that ordinary generalizations do. The connection between logical principle and a particular instance of it must be mediated by some principle of truth.

1. Every proposition of the form *not both P and not P* is true.
2. "Copper does not both conduct electricity and not do so" is of the form *not both P and not P*.
3. So, "Copper does not both conduct electricity and not do so" is true.
4. "Copper does not both conduct electricity and not do so" is true if and only if copper does not both conduct electricity and not do so.
5. So, copper does not both conduct electricity and not do so.

Line (4) in this argument is a relevant instance of the schema "*x* is true if and only if *p.*" There are infinitely many relevant instances of this schema. A finite theory of truth conditions must imply each of these instances if we are to use that theory in giving a general account of the way in which logical principles account for their instances.

I see no way to justify either the stronger or the weaker requirement (that analyses of logical form must make possible accounts of truth conditions) without getting involved in the sorts of speculations I have discussed. It is sometimes said that a theory of meaning must include such a theory of truth conditions. But, as I have argued elsewhere, such a theory of truth conditions offers no nontrivial account of the meaning of nonlogical elements of sentences (since it tells us only such things as that "horse" denotes horses—cf. "heffalump" denotes heffalumps) and says something about the meaning of logical elements only on the supposition that the meaning of logical elements depends on their special role in reasoning, which is to say it depends on their special role in argument, the relevant principles of which are truth preserving (see Harman, 1974).

I have no way of knowing whether the speculations advanced here are in any way correct. Recall that I began with two questions: (1) Does logic play any role in the actual reasoning people do? and (2) Do sentences of a natural language like English have logical forms? My point has been that a consideration of such questions immediately involves one in this sort of speculation (discussed at greater length in Harman, forthcoming a,b,c,d).

REFERENCES

Carroll, L. 1895. What the tortoise told Achilles. *Mind* 4.
Harman, G. 1973. *Thought*. Princeton: Princeton University Press.

Harman, G. 1974. Meaning and semantics. In *Semantics and philosophy*, ed. M. Munitz & P. Unger. New York: New York University Press.

Harman, G. 1975-76. Practical reasoning. *Review of Metaphysics* 29: 431-63.

Harman, G. 1979. If and modus ponens. *Theory and Decision* 11:41-53.

Harman, G. The logic of ordinary language. In *Philosophies of existence*, ed. P. Morewedge, forthcoming a.

Harman, G. Logic and reasoning. In *Proceedings of the 1980 New York Logic Conference*, ed. H. Leblanc et. al., forthcoming b.

Harman, G. A possible rational for Davidson's convention T. in *Donald Davidson*, ed. B. Vermazen and M. Hintikka, forthcoming c.

Harman, G. *Reasoning*. In *Encyclopedia Americana*, forthcoming d.

Hempel, C. G. 1965. *Aspects of scientific explanation and other essays in the philosophy of science*. New York: Free Press.

Quine, W. V. 1966. Truth by convention. In *The ways of paradox*, ed. W. V. Quine. Rev. ed. 1976. New York: Random House.

Quine, W. V. 1972. *Philosophy of logic*. Englewood Cliffs, N.J.: Prentice-Hall.

Wason, P. C., & Johnson-Laird, P. N. 1972. *Psychology of reasoning: structure and content*. Cambridge: Harvard University Press.

2 Variable-Free Semantics with Remarks on Procedural Extensions

Patrick Suppes
Stanford University

In earlier publications (Suppes, 1976, 1979; Suppes & Macken, 1978), I have emphasized the development of a model-theoretic semantics for English sentences, which uses neither quantifiers nor variables, but only constants denoting given sets and relations, and operations on sets and relations. I first want to survey these developments and then consider some extensions to procedural semantics.

The set-theoretical apparatus is that of what I call *extended relation algebras*. To the ordinary concept of a relation algebra with Boolean operations and operations on relations such as converse and relative product, the standard operation of forming the image of a set under a relation is added. (There are important features of natural language that this framework does not easily account for. A good example would be the semantics of prepositional phrases.)

There is one strong computational advantage of the kind of "algebraic" semantics I am proposing. A full Zermelo-like hierarchy of sets is not needed for the model structure as it is, in principle, for Montague semantics. Some aspects of the analysis run contrary to many standard linguistic ideas. This is perhaps especially true of my insistence that such expressions as *every man, all sophomores,* and *some lovers* are not noun phrases. As should be evident from what has been said, the English quantifier words *every, all, some,* etc., do not denote at all but function as control structure words.

In the matter of the denotation or lack of it of *every man,* or *all men,* we can prove in a simple way that the conventional production rules will not permit a semantic account of the syllogism at the level of Boolean algebra, that is, at the level of subsets of the domain, but require what from a semantical or set-theoretical standpoint is to be regarded as an artificial escalation of type. This proof, which is meant to be a strong substantive argument against assigning a denotation to *every man,* is given at the end of Section I. (Arguments in favor of this viewpoint and the proof of the theorem are given in Suppes, 1976, but I amplify here some of the details in order to make the proof more explicit.)

I. GENERATIVE GRAMMARS AND THEIR SEMANTICS

A couple of examples will illustrate the framework I have in mind and provide an introduction to the concept of semantic trees for context-free grammars.

Consider the tree for the sentence *Some people do not drink some wines,* shown in Fig. 2.1. On the left of the colon at each node is shown the terminal or nonterminal label. The nonterminal grammatical categories should be obvious: S = sentence, EQ = existential quantifier, NP = noun phrase, Aux = auxiliary, etc. To the right of the colon at a node is shown the denotation of the label if it has one. Thus, in the semantic tree of Fig. 2.1, *people* and its ascendant NP node have the set P of people as denotation; *drink* and its ascendant TV (transitive verb) node have the binary relation D of drinking as denotation; *wines* and its ascendant NP node have the set W of wines as denotation. The VP (verb phrase) node has a denotation composed of set-theoretical operations on D and W. Intuitively the denotation is just the set of people who do not drink some wines. The notation $\check{D}$ is for the *converse* of the relation D, $\neg\check{D}$ is the *complement* of the relation $\check{D}$, and $(\neg\check{D})''W$ is the *image* of the set W under the relation $\neg\check{D}$. At this point I take the root of the semantic tree of a sentence to denote the value T or F in a standard Fregean manner; an explicit Boolean function is introduced later. Most of this notation is standard in elementary set theory (see, e.g., Suppes, 1960). Some subtleties about complementation are discussed later.

I give now a quick overview of the relevant formal concepts. First, a structure $G = (V,N,P,S)$ is a *phrase-structure grammar* if and only if V and P are finite,

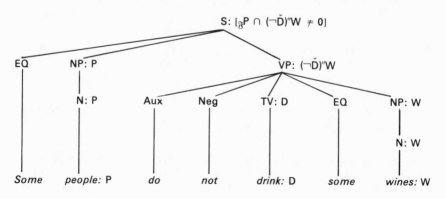

FIG. 2.1.

nonempty sets; N is a subset of V; S is in N; and $P \subseteq N^* \times V^+$, where N^* is the set of all finite sequences whose terms are elements of N and V^+ is V^* minus the empty sequence. The grammar G is *context-free* if and only if $P \subseteq N \times V^+$. In the usual terminology, V is the vocabulary, N is the nonterminal vocabulary, S is the start symbol of derivations or the label of the root of derivation trees of the grammar, and P is the set of production rules. I assume as known the standard definitions of one string of V^* being G–*derivable* from another, the concept of a *derivation tree* of G, and the language L(G) generated by G. (For a detailed treatment of these concepts, see Hopcroft & Ullman, 1969.) A context-free grammar G is *unambiguous* if and only if every terminal string in L(G) has exactly one derivation tree (with respect to G).

Semantics may be introduced in two steps. First, the grammar G is extended to a *potentially denoting* grammar by assigning at most one set-theoretical function to each production rule of G. We may show these functions in general by using a notation of square braces; for example, [NP] is the denotation of NP. In the case of Fig. 2.1,

Production Rule	*Semantic Function*
S → EQ + NP + VP	$[S] = [\frac{}{\delta}[NP] \cap [VP]] \neq 0]$
VP → Aux + Neg + TV + EQ + NP	$[VP] = (\neg[\tilde{TV}])''[NP],$

where the Frege function $[\frac{}{\delta}\phi]$ is defined for any (extensional) sentence ϕ as follows:

$$[\tfrac{}{\delta}\phi] = \begin{cases} T \text{ if } \phi \text{ is true (in the given model)} \\ F \text{ otherwise.} \end{cases}$$

(This definition is slightly reformulated below, in order to make it explicitly Boolean.) And in the case of the other nodes with only one descendant, the semantic function is identity if there is a denotation. For example,

TV → *drink*   [TV] = [*drink*].

The second step is the characterization of model structures. In the general theory of model-theoretic semantics for context-free languages, I use the concept of a *hierarchy* $\mathcal{H}(D)$ of sets built up from a given nonempty domain D by closure under union, subset, and power set "operations," with T and F excluded from the hierarchy and $T \neq F$. A *model structure* for a given grammar G with terminal vocabulary V_T is a pair (D,v) where D is a nonempty set and v is a partial function from V_T^+ to $\mathcal{H}(D)$. Explicit details are to be found in Suppes (1973b). The treatment here is restricted. First, only terminal words, not terminal phrases, are permitted to denote, so that the domain of the valuation function v is V_T, not V_T^+. (The function v remains a partial function because many terminal words—e.g., quantifier words—do not denote.)

The more important restriction is in the hierarchy. In line with my earlier paper (Suppes, 1976), I restrict the model structures to the power set $\mathscr{P}(D)$ of the domain D, that is, the set of all subsets of D, and the power set of the Cartesian product D × D—thus, only binary relations are considered. Formally, I define

$$\mathscr{E}(D) = \mathscr{P}(D) \cup \mathscr{P}(D \times D).$$

using "$\mathscr{E}$" for extended relation algebras of sets, a terminology introduced in the earlier paper. The valuation function v is then a partial function from V_T to $\mathscr{E}(D)$.

The "algebraic" operations on elements of $\mathscr{E}(D)$ have mainly already been mentioned: union, intersection, and complementation on arbitrary sets; the converse of relations; and the image of a set under a relation, R″A. In addition, we need the restriction of the domain of a relation R to a set A, R|A, which is defined as:

$$R|A = R \cap (A \times \mathscr{R}(R)),$$

where $\mathscr{R}(R)$ is the range of the relation R.

As always, complementation is relative to some given set. From the standpoint of $\mathscr{E}(D)$, the natural set-theoretical choice is D ∪ (D × D), but conceptually this is not very intuitive. For instance, if L is the relation of loving, then ¬L should be the *relation* of not loving, that is.

$$\neg L = (D \times D) - L.$$

Consequently, complementation is here taken to mean complementation with respect to D × D in the case of relations and with respect to D in the case of sets that are subsets of D. The only point of ambiguity concerns complementation of the empty set or relation, and the context will make clear which is meant.

In the earlier paper on these matters (Suppes, 1976). I introduced the notation

$$\cap(R,A) = \underset{a \in A}{\cap} (R''\{a\})$$

for the appropriate denotation when a verb phrase uses a universal quantifier in object position. This use may be seen in the semantic tree (Fig. 2.2) for *Some people drink all wines.* I note that UQ is the nonterminal symbol for the universal quantifier *all.* In direct analogy with O syllogistic propositions being the contradictory of A propositions, we may define $\cap(R,A)$ in the following manner (Suppes, 1979) for R ⊆ D × D and A ⊆ D,

$$\cap(R,A) = (\neg((\neg R)''A)).$$

Note that the "inside" complementation is with respect to D × D and the "outside" one with respect to D.

I now apply these ideas to prove the theorem mentioned earlier. To prove the theorem we need to define two grammars, one, G_1, that does not assign a denotation to *all men,* etc. The grammar G_2, in contrast, is meant to capture the

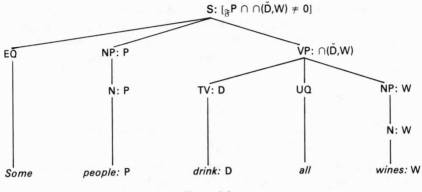

Figure 2.2.

widely accepted linguistic idea that *all men* is a noun phrase and has a denotation. (In both grammars I use only plural verbs and nouns in order to avoid problems of inflection.)

To keep the grammars simple, I shall restrict them to generating sentences of the standard A, E, I, and O forms used in the classical syllogism. It is apparent that the results can be generalized to the kinds of relational examples discussed earlier.

Grammar G_1 has the following structure. The set N_1 of nonterminal vocabulary consists of S, NP, VP, UQ, EQ, NQ, N, Cop, Adj, and Neg, each with its nearly classical grammatical meaning, for example, NP for noun phrase. Also the lexical production rules for function words are these: UQ $\rightarrow$ *All*, EQ $\rightarrow$ *Some*, NQ $\rightarrow$ *No*, Cop $\rightarrow$ *are*, Neg $\rightarrow$ *not*. The many lexical rules for N and Adj are left open, and so the set V of vocabulary is left unspecified but will be taken to be the same for both grammars considered.

The set P_1 of production rules, minus the lexical rules, is as follows, where the associated semantic function for each rule is also given, although the semantic functions for the three top-level rules are made explicitly Boolean later:

$$S \rightarrow \quad UQ + NP + VP \, / \, EQ + NP + VP \, / \, NQ + NP + VP$$
$$[S] = \quad [_\Im[NP] \subseteq [VP]] \, / \, [_\Im[NP] \cap [VP] \neq 0] \, / \, [_\Im[NP] \cap [VP] = 0]$$
$$NP \rightarrow \quad N$$
$$[NP] = \quad [N]$$
$$VP \rightarrow \quad Cop + N \, / \, Cop + Adj \, / \, Cop + Neg + N \, / \, Cop + Neg + Adj$$
$$[VP] = \quad [N] \, / \, [Adj] \, / \, \neg [N] \, / \, \neg [Adj]$$

(The slash "/" is used to present several rules that have the same nonterminal symbol on the left; thus there are eight rules given here.)

The grammar G_2 has the same nonterminal vocabulary as G_1, so $N_2 = N_1$, and, as already stated, the same terminal vocabulary. The production rules, however, are different, to reflect the different treatment of quantifiers. No semantic rules are shown for S and NP rules; rather, the possibilities are examined in the proof of the theorem. Because the semantics of the restricted verb phrases permitted by G_1 and G_2 are not at issue, the semantic rules are the same as for G_1. Thus, the set P_2 is specified as follows:

$$S \rightarrow NP + VP$$
$$NP \rightarrow UQ + N \mathbin{/} EQ + N \mathbin{/} NQ + N$$
$$VP \rightarrow Cop + N \mathbin{/} Cop + Adj \mathbin{/} Cop + Neg + N \mathbin{/} Cop + Neg + Adj$$
$$[VP] = [N] \mathbin{/} [Adj] \mathbin{/} \neg [N] \mathbin{/} \neg [Adj].$$

To state the desired theorem, some additional general concepts are needed.

A context-free grammar $G = (V,N,P,S)$ is *unambiguous* if and only if every terminal string in $L(G)$ has exactly one derivation tree (with respect to G). A context-free grammar $G' = (V',N',P',S')$ is a *conservative extension* of an unambiguous grammar $G = (V,N,P,S)$ if and only if (1) $V \subseteq V'$, $N \subseteq N'$, and $P \subseteq P'$ and (2) every terminal string in $L(G)$ has exactly one derivation tree with respect to G'. The concept of conservative extension is useful for showing why the conventional linguistic treatment of quantifiers leads to an unnecessary escalation of type semantically. A conservative extension of an unambiguous grammar does not open up a new route to avoid semantic escalation of type.

A model structure (D,v) of a grammar G is *Boolean* if and only if for any string s of V_T^+ for which v is defined, $v(s)$ is a subset of D. A potentially denoting context-free grammar G is *Boolean* if and only if for any Boolean model structure (D,v) of G, every semantic function of G has as its value a subset of D whenever its arguments are subsets of D. Making explicit the Boolean semantic functions that make G_1 Boolean is routine based on the examples given, and the details will not be repeated, but it is worth making explicit the Boolean formulation of the Frege function—rather functions, for we now have different Boolean functions for different top-level rules.[1] In particular, for grammar G_1, using mnemonically U for the universal quantifier function, E for the existential quantifier function, and N for the negative quantifier function, we have for any set A

$$U(A) = \begin{cases} D \text{ if } A = D \\ 0 \text{ if } A \neq D \end{cases}$$

$$E(A) = \begin{cases} D \text{ if } A \neq 0 \\ 0 \text{ if } A = 0 \end{cases}$$

$$N(A) = \begin{cases} D \text{ if } A = 0 \\ 0 \text{ if } A \neq 0. \end{cases}$$

---

[1] I am indebted to Barbara Partee for pointing out to me the need for a more explicit treatment of these matters than I gave in Suppes (1976).

Thus, explicitly, for the top-level rules of G_1

$$S \rightarrow \quad UQ + NP + VP$$
$$[S] = \quad U(\neg[NP] \cup [VP])$$
$$S \rightarrow \quad EQ + NP + VP$$
$$[S] = \quad E([NP] \cap [VP])$$
$$S \rightarrow \quad NQ + NP + VP$$
$$[S] = \quad N([NP] \cap [VP]).$$

It is important for later purposes to note that for a two-element Boolean algebra

$$U_2(A) = E_2(A) = A$$
and
$$N_2(A) = \neg A,$$

where the subscript has been introduced to denote the number of elements in the Boolean algebra. A Boolean grammar is *semantically correct* if and only if it has a semantically valid model theory of the syllogism. The theorem I want now to prove is a negative one about grammar G_2. I interpret the theorem as being a semantically based argument against the possibility of having both a standard linguistic parsing of quantifiers and an appropriately simple model theory of the syllogism.

THEOREM. *The grammar G_1 for the syllogism is Boolean and semantically correct. In contrast, neither grammar G_2 nor any of its conservative extensions can be both Boolean and semantically correct.*

PROOF. The proof for G_1 is obvious. I therefore give only the negative proof for G_2. To begin with, I shall assume that UQ and EQ do not have a denotation. Later it will be apparent that the same argument works when they do denote. Also, for the proof it is necessary to consider only two of the three quantifiers and so I omit any consideration of NQ.

In general, for the rule $NP \rightarrow UQ + N$ we have a semantic function f such that

$$[NP] = f([N]),$$

on the assumption already made that UQ does not denote. Similarly, for the rule $NP \rightarrow EQ + N$ we have a semantic function g such that

$$[NP] = g([N]).$$

It is required that these semantic functions be Boolean. There also must be a Boolean semantic function ϕ for the top-level rule $S \rightarrow NP + VP$. At this point we specialize to a two-element Boolean algebra to provide a simple counterexample to the semantic validity of G_2. We must then have for the universal quantifier

$$(1) \quad \phi([NP], [VP]) = \phi(f([N]),[VP]),$$

and so in the two-element model we must have the following results for the various possible values of [N] and [VP] in accordance with the standard semantics of A propositions:

$$(2) \begin{cases} \phi(f(0),0) = 1 \\ \phi(f(0),1) = 1 \\ \phi(f(1),0) = 0 \\ \phi(f(1),1) = 1, \end{cases}$$

and correspondingly we must have for I propositions:

$$(3) \begin{cases} \phi(g(0),0) = 0 \\ \phi(g(0),1) = 0 \\ \phi(g(1),0) = 0 \\ \phi(g(1),1) = 1. \end{cases}$$

We must show that the eight Boolean functional equations of (2) and (3) do not have a simultaneous solution, that is, there are no Boolean functions ϕ, f, and g that simultaneously satisfy these equations.

First, we note from the first and third equations of (2) that f cannot be a constant function, that is, we can have neither $f(0) = f(1) = 0$ nor $f(0) = f(1) = 1$. The second and fourth equations of (3) show that g also cannot be a constant function. Next, we note from the first equations of (2) and (3) that $f(0) \neq g(0)$, so f and g must have "opposite" values for the same argument. We are thus left with two possibilities: Either

$$(4) \quad f(0) = 0, f(1) = 1, g(0) = 1, g(1) = 0,$$

or

$$(5) \quad f(0) = 1, f(1) = 0, g(0) = 0, g(1) = 1.$$

Consider, first, (4). Then we must have:

$$\phi(f(0),0) = 1 = \phi(0,0)$$
$$\phi(g(1),0) = 0 = \phi(0,0).$$

which is a contradiction. The same kind of analysis shows (5) cannot lead to a solution, for we have:

$$\phi(f(0),0) = 1 = \phi(1,0)$$
$$\phi(g(1),0) = 0 = \phi(1,0).$$

The conceptual situation is not changed by permitting UQ and EQ to denote, for they would need to be constant denotations, and they could do no more than select functions f and g as just analyzed. Thus we conclude that G_2 cannot be both Boolean and semantically correct. This conclusion also clearly holds for its conservative extensions.

A quite different sort of application of variable-free semantics to prosodic variations of negation is given in Suppes (1979).

II. PROCEDURAL SEMANTICS

It is obvious to anyone that the kind of set-theoretical semantics described thus far in this chapter cannot hope to offer a direct psychological model of speech production or comprehension. I have recently outlined my approach to procedural semantics, which is meant to move a step toward a more psychologically realistic theory (Suppes, 1980). Without repeating the general themes of that paper here, I want to sketch how I currently view the problems of moving from a set-theoretical to a procedural version of the highly restricted fragment of language encompassed by grammar G_1. Certainly from a psychological standpoint this grammar is not really interesting because it is far too restricted in its range, but it can serve as a kind of toy example for the discussion of the problems of working out in partially satisfactory form a procedural approach.

What is Procedural Semantics?   Without giving a general definition or a systematic characterization of expected properties, I would like in an informal way to describe how I think about procedural semantics. The basic and fundamental psychological point is that, with rare exception, in applying a predicate to an object or judging that a relation holds between two or more objects, we do not consider properties or relations as sets. We do not even consider them as somehow simply intensional properties, but we have procedures that compute their values for the object in question. Thus, if someone tells me that an object in the distance is a cow, I have a perceptual and conceptual procedure for making computations on the input data that reach my peripheral sensory system, and as these data change with the shortening of the distance between the object and me, my computations change and I come to a firm view as to whether the object in question is indeed a cow. In the same way, if someone says to me that the sum of 653 and 742 is 1,395, I do not have an abstract, set-theoretical way of deriving the answer but an algorithmic procedure that I learned early in school, and that perhaps I have since modified to some degree but that in essence is similar to an algorithm taught throughout the world to children of about 8 to 10 years of age. Fregean and other accounts of number scarcely touch this psychological aspect of actually determining by application of a specific algorithmic procedure a truth claim about the sum of certain numbers. As a third example, if someone asks me: Have you ever been to Katmandu, I am able to make a very quick computation and respond almost immediately, "No." On the other hand, if I am asked whether I have ever been to Paris, I can with at least as great an ease compute a positive answer. These three examples certainly do not exhaust the range of computational procedures but they are typical cases, and a psychological theory of computation is required in order to give a serious account of how utterances or parts of utterances are processed either by speakers or by listeners.

In the paper mentioned earlier (Suppes, 1980), I try to give a somewhat detailed account in the final section of how to approach, from a procedural standpoint, the meaning and proof of declarative statements, commands, or questions about elementary arithmetic.

Properties as Abstractions of Procedures.   It has been a familiar point in philosophy since the last century that classes are abstractions of properties. The point relevant here is that properties stand in the same relation to procedures that classes stand to properties. For example, the property of a number being prime can be tested by quite different procedures, and among this indefinitely large number of procedures some will of course be much more efficient or faster than others. It is part of the thesis of the earlier paper on procedural semantics that I have mentioned to claim that the procedures used by each of us in talking and listening, or indeed in perceiving and moving about, are private and individually idiosyncratic. These private procedures are behind public talk about properties. Two of us can agree that a given object has the property of being heavy but we may compute this in quite different ways, for example, by comparison with different reference objects.

In general, intensional logic has made the move from classes to properties but not the additional move from properties to procedures. The line of attack for moving from classes to properties, in terms of the grammar G_1 and its associated semantics, is straightforward and scarcely needs detailed discussion here. I shall restrict myself to sketching one way of approaching this step. Each of the non-functional lexical items, that is, adjectives and nouns, as introduced by the unstated lexical rules of G_1, is represented by a set of properties, based upon some primitive list, perhaps. This list of properties, for example, the list of properties of cows or of numbers, is not something we always consciously know but is part of our psychological—in particular of our linguistic—development. Of course, there are immediate questions that arise about the list of properties that belong to a given adjective or noun. Is the list composed entirely of essential properties or are there also accidental properties? And under what formal operations do we think the list of properties is closed? In other words, what do we maintain is the algebra of properties? Once we start talking about closure properties of the algebra of properties, it is also easy to move away from a psychologically realistic model, just as it is unrealistic to believe that any logical consequence of our beliefs must also be a belief. On the other hand, some kinds of highly constructive closure properties seem natural and psychologically relatively acceptable. Thus, if an object that falls under some noun has two properties, we would ordinarily think of it as having the property consisting of the conjunction of these two properties.

When we are prepared to make an explicit commitment to the list of properties, then the logical structure of sentences and their relationships can be studied in a formal manner, a topic that is rather removed from a psychological model of speech. For example, when the property lists are explicit, then those universal propositions that are necessary are easily identified, namely, just those sentences generated by grammar G_1 for which the properties of the subject are a subset of the properties of the predicate.

The formal generalization of the semantics of Section I to properties is obvious: The denotations of individual lexical items are replaced by functions from possible worlds to subsets of each world in the standard manner of possible-world semantics, and the set-theoretic operations of combination as we move up the semantic tree of a sentence are modified accordingly. The totally unrealistic computational aspects of this procedure make it unreasonable to pursue further in the present context.

Procedures and Computations.   As we move from properties to procedures, the steps should be obvious. We replace the functions just described, which in turn replace the standard sets, by procedures, and the procedures are combined into a program in accordance with the structure given by the semantic trees considered earlier. But there is now another difficulty. What are the input data for the procedures, and is there more than one way to convert a semantic tree in the sense of Section I into a procedural tree? Both questions have answers that lead to difficulties.

Avoiding these difficulties for the moment, let me try to illustrate in a schematic way how procedural ideas might be developed from the simplest sort of example. Suppose that we are in a room with a fair number of objects and somebody asserts "Some balls are green." The sentence is uttered in such a context that it refers to balls in the room and not to balls elsewhere. We might describe in English the following program or procedure that tests for the truth or falsity of this sentence.

> Look at the first object on the left.
> Is it round? If yes, is it green?
> If yes, stop and answer "true."
> But if not round or not green, look for a next object.
> If there is a next object, proceed as before.
> If there is no next object, stop and answer "false."

Here the assumption is that the predicate *round* has an underlying procedure that provides an adequate test for an object being a ball in the present context, and also there is a perceptual procedure back of the color word *green* that tests whether an ordinary object in direct perception is green or not. Thus, in this example we need two lexical procedures, the one for *round* and the other for *green*. The program then provides a way of determining the truth or falsity of the statement "Some balls are green" in the context in which the statement is made.

This example illustrates several features of my current thinking about these matters. The most important idea is that there is no attempt to spell out a primitive machine language that the individual uses, for it is my claim that this machine language is private and unknowable. Moreover, there is no reason to introduce a technical language. It is very likely that the ordinary use of English is deeply intertwined for speakers of English with their private machine language, and it is better to use English than an artificial language for describing procedures because it is in this language that we give one another instruction on how to construct new procedures. Second, the program that I have written down is meant to be only an example of the way that the ideas are organized, and a given individual will not follow this exact setup, in accordance with my claim of privacy. Third, although English words are used extensively in the giving of instruction and in the putting together of new and more complex procedures from simpler ones, once a complex procedure is learned the English-labeled "subroutines" illustrated in the example are almost surely eliminated and a more efficient internal procedure is used without reference to the kinds of English phrasing I have used. Roughly speaking, this corresponds to compiling into machine language a procedure written in a high-level language in standard computer practice. Fourth, there are no procedures that we describe in English that are primitive. The primitive procedures are in a machine language we cannot get our hands on precisely, although we might make some naive guesses from psychophysiological studies. Thus, any sentence, no matter how simple, can be explained in words we as English-speaking adults already understand. The procedures that are called by English phrases can be used to interdefine appropriate procedures for one another. It is also apparent that I have not really specified a general constructive way in which the objects in the room are scanned. It is certainly an unnecessary convention to begin by looking at the first object on the left.

One thing is evident. In the case of sentences as simple and as qualitative in character as "Some balls are green," much of the computing required is called for by the procedures denoted by lexical substantives, *round* and *green* in the present instance. In other cases the computation can be a good deal more difficult just because of the complexity of the structure of the sentence. Another point is that I have presented the procedure as a linear program rather than as a procedural tree. Just as in the case of grammatical derivations for context-free grammars, there is a natural relation between linear programs and procedural trees, but I shall not pursue technical details here, which do need to be worked out. It seems likely that a realistic computational model of speech processing will be structurally more complex than either linear programs or semantic trees.

Procedures and Variable-Free Semantics.   Something needs to be said about the way in which the two main sections of this chapter are related. The variable-free set-theoretical semantics outlined in Section I is, in my view, a natural abstraction of the procedures sketched in Section II. The algebraic character of the semantics of Section I and the highly constructive character of the representations, due to the absence of variables, make a computational model already implicit in the formalism. Second, the set-theoretical semantics is meant to fit hand in glove with the structure of the English sentences, and this, too, accords well with the intertwining of the procedural approach I have described to the surface structure of English.

If I were willing to commit to a specific machine language, it would then be straightforward to prove some representations of procedures at an abstract level in terms of the set-theoretical semantics of Section I, but I have come to view such a commitment as a mistake. On the other hand, because of the complexity of working out details of the procedural approach, the greater abstraction and simplicity of the set-theoretical approach will continue to be of value as an intermediate step of analysis. However, I do want to insist on the point that it should be regarded as an intermediate step and not in any sense as providing a fully satisfactory theory of the semantics of language as actually used.

Procedures and Meaning.   This takes me to my final point. In the paper mentioned earlier (Suppes, 1980) I have defended the thesis that the meaning of a sentence is a procedure or a collection of procedures and that this meaning in its most concrete representation is wholly private and idiosyncratic to each individual.[2] This private representation is the most detailed sense of meaning. Thus, for example, the meaning of a proper name is a procedure—or, better yet, a private collection of procedures—that each of us uses in various contexts for recognizing the person or object denoted by the proper name. Public meaning is obtained by abstraction from the great variety of private meanings. Sufficiently coarse congruence relations take us all the way back to set-theoretical semantics. I have outlined the beginnings of a theory of congruence for set-theoretical semantics in Suppes (1973a), but a psychologically realistic theory of congruence that takes into account not only procedures but also intentions and emotional states of speakers and listeners is needed as part of any empirically satisfactory theory of communication.

REFERENCES

Hopcroft, J. E., & Ullman, J. D. 1969. *Formal languages and their relation to automata.* New York: Addison-Wesley.
Suppes, P. 1960. *Axiomatic set theory.* New York: Van Nostrand.
Suppes, P. 1973a. Congruence of meaning. *Proceedings and Addresses of the American Philosophical Association, 46:* 21–38.

---

[2] I hold a similar thesis about each individual's grammar.

Suppes, P. 1973b. Semantics of context-free fragments of natural languages. In *Approaches to natural language,* ed. K. J. J. Hintikka, J. M. E. Moravcsik, & P. Suppes. Dordrecht: Reidel.

Suppes, P. 1976. Elimination of quantifiers in the semantics of natural language by use of extended relation algebras. *Revue International de Philosophie, 117-118,* 243-259.

Suppes, P. 1979. Variable-free semantics for negations with prosodic variation. In *Essays in honour of Jaakko Hintikka,* ed. E. Saarinen, R. Hilpinen, I. Niiniluoto, & M. Provence Hintikka. Dordrecht: Reidel.

Suppes, P. 1980. Procedural semantics. In *Proceedings of the Fourth International Wittgenstein Symposium,* August 28-September 2, 1979, Kirchberg, Austria, ed. R. Haller & W. Grassl. Vienna: Hölder-Pichler-Tempsky.

Suppes, P., & Macken, E. Steps toward a variable-free semantics of attributive adjectives, possessives, and intensifying adverbs. In *Children's language* (Vol. 1), ed. K. E. Nelson. New York: Gardner Press, 1978.

3 Speaking of Imagination

Zeno Vendler
University of California, San Diego

It is important to know what one is talking about—and not just in philosophy. Thus when psychologists tell us things about knowledge and memory, when linguists expound their views on understanding, when computer scientists discuss simulations of reasoning and decision, we have the right to expect that they mean what we mean by these terms, unless they tell us otherwise. And even then, the original notions are at least presupposed, as a fixed frame of reference against which the conceptual deviation is to be assessed. But what do *we* mean by such terms? There has to be something in common between us, otherwise we would not understand each other even in our ordinary conversations, and, sometimes at least, we do.

The analysis of such key concepts, which are not the products of science but precede it, is the philosopher's task. And he is expected to produce no mere subjective impressions, but results of inter-subjective validity. Just like a scientist—one would like to say. But, alas, this poor "scientist" has no laboratory: no microscopes to view his concepts, no microtomes to cut them up, and no experiments to make them kick. Concepts, unlike crystals and bugs, are not subject to inspection—not even to introspection.

Yet the situation is not without hope. As we just said, we understand each other; moreover, children and foreigners are able to learn the words expressing these concepts. Thus there must be some restrictions on the use of the word to fit the concept, to make the word a suitable means to express it. The phonetic shape is quite useless in this respect; the grammar, including selection restrictions, begins the story.

In the following I offer an example of how such a story might go. The subject

35

is a neglected child in the domain of philosophical analysis: the notion of the imagination.

We are looking down upon the ocean from a cliff. The water is rough and cold, yet there are some swimmers riding the waves. "Just imagine swimming in that water" says my friend, and I know what to do. "Brr!" I say as I imagine the cold, the salty taste, the tug of the current, and so forth. Had he said "Just imagine yourself swimming in that water," I could comply in another way too: by picturing myself being tossed about, a scrawny body bobbing up and down in the foamy waste. In this case, I do not have to leave the cliff in the imagination: I may see myself, if I so choose, from the very same perspective. Not so in the previous case: if I indeed imagine being in the water, then I may see the cliff above me, but not myself from it.

I shall call the act of imagination involved in the first exercise subjective, and the one in the second objective. As the swimming example shows, the second kind consists in the inner representation (see Pribram, this volume) of one's body (or voice) from a certain perspective. This task is no different from the representation of other bodies; after all I can imagine you floating in the ocean with equal ease. The other kind does not call for the representation of my body from a distinct point of view, it merely consists in the representation of the experiences I would have if I were in some situation or other. To put it another way: In the objective case I fancy to see (or hear) what *I* would look (or sound) like in a given situation, whereas in the subjective case I fancy to experience what *it* would be like to be in such a situation.

In order to familiarize yourself with this distinction, imagine eating a lemon (sour taste), and then imagine yourself eating a lemon (pinched face); imagine being on the rack (agony), and then yourself being on the rack (distorted limbs); imagine whistling in the dark (sensation of puckered lips), and then yourself whistling in the dark (distance uncertain, but coming closer); and so forth.

Consider once more the two injunctions we mentioned at the beginning:

(1) Imagine swimming in that water.

(2) Imagine yourself swimming in that water.

I have suggested that (1) demands the subjective reading, but (2) requires, or at least permits, the objective. Yet the two sentences differ only in the word *yourself*. Moreover, one might argue, this difference is no difference, since the verb-complements in both (1) and (2) are derived from the same sentence in the deep-structure, to wit:

(3) You (are) swim(ming) in that water.

This suggestion is supported by the intuition that in both cases it is the subject's own swimming that is the object of his imagination. This is obvious in (2), since the reflexive marker, *self*, is affixed to *you*, which indicates the identity of the imaginer and the swimmer. It is true, of course, that *you*, the subject of *imagine*, is missing from (2), but this is a standard feature of the imperative; think of

Shave yourself! Notice, moreover, that even *yourself* can be omitted without much loss; *Shave!* normally means shave yourself. So it is possible to argue that in (1) too, not only the *you* before *imagine,* but *yourself* after *imagine,* are omitted on the surface. This line of argument is strengthened by the fact that in the sentence

Imagine shaving yourself.

the *self* indicates the suppressed presence of *you* as the subject of *shave.* For that *self* cannot reflect the *you* belonging to *imagine,* because in that case the following sentence would be grammatical:

*Imagine him shaving yourself.

Which it is not.

Yet these arguments cannot be right. (1) and (2) do require (or allow for) different readings, therefore, if linguists are right, they cannot have the same underlying structure. And this can be shown by a more obvious proof as well. *Imagine* in (2) can be replaced by the verb *picture* without loss of meaning or grammaticality:

Picture yourself swimming in that water.

A similar substitution spoils (1):

*Picture swimming in that water.

It follows, therefore, that the two verb-complements:

. . . swimming in that water

. . . yourself swimming in that water

have different verb-demands, consequently the verb *imagine* must figure differently in (1) and (2). And, of course, it does: As we explained before, (2) calls for an objective representation, a picturing in this particular case, but (1) does not.

It seems, therefore, that (3) correctly represents the source of *yourself swimming in that water* in (2). This accounts for the fact that the subject of *swim* can be raised out of similar sentences in such emphatic forms as

It is myself (and not you) that I imagined swimming in
that water.

Sentences like (1), on the other hand yield the following emphatic version:

It is swimming (and not wading) that I imagined doing in
that water.

The emergence of *do* after *imagine* is very revealing. In complying with (1) you imagine doing something, in complying with (2) you imagine yourself (or, in other cases, somebody else) doing something.

In the light of this difference, it is not too difficult to account for the structure of (1). There are groups of aspectual verbs that show the same behavior as the subjective *imagine.* I have in mind *start, stop, continue* and *resume* on the one hand, and *appear* and *seem* (to be) on the other. Consider the following sentences:

He started running.
He resumed talking to the crowd.
She appeared to be floating over the water.
and so forth. Then notice that these verbs also behave like the subjective *imagine,* when followed by a reflexive construction:
He started shaving himself.
She appeared to be hitting herself.
Obviously, the subject of *shave* is *he* and the subject of *hit* is *she,* notwithstanding the intervening aspectual verbs, *start* and *appear.* Even the emphatic forms follow suit nicely:
It is shaving himself that he started doing.
It is floating over the water that she appeared to be doing.
Let us assume, then, that the verb *imagine,* at least sometimes, functions as an aspectual verb. Accordingly, the subject of *swim* in (1) is *you,* and the verb *imagine* is nothing but an aspectual modifier of *swim.* In the following discussion I am going to show that this hypothesis is an illuminating and fertile one.

First of all, inspired by the spirit of Ockham's famous dictum, we may ask the question whether there are indeed two senses of the verb *imagine,* i.e. the subjective and the objective, or can we get by with the subjective one alone, with which we have just learned to cope? Is there a way, in other words, to reduce objective occurrences to subjective ones? Compare, once more, (1) and (2). How can we derive something like (2) from something like (1)? Well, what, exactly, does (1) call for? Earlier, we said this: It calls for "the representation of the experiences I would have if I were in a certain situation," in the water that is, in that case. What are these experiences? We mentioned feeling cold, tasting salt, and seeing the cliff above. This last one holds the key to the magic box. Because, for sure, imagining being in some situation or other involves not merely fancying tactual, muscular, or kinesthetic sensations, but auditory and visual ones as well. Consequently imagining myself swimming in that water, or imagining you running on the field, can be understood in terms of imagining seeing myself swimming in that water, and imagining seeing you running on the field. And what about imagining you (or myself) whistling in the dark? Obviously, what this means is imagining hearing your (or myself) whistling in the dark. If this is true, then (2) is nothing but an elliptical product of
Imagine seeing yourself swimming in that water.
Seeing simply drops out by the familiar process of removing redundancy.

In some cases, however, the deletion of the perceptual verb might lead to ambiguity, which may be resolved by supplying the omitted verb. Suppose you tell me "Imagine Rubinstein playing this piece." "Yes, I see him sitting straight, his fingers running over the keyboard." "No, that is not what I mean; imagine hearing him play it on the radio."

Deletions of the same kind often occur with some of the other aspectual verbs mentioned above. For example:

Tolstoy started *War and Peace* in 1865.

The crew finished the road two weeks ago.

It is clear that what Tolstoy started was *writing War and Peace* and what the crew did was to finish *building* the road. Even ambiguities can occur, for the same reason as with *imagine*. If I say

I started *War and Peace* two weeks ago

people who are familiar with literature will understand that, unlike Tolstoy, I started reading, and not writing, *War and Peace*.

The suppressed presence of the perceptual verb (mainly *see* or *hear*) can also be demonstrated by the manner-adverbs such sentences can take. Consider the following examples:

Imagine the battlefield from above.

Imagine this statue sideways.

Imagine the music coming from a distance.

It is clear that what is meant here is seeing the battlefield from above, the statue from the side, and hearing the music coming from a distance. For, if these adverbs were to modify the verb *imagine* itself, rather than the deleted perceptual verbs, then nothing would prevent the formation of such sentences as

*Imagine a thunderbolt from the side.

*Imagine the taste of lemons from above.

The verb *imagine* can indeed take adverbs on its own. The most notable one is *vividly*. And, notice, *vividly* does go with *imagine* regardless of the kind of perception involved. One can imagine vividly the battlefield, the thunderbolt, the taste of lemons, and what not.

It is particularly important to realize that the element of perspective involved in visual and auditory phantasy is due to the perspective nature of vision, and, to a lesser extent, of hearing. These senses, unlike, say, taste and smell, are eminently "objective" in the etymological sense of the word. They put the perceiver in a spatial relation to the object (see Boden, this volume). Hence one can see, and imagine seeing, a lion *coming* towards one, a building *towering above* one, and one can hear, and imagine hearing, the church-bells *far-away*, the sound of the train *coming close*, or *fading away in the distance*.

It will be objected that the verb *picture*, which we could substitute for *imagine* in (2), does not tolerate the addition of a perceptual verb. We do not have, for instance.

*Picture seeing John in the water.

This fact can be explained by the assumption that this use of *picture* simply amounts to *imagine seeing*. If so, then it is not surprising to find that *picture* is out of place with auditory phantasy, e.g.,

*Picture a thunderbolt.

and with the subjective imagining of (1):

*Picture swimming in the water.

Picture, therefore, is a real verb, albeit with an aspectual element added. Not so *fancy.* It is a near synonym to *imagine,* as can be shown by the possibility of such sentences as

Just fancy driving that car.

Fancy hearing Caruso singing that aria.

Finally, one might ask the question whether it is indeed *see,* rather than *look at,* which is the perceptual verb deleted from the sentences calling for or report- ing feats of visual imagination. By using the appropriate adverb test, we can show that *look at* would hardly fit. Typical adverbs to *look at* are *intently, carefully, from left to right,* and the like. Indeed, one can imagine looking at the Escorial intently, carefully and from left to right. Nothing surprising in this, since looking, like swimming and shaving, is an action one can imagine doing. The point is, however, that the adverbs alone won't do; the sentences;:

Imagine the battlefield intently.

Imagine the Escorial from left to right.

are marginal at best. Thus whereas there is nothing wrong with imagining the Escorial from above, since one can see the Escorial from above, there is some- thing funny about imagining the Escorial from left to right, because there is something funny about seeing the Escorial from left to right. It appears, then, that *imagining the Escorial* comes from *imagining seeing the Escorial* rather than *imagining looking at the Escorial.*

What can you imagine? I shall start out with considering the feats of imagina- tion that we called subjective. These, as we remember, consist in imagining doing something or being in some situation or condition: We mentioned swim- ming, walking, looking at something, being in the water, and, of course, seeing, hearing, etc. Will any action do? Obviously not. We cannot imagine, for in- stance, thinking about something, remembering the past, realizing that some- thing is the case, and, interestingly enough, one cannot imagine imagining some- thing. Furthermore, one cannot imagine being sound asleep, or being dead. Can one imagine having purple eyes? Not directly; the closest one can get to it is imagining seeing oneself in a mirror, or, objectively, from a detached point of view, with purple eyes. What about imagining being tall? This is an interesting case, since being tall has all sorts of consequences for the quality of one's experience: looking down on other people, seeing better in the cinema, and the like. What these examples show is that the necessary condition for imagining performing certain actions, or being in certain conditions, is the existence of an experiential content attached to these things. It must make sense, in other words, to ask the question: What would it be like doing such a thing, or being in such a state. One can imagine being dead only if one assumes, falsely I think, that being dead is compatible with, and is characterizable by, having certain experiences. Thus it is possible to imagine being blind, deaf, numb, etc., but not being without any perceptions at all, which would be required to imagine being really dead, or sound asleep.

Once this condition is satisfied, the sway of imagination knows no boundaries: One can try to imagine being a king, a beggar, a cripple, a child, or a cat. Not even the limits of personal identity are observed: in reading history or fiction, we find ourselves imagining being Caesar, Napoleon, Hamlet, or even being Napoleon at the battle of Waterloo, and so forth. What is impossible is to imagine being a thing with no experience: a stone, or a coffee-pot. "But pots often talk in fairy-tales" you say. True, I answer, but look at the picture: The pot has eyes and ears. . . . The limits of imagination are the limits of experience, and to say that some individual is a subject of experience is to allow for the possibility of imagining being that individual. In other words, subjective imagination is the only way to represent a conscious being, a subject of experience, as such.

Is it possible for me to imagine doing exactly the thing I am currently doing, or being in the very state in which I actually am? The answer is clearly no: The actual experience preempts the vicarious one. Nothing prevents, of course, the corresponding objective exercise: The fashion-model walking down the aisle is intensely conscious of what she must look like from various angles; she sees herself, with the mind's eye, walking down the aisle, while walking down the aisle.

We just said that actual experience can preempt the vicarious one. It is also true that the actual exercise of the bodily senses often interferes with the exercise of the imagination. One is likely to close one's eyes to allow the mind's eye to do its job, and it is quite hard to imagine listening to a Chopin nocturne while being exposed to a full blast of hard rock. Common experience further shows that vivid imaginings are able to produce the same psychological, or even physiological reactions as their real counterparts. Imagining eating tasty food, or lemons, produces salivation, and the lecher's dirty mind is aimed at providing vicarious *delectatio morosa*. It seems, therefore, that from a phenomenological point of view there is no specific difference between real experiences and imaginary ones. There is, presumably, a difference in intensity, and, of course, the more important fact that the exercise of the imagination does not involve conscious use of the sense organs: One does not have to look to see, listen to hear, touch to feel, and so on. It is reasonable to assume, however, that at least the same functions of the central nervous system are being activated in either case: by sensory input in the one, and by some inner stimulus, often sheer "will," whatever it is, in the other.

We may remember that the imagination we earlier called objective is mediated by the data of such objective perceptions as sight and hearing. To imagine an elephant is to imagine seeing an elephant, and to imagine a thunderbolt is to imagine hearing a thunderbolt. This fact imposes an obvious restriction on the domain of things that can be thus imagined. As the practice of subjective imagination is confined to actions and states with experiential content, so the exercise of objective imagination is restricted to the representation of objects with visual, auditory, or otherwise sensory aspects. For this reason one cannot imagine numbers, classes, human rights or moral virtues. Thus not everything that exists, or is logically possible, is imaginable. Even the "pure" imagination, often evoked in geometry, is but an abstraction. You know that the straight line touches the circle at one point only in the plane, you know that the chiliagon has one thousand sides, you know that the hyperbola meets its asymptotes in infinity, and then you try to sharpen your mental vision by "zooming on," as it were, to reveal finer and finer details . . . till you stop. And as you do not need eyes to imagine, you do not need microscopes to see the minutiae: Whatever can be seen (heard, felt, etc.) can be imagined. But no more. As the limits of subjective experience are the limits of subjective imagination, so the domain of objective imagination exhausts the world of possible experience.

The verb *to imagine* is often used in a way which does not fit into the pattern sketched thus far. Consider the following occurrences:

Can you imagine what would have happened if Goldwater had been elected president?

Imagine we had found life on Mars.

Imagine that there is life outside the Solar System.

It is immediately obvious that these sentences do not evoke the "vicarious experience" of sensory imagination; what they do call for is an exercise of reasoning: to think of the consequences or implications of certain possible states of affairs. Accordingly, there is no way of inserting a perceptual verb after *imagine* in these examples. *Imagine there is life out there* does not mean *Imagine seeing there is life out there*. For this reason, the typically perspectival aspect of sensory imagination is absent too: What would it be like to imagine Goldwater's having been elected from above, sideways or from a distance? Even the characteristic adverb, *vividly,* fares ill in these contexts. Many things would have happened if Goldwater had been elected. Now which of these things do you imagine vividly when you imagine what would happen in that case? *Imagine,* therefore, does not function here as an aspectual verb, but rather as a propositional verb on its own, semantically quite similar to *suppose, think of, consider the possibility,* etc.

There is nothing surprising in such an extended employment of *imagine*. It is well known that many straight perceptual verbs, particularly *see, hear* and *feel* have similar propositional uses. "Now I see that you are right"; "You lost your job, I hear"; "He agreed, but I felt otherwise"; and so forth. Now since the primary sense of *imagine* is tied to the primary senses of perceptual verbs, it is quite natural to see it follow them into the propositional domain. Consider the following exchange in which the propositional *see* matches the propositional *imagine:* "Imagine what would have happened if Goldwater had been president"; "I can pretty well see what would have happened. . . ."

This, then, is how a conceptual story might begin and proceed. Needless to say, it is not the whole story, nor the only possible beginning. Philosophers themselves may disagree, and offer alternatives. In doing so, however, they have to give reasons for their dissent, and these will be of the same kind as the ones I collected. But even when (or if . . .) they are through with the notion, the story is by no means over: It is up to the scientists to complete it. How, for example, imagination is realized in the human organism, what laws govern its employment, and so forth, are questions beyond the domain of philosophy, to be answered by the various sciences. It may even happen that the scientific view thus emerging will have an effect on our common notions and common speech. So be it, it has happened before. "Ordinary language is *not* the last word: in principle it can everywhere be supplemented and improved upon and superseded. Only remember, it *is* the first word" (Austin, 1961, p. 133).

ACKNOWLEDGMENT

This chapter incorporates part of my article, "Vicarious Experience," which appeared in the *Revue de Métaphysique et de Morale* (No. 2, 1979), and is here reprinted with the permission of the editors of that journal.

REFERENCE

Austin, J. L. 1961. A plea for excuses. In *Philosophical papers* (Ed.) J. O. Urmson & G. J. Warnock. Oxford: Clarendon.

4 Artificial Intelligence and Semantic Theory

Martin Ringle
Computer Science Department
Vassar College

TWO APPROACHES TO SEMANTICS

A theory of semantics, in the broadest sense, explains how a set of symbols may be said to represent a particular "meaning." The semantics of an artificial or formal language generally consists of a set of interpretation relations for mapping a symbol string onto a particular state of affairs which holds within an explicitly defined domain. The meaning of a symbol string of a formal language, therefore, is defined in terms of the truth conditions for reference to a state of affairs.

Success in the area of formal language has led some philosophers and linguists to attempt to build a similar theory of semantics for natural language. In essence, such a theory presupposes that the meaning of ordinary language terms and sentences can be given by eliciting the mapping(s) between words and the world. This mapping would involve a discrete, two-place relation between linguistic symbols and states-of-affairs and should, therefore, be susceptible to finite computation.

The problem with this approach is that the domain of "states-of-affairs" in the world seems to be inherently open-textured with respect to natural language. What counts as a state-of-affairs seems to depend crucially upon the constraints placed upon reality by a conscious agent and the linguistic interactions of a community of such agents. The meaning of any symbol string in natural language, therefore, involves an intentionalist perspective as well as a symbol string and a set of external, physical conditions. The meaning relation is a triadic one among symbol, intentional framework, and target domain.

Given this fact, we have (at least) two choices for the development of a semantic theory for natural language: (1) We can attempt to assimilate the factors

45

present in the intentional framework to the "state-of-affairs" repertoire of the target domain and continue the attempt to develop a general word-to-world mapping for natural language; or (2) we can try to develop a procedural model of semantic interpretation whereby a mechanism (program) for identifying contextual elements is substituted for a static description of all possible intentional states and their relationship(s) to words and states-of-affairs in the external world. The research strategy of artificial intelligence (AI), in the area of natural language processing, has focused mainly on the second alternative.

It might be said that the two alternatives actually address two rather different sorts of questions. We might state the differences as follows:

1. What does a particular symbol string mean in a given language?
2. What does a particular linguistic agent mean by using a symbol string of a given language?

In (1) we seem to be interested in a question of semantic interpretability, a proper question for semantic theory; in (2) we seem to be concerned with a psychological question of language *use,* that is linguistic production and comprehension. Some philosophers and linguists, such as Fodor (1978) have argued that the two questions belong to separate lines of inquiry, though they are related insofar as the psychological question presupposes that a solution to the first question is, in principle, attainable. Put another way, we must assume that there is an explanation of how words in general have meaning if we are to explore the question of how people can manipulate those meanings in order to communicate. Fodor, as a spokesman for a substantial part of a formalist tradition in linguistics and philosophy of language, contends that whatever AI seeks to do in the area of natural language processing will have no direct bearing on a theory of semantics per se; at best it will shed some light on the mechanics of language production and comprehension (though even there he is somewhat skeptical). His primary reason for saying this is that he sees nothing within the programming approach of AI that will either advance our understanding of semantic interpretability as a matter of mapping (from a lexicon to a world domain) or will replace it with something more enlightening.

AI workers such as Wilks (1976), on the other hand, take the position that elements of linguistic, intentional, and perceptual context are critical to the very notion of "semantic interpretation," that they cannot effectively be omitted from a semantic theory, and that a dynamic (i.e., programmatic) approach is appropriate if we are dealing with genuine natural language rather than some attenuated abstraction. In effect, then, the so-called psychological question of language use cannot (or, minimally, *need not*) be separated from the general question of the nature of a semantic theory. The mechanisms employed at the individual level by an agent in the process of producing or comprehending language, must be taken into account and generalized as part of the explanation of semantic interpretability at the theoretical level. The overall thesis may be stated thus: Apart from context, words have no meaning and without dynamic processes, context can neither be discerned nor utilized. An explanation of how words have meaning, therefore, must include an account of how human beings detect and inject context into their writing, discourse, and other linguistic activities.

This is the position I would like to explore in this chapter. The pivotal question to consider is whether or not the computational approach of AI has anything new to say about the problem of semantic interpretation.

PROCEDURAL SEMANTICS

In his paper on procedural semantics, Johnson-Laird (1977) enunciates a viewpoint that has enjoyed considerable commerce in AI discussions for the past ten years or so. He focuses on the fact that there is a rather straightforward analogy between the syntax/semantics analysis in natural language and the compile/execute dichotomy in computer science. According to traditional linguistic theories such as Chomsky's (1965) semantic interpretation involves the selection of appropriate "readings" of a sentence after the deep structure phrase marker has been generated from the surface structure. In contemporary computer systems, an instruction is input in a high-level language, such as FORTRAN or COBOL; it then becomes translated or "interpreted" by a program known as a *compiler* into a machine language instruction, which may then be executed. The execution of a machine level instruction is frequently referred to as the "semantic interpretation" of the high level statement in the user language. It is, as it were, the domain to which a symbol string may be mapped and for which appropriate truth and reference conditions may be specified.

Johnson-Laird suggests that we may view semantic interpretation in humans (for natural language) along the same lines as we view it in computers. English sentences (for example) would be compiled (or translated) into the "machine level" language of the brain and the execution of the subsequent procedures would constitute the "semantic interpretation" of the initial input. (During language production, the process would simply be reversed.)

Fodor happily concedes that it makes sense to speak about the execution of machine level instructions as semantic interpretations for programming languages, but he sees no reason to believe that internal processing configurations can shed light on the semantic interpretation of natural language terms. Presumably, the meaning of a word like "grandmother" or a sentence like "This is my grandmother" has to do with states-of-affairs in the world—not states-of-affairs in people's brains (much less in their digital computers). A programming language term like "GOTO," on the other hand, does have to do with a specific configuration of internal machine states, hence we can talk about the execution of the routine that produces those states as the semantic interpretation of the term.

Perhaps, though, we can add something to the notion of "internal state" that will make it easier for us to connect it to semantic interpretation in natural language. Suppose that we provide a computer with various sensory devices so that it assumes internal states that correspond to different states-of-affairs in the world. Thus, it will assume a unique internal state when presented with a spherical solid at its visual receptor. We might then go on to create a link between this internal state and another internal state that is produced whenever the word "ball" is being processed. By appropriately associating the two internal states we can insure that the procedure executed when the high level term "ball" is being processed is causally attached to the sensed properties of balls in the world.

The problem with this approach, as Fodor correctly observes, is that it drastically oversimplifies both the nature of the world (by reducing it to a set of determinate, integrated, sense data) and the nature of natural language (by restricting words and sentences to unambiguous nominals for concrete objects). The deficiency of this approach may be further clarified by citing an example Dreyfus (1979) uses in his critique of Winston's "concept learning program." Winston (1970) devised a program to demonstrate how the concept of an "arch" could be developed algorithmically in a computer by successive refinements of object and relation descriptions. A descriptive feature list, including such things as the position, orientation, and support-relation of brick- and wedge-shaped solids, is input to the program along with a determination of whether or not the feature list is indicative of an arch or a "near-miss." The program augments or refines its internal feature list for arches by deducing whether newly input features are required or prohibited for arches. (The selection of the input feature list is done by the programmer/operator but it could, in fact, be done by a visual pattern recognition program of the sort written by Waltz, 1975.)

Dreyfus' point is that the meaning of the term "arch" is immeasurably richer than the feature list of sense-data properties that Winston uses to identify arches. There will be cases where the features are absent (e.g., a rainbow), yet we would be correct in using the term, and there are cases where the features would be present (e.g., in a chromosomal configuration) where we would be reluctant to apply the term. Dreyfus argues that the meaning of even a relatively "simple" term like "arch" involves knowledge of how arches come to exist, what they are typically used for, where one ordinarily finds them, and so forth. Even if perceptual features are relevant, he avers, they are not exclusively determinate of arches nor are they immune from significant variation (as in the case of rainbows and masonry arches).

If Dreyfus' observation is valid for concrete nouns like "arch" it is even more so for abstract nouns, adjectives, and especially for verbs. The meaning(s) of action words are infinitely less tractable to feature list descriptions in terms of sense-data than the meaning(s) of nominals.

What then are we to make of the notion that execution of machine level code can count as semantic interpretation for natural language terms? Fodor concludes that, at best, we have succeeded in moving the question of interpretation from one level of organization to a lower level, but that we have not answered it. Even if, he argues, we can map high level terms (as high as natural language words, if you wish) onto machine level states, we have still shed no light on the problem of identifying the semantic content of those words (or associated states) and we have no new clues to help us unravel the nature of synonymity, paraphrase, anomalousness, etc. If this is all that is meant by "procedural semantics" then, indeed, we have not advanced beyond traditional interpretive semantics. But perhaps there is more to it than this.

One popular use of the term "procedural" in natural language processing occurs as a contrastive term for "declarative." This is *not* a use which is relevant to the present concern, but it is worth mentioning it briefly in order to avoid potential confusions.

Winograd (1975) repeatedly draws attention to the fact that many action words in his processor do not have static representations in a "semantic marker" type of lexicon; rather, the action words when compiled, serve as function headers and invoke specialized sub-routines. Thus a word like "hold" will not appear in a data structure accompanied by semantic and syntactic markers; instead it will be the name of a sub-routine that will then explore the other parts of the sentence in which the word occurs to locate nominals that are required for the (potential) execution of an act (of "holding"). This, of course, has interesting implications for linguistic theory since it suggests that the meanings of some words involve procedures, rather than descriptions or definitions, and that an understanding of the meaning of such words entails dispositions to behave, rather than conceptual knowledge of some sort.

Of course, this is anything but new in the philosophy of language. The perspective taken here is little different from the traditional *operationalist* approach to meaning espoused by numerous philosophical schools as well as the majority of behaviorists in the Skinnerian tradition. Whether one accepts this view or not is irrelevant to the question of the nature of a semantic theory. Proceduralism (or operationalism) in this sense has to do with *what* words mean, not *how* words can have meaning. The two questions cannot be (validly) conflated unless we are willing to take the position that *all* words are susceptible to operationalist analysis and I think there are few today who would wish to take this as a serious possibility.

If procedural semantics is not simply the execution of machine level instructions transparently linked to sensory input configurations, nor the operationalist analysis of terms, then what else might it be? The answer is explicitly supplied by Johnson-Laird (1977):

> a lexical concept interrelates a word, rules governing its syntactic behaviour, and a schema. A schema is made up from both *functional* and perceptual information,

and may well include information that has *no direct perceptual consequences*. Moreover, lexical concepts are interrelated to one another. They are organized into semantic fields that have a *conceptual core* which reflects a deeper conceptualization of the world and integrates the different concepts with the semantic field. [p. 203; italics in the first two instances are mine.]

To unpack this, let us reconsider for a moment the traditional notion of "semantic interpretation" as it occurs in the interpretive theory of Fodor and Katz (1964). According to Katz the semantic component interprets a deep structure phrase marker by inserting readings from the lexicon for each item at the terminal nodes of the marker. Selectional restrictions prune the number of possible readings as the interpretation is carried up the branches of the marker, creating larger meaning structures in the ascent. At the root level, the interpretations are complete (although there may still be more than one possible reading, depending upon the inherent degree of ambiguity of the phrase). The crucial semantic information contained in the lexicon takes the form of semantic markers that identify concepts; the meaning of a word is completely given by its lexical set of such markers and the meaning of a phrase or sentence is uniformly constructed by the amalgamation of word meanings.

The problem with this account is that no accommodation is made for the role that context plays in the determination of phrase and sentence meaning. To some extent, different possibilities for speaker/listener intentions, perceptual environment, and state-of-the world descriptions are packed into the choice of semantic categories of the lexicon. Yet it is difficult to imagine a lexicon that could handle novel extensions of word meaning, as in the case of metaphor or neologism, by means of static semantic marker assignments. It is also doubtful that markers for state descriptions of the world (or perceptual conditions) could be assigned to anticipate the vast number of novel possibilities within which language use occurs. A lexicon for even a small subset of natural language (say, 50 words) would be astronomical in size if it included selectional restrictions that were sensitive to language users' intentions and possible states of the world.

Yet, if contextual elements do play a role in determining the meaning of a phrase or sentence, then they have to be included somehow in the account of semantic interpretation. Let us take a closer look at what Johnson-Laird is saying. A lexical concept (i.e., the semantic interpretation for a word) involves syntactic rules governing its compatibility with other words and a *schema*. A schema includes functional information, perceptual information, and information that may have no perceptual consequences. What can this mean? Let us try an example.

A concrete noun like "arch" involves some (perhaps an indefinite) set of perceptual properties, plus some (again a possibly indefinite set of) functional properties, plus some other things as well, such as knowledge about origins, dispositions to behave, etc. All of this information may be entailed by the word "arch" and different parts of it may be available at different times to be used to interpret the word "arch" in different contexts. We can include this information in our semantic component in two ways: Either we can specify every possible combination of intentional, perceptual, conceptual, etc., contextual properties for the term and then identify meaningful combinations via some set of selectional restrictions or we can define procedures that will be executed to detect and weigh intentional, perceptual, conceptual (etc.) properties and to define interpretations "on the fly" as it were.

In the case of the word "arch," this might mean something like the following. Suppose we consider this sentence:

1. The stellar *arch* marked the way to the New World.

In order to make sense of it from the point of view of an interpretive, i.e., compositional semantic theory, we would find the word "arch" in our lexicon, examine the different readings, and see which markers and restrictions would be compatible with those for neighboring words such as "stellar" in the noun phrase and, if that were successful, "mark(ed)" in the verb phrase.

It is unlikely, though, that our lexicon would be able to produce any coherent reading for "stellar arch" if we had a semantic marker analysis suitable to man-made arches or even natural occurrences like rainbows. Indeed, it takes a moment for one to realize that the phrase "stellar arch" means something like a "configuration of stars resembling a horseshoe." What permits us to generate this paraphrase, presumably, is our ability to take the information that we have about arches and the information that we have about stars and *synthesize* a meaningful semantic interpretation from the phrase. In this case, the synthesis might involve a piece of analogical reasoning based specifically on the perceptual (or possibly the behavioral) properties of stars and the perceptual properties of arches. In a sentence like:

2. His insurance policy formed an *arch* to protect him from an avalanche of lawsuits.

a similar inferential procedure might be undertaken to produce a semantic interpretation for the word "arch." In this case, however, the inference might focus on functional, rather than perceptual, properties.

Notice that we are not concerned here with a pragmatic question of linguistic comprehension or production for individual, idiosyncratic cases; we are talking about a generalizable procedure, involving inference, memory manipulation, etc., which is required for context identification in a broad range of cases. The two examples just cited illustrate the resolution of linguistic (or lexical) context, but, as we shall see in a moment, the same sort of argument may be applied to perceptual, situational, or intentional context elements as well. It must also be emphasized that, despite the fact that the examples appeal to senses of "arch" that are unusual or metaphorical, the claim is not restricted only to cases of metaphorical usage. I am presupposing that virtually all natural language use involves a high degree of flexibility, thus making the "normal use/metaphorical use" dichotomy really a matter of degree rather than categorical difference. (A discussion of this point lies far beyond the scope of this paper; for a defense of the position cf. Lakoff & Johnson, unpublished manuscript.)

This, then, is the meaning of "procedural semantics," which I believe that Johnson-Laird and others in artificial intelligence wish to espouse. It stands in contrast to compositional semantic theories that rely on static semantic interpretations taken from explicit, descriptive lexicons; it places great importance on the holistic role that context plays in the determination of phrase and sentence meaning, and it holds that context identification depends upon the execution of various procedures. Defining these procedures in terms of computer algorithms, thus, is the research strategy that AI follows for analyzing the nature of semantic interpretation.

We can explore the applicability of this procedural approach by looking at other cases where context identification plays a critical role in semantic interpretation.

HETEROGENEITY IN LEXICAL SCHEMATA

Consider the meaning of the word "address" in the following sentence:

3. Give me the *address*.

Unlike sentences (1) and (2) above, we have no prima facie reason to believe that the focal term is being used in an extended or metaphorical way. The sentence is ambiguous, however, because there are several possible readings for both "address" and "give." Alternate paraphrases such as the following are plausible:

3a. Hand me the speech.

3b. Recite the speech for me.

3c. Inform me of the location.

We might conclude that a traditional interpretive approach would pass all such interpretations along during processing and that disambiguation would occur as a result of the application of contextual knowledge that might be derived from other lexical cues or situational cues. Such contextual information might reside in a sort of "context lexicon" or a set of "context-detecting procedures" but, in either case, the interpretive component would be autonomous with respect to the mechanism for disambiguation. Put another way, complete semantic interpretability would be possible without appealing to context analysis; the role of context, in this model, would be to disambiguate, not to interpret.

However, suppose we complicate the example slightly by locating the sentence in two, rather different, situations:

4. John and Mary are seated next to one another in the living room, discussing the whereabouts of Jesse. Mary informs John that she has Jesse's new address written on a slip of paper in her purse. John says, "Give me the address."

5. John is in Boston, having a telephone conversation with Mary, who is in Seattle. They are discussing the whereabouts of their friend, Jesse, who has recently moved. Mary informs John that she has Jesse's new address written on a slip of paper in front of her. John says, "Give me the address."

A paraphrase of the occurrence of sentence (3) in case (4) might be (3c), namely, "Inform me of the location." It might, however, also be paraphrased as:

6. Hand me the slip of paper.

The occurrence of (3) in case (5) might also be paraphrased as in (3c), but it could not possibly be paraphrased as (6). More precisely, the term "address," might in case (4) be interpreted to mean "the slip of paper that bear's Jesse's address." The term "give," in that case, would be equivalent to "hand over." Such an interpretation would not be possible for case (5). In case (4) we do not find that a comprehensive set of readings is passed along to a separate context component for purposes of disambiguation; rather, we find that contextual information is instrumental in the production of the interpretation itself.

The point here is that the term "address" can assume interestingly different meanings in novel situations. Finding an appropriate semantic interpretation for the term requires us to actively apply context-detection and inference procedures to prototypical information that we have about lexical items. (Note that I am not advocating an elimination of the lexicon; I am, instead, suggesting that: (1) it should include prototypical (rather than categorical) markers, and (2) that it be integrated with context-detection procedures at a fundamental level.)

We may, at this point, raise three central questions: First, what kind(s) of information do we wish to store in our lexicon as "prototypical markers?" In terms of Johnson-Laird's account, what are the ingredients of the lexical schemata that form the conceptual core (reflecting a deeper conceptualization of the world)? Second, what are some of the contextual cues that play a vital role in semantic interpretation and what sorts of procedures may be used for detecting them? Third, how does current research in artificial intelligence (and natural language processing) bear on these problems?

In the lexicon of traditional semantic theories the "content" of a term is configured by a set of semantic markers, representing generalized concepts (such as "animate," "male," etc.) and a distinguisher (such as "never married" [in one reading of the term "bachelor," cf. Katz, 1966]). This approach falls short for two reasons: (1) It makes no provision for "borderline" usage of terms, since the semantic categories are determinate and discrete; (2) it is insensitive to the differences among taxonomic concepts, functional concepts, sensory concepts, and so forth. It is, in effect, a shorthand method for marshalling concrete properties into abstractive categories. It would appear, however, that human beings can refer to flexible representations of the concrete properties themselves, when determining the interpretation of a word. What I mean is this: A traditional semantic marker approach might store the information that the term "fire-engine" is catalogued with the concepts "red," "used for fighting fires," and so forth. A person, on the other hand, might have pointers from the term "fire-engine" to visual memory representations of the perceptual features of fire-engines and to event memory representations of fire-engines in action. Being able to access these sorts of memories, the person is able to *elicit* the categorization of "red" and "used to fight fires" but one might also elicit a host of other categorizations from the raw material of the memories. Borderline usage, under this model, becomes far more susceptible to explanation.

The information that may be accessed for the interpretation of a lexical item need not be homogeneous. In some cases, it would not even be appropriate to refer to what is stored as "information." Minimally, I would include the following types of properties as items that might be available in human semantic interpretation:

A. Perceptual properties of objects

B. Functional properties of objects and organizations

C. Physical and logical relations among objects

D. Properties of episodes and events

E. Dispositions to behave (of the subject or agent)

F. Qualitative aspects of sensation

G. Higher order properties of semantic conceptualizations

This list is not by any means exhaustive; it is intended only to demonstrate that the diversity of word uses may be matched by a similar diversity of ontological elements. The meaning of a term like "arch" (in its nominal sense(s), might not be analyzable in terms of perceptual properties alone, but a flexible combination of perceptual, functional and logical properties, together with perhaps the dispositions one might have towards behaving in the presence of the object, might provide us with a workable interpretation. This is not to say that a cross-listing of all of these properties will produce an unequivocal *definition* for the term "arch." Indeed, in this approach, definitions (which are abstractions) would have nothing to do with the problem of semantic interpretation. The ability for two people to effectively communicate by using the word "arch" would depend on their having access to stored property representations that were similar in many ways. Here, of course, we run into the problem of how "similarity" is to be judged and measured. How can we determine that the properties you use to interpret a word are the same or similar to the ones I use?

The answer to this question is long and difficult and a full treatment cannot be given in a paper of this size. Let me instead give the short reply: We presuppose that items such as perceptual properties, dispositions to behave, and qualitative aspects of sensation, are dependent upon the nature of our physiology and its causal connections with the environment. We assume, therefore, that having the same type of body will result in similar perceptions, action abilities, and qualitative sensory experiences. Likewise, we presuppose that conceptualizations are largely determined by culture-dependent processes, hence we assume that persons who share cultural backgrounds will share similar modes of conceptualization. These two suppositions, shared physical and shared cultural elements, provide us with the foundation for the belief that internalized properties are similar in human language users.

The variation that likely exists in stored properties from one individual to the next suggests that communication is always based on the *proximity* of semantic interpretation among individuals, not upon shared, univocal definitions. When physical or cultural variation goes beyond the norm, as in the case of a robot composed of solid-state circuitry, we assume that stored properties are *not* similar to our own and we withhold the belief that such an entity could give a semantic interpretation to a word or phrase comparable to that given by a human. (I believe that this is the justification for the argument made by Dreyfus, 1979, and Searle, 1980, that a protoplasmic body is a prerequisite for human *understanding;* Cf. also Ringle, 1980.)

We can follow the same line of argument when considering the semantic interpretation of words such as "pain." There have been attempts to assimilate the meaning of this term to operational features of pain (viz., pain behavior in the presence of certain observable stimuli), to dispositions to behave, to internal sensations, and to mere conventions of usage. None of these attempts have been successful. Identifying the meaning of the term with an internal state is unilluminating because we do not have access to one another's sensations. Identifying it with observable behavior alone is equally unilluminating because it overlooks the relevance of the felt experience totally. The most reasonable approach to such a word is to assume that it draws upon both behavioral (and perceptual) information, as well as felt experience (what I have referred to as "qualitative aspects of sensation"). Indeed, this permits us to speak about differences in what is meant by the term without thereby reducing the question of meaning to pure idiosyncrasy on the part of linguistic agents.

The relationship, moreover, between words and the stored property representations listed above, is most likely a nondeterministic one. That is to say, a pointer from a word to a property representation may be *weighted* in correspondence to the strength of the association. For some people, a word like "arch" may have heavily weighted pointers to perceptual properties, for others the greatest weighted pointers may lead to functional properties. By making the pointers nondeterministic, we can produce a model of semantic interpretation that will move quickly to "preferential" readings of a term, but will still be able to move away from those readings if they do not succeed in generating a workable interpretation. Thus, in the case of (2) above ("His insurance policy formed an arch to protect him from an avalanche of lawsuits.") one might be inclined to first consider, and then reject, the perceptual properties of arches as relevant to the meaning of the term. Exploration of the functional properties, on the other hand, would provide the information needed to make the analogical inference that an "arch" is something that a person may stand under to protect himself from falling objects. The remainder of the metaphorical interpretation of the sentence then follows without too much difficulty.

To return to the passage cited earlier from Johnson-Laird, the schema to which a word is linked may involve all of the types of information in the list of properties (given above) and perhaps other types as well. In addition, preferred properties may be marshalled at higher levels of representation to constitute semantic categorizations that would correspond roughly to our intuitions about canonical meanings (viz., definitions) of words. This, I believe, is what Johnson-Laird has in mind when he speaks of a *conceptual core* that reflects our deeper conceptualization of a word's meaning.

Let us turn our attention to the second question of the mechanisms that might be used to exploit this information in the determination of context.

DIMENSIONS OF CONTEXT

Each of the elements of the triad I have proposed as essential to a semantic theory, namely *words, world,* and *intentional agent(s),* has its own contextual constraints, which we may refer to as follows:

A. Linguistic Context

B. Situational Context

C. Intentional Context

Linguistic context refers to the constraints that words place upon each other in phrases and sentences; traditional interpretive semantics deals with this aspect of context via selectional restrictions. The difference here, between a descriptive and a procedural approach, is that the descriptive approach assumes that all possible semantic compatibilities (i.e., readings) can be predetermined on the basis of some finite set of semantic categories, while the procedural approach assumes that readings may be generated by such means as analogical inference from stored properties (e.g., the case of "stellar arch" described earlier). The contribution that artificial intelligence could make in this area is the development of programs for searching associative networks of stored properties in order to make proximity decisions that would produce coherent readings for phrases such as "stellar arch." First steps in this direction have already been taken by Russell (1976) and Gentner (1981) in their analyses of metaphor resolution. In both cases, the inference procedures are somewhat restricted, tending more towards slot-filling than open-textured analogical reasoning; nevertheless, their research points the way to the development of more flexible, generalized procedures that could operate effectively in a minimally structured relational database.

Traditional semantic theories have paid a great deal of attention to the question of "linguistic context" and have largely ignored the constraints placed upon interpretation by the situation in which the language occurrence arises. (For the most part, this question has been relegated to the domain of sociolinguistics.) Yet it seems evident that states of the world will have a great bearing on the possible interpretations of a lexical item (or a phrase). This is obviously the case for deictic terms such as "here," "now," etc., but it also seems to apply to non-deictic terms. Consider the following:

7. John and Mary are arguing. John wishes to shoot Peter (who happens to be Mary's lover). John says to Mary, "Don't stand in my *way!*"

What does the word "way" mean in the utterance? We cannot tell unless we know something more about the situation. Is Peter in the room? Does John have a gun? Is Mary able to physically position herself between John and Peter? If John is pointing the gun at Peter and Mary is standing between them, "way" will have a totally different meaning than it would if Peter is not in the room, or Mary is tied to a chair. In such a case, knowledge of the situation is crucial for obtaining the correct interpretation.

Can this sort of information, i.e., knowledge about the context in which an utterance (or a written statement) occurs, be codified in a descriptive fashion? I think the answer is no. Given the extraordinary variability of real-world situations, it seems far more plausible to suppose that we continually assimilate (via inference procedures) our current perceptual information to interpretive criteria. These criteria themselves may (perhaps *must*) be susceptible to some codification, but this is a question we have barely begun to explore. Many programs in natural language processing have, in the past, skirted this problem by artificially constraining the potential number of real-world situations through the expedient of micro-worlds (Cf. Winograd, 1972); it is likely that this approach will dominate AI for some time to come. Yet at least some researchers have started to explore the role of situational context in the acquisition of lexical concepts. Salveter (1979), for example, is developing a system that infers property representations (conceptualizations) for verbs based on successive "perceptual snap-shots," that is descriptions of action-states, which are associated with different verbs. Multiple presentations of "before-and-after" descriptions for an action (associated with a verb) help the system to infer generalizations about situational states of the world that delimit the interpretation of a verb. Presumably, the schemata developed during concept acquisition could later be applied to mechanisms for context detection (though this has not yet been attempted).

Clearly, the notion of *situational context* seems to have greater applicability to spoken than to written language. Spoken language is, after all, governed by space and time in a way in which written language is not. Yet it is illusory to imagine that written language is actually free of situational context. Written language is largely parasitic on situational conventions established in spoken language; these conventions are imported in written language either explicitly (as in the case of narrative) or implicitly (as in the case of letters or speeches). We should not be mesmerized by the apparent context-neutrality of written language into believing that it can be semantically interpreted apart from the situational presuppositions that we induce from it.

The third sort of context, *intentional context,* is in some ways the most interesting and yet least examined aspect of language. Wittgenstein based most of his later philosophy of language on this notion (1953) and Searle has done extensive work in speech act theory based on the presupposition that the beliefs and purposes of linguistic agents play a crucial role in the significance of utterances (Cf. Searle, 1959, 1976). In essence, the point is this: In order to obtain the correct semantic interpretation for a phrase (and the words of which it is composed) we have to make appropriate inferences about the beliefs and purposes of the linguistic agent who issued it. (Conversely, we assume that the production of meaningful utterances depends upon the selection of words and locutionary forms in response to underlying beliefs and purposes held by the speaker.) In the absence of the relevant beliefs and purposes we would not merely say that an utterance was ambiguous or vague; rather we would say that it was meaningless, in a special sort of way. For example, consider the following sentence:

8. I was lying to you.

If sentence (8) were uttered by an adult human we should have little trouble understanding it. If, on the other hand, it was uttered (or printed out) by a computer, we would be reluctant to view it as a meaningful locution at all. The reason is that we ordinarily understand the word "lie" (in this sense) to involve an intent to deceive by means of a false utterance that the speaker believes that the hearer will accept. In order to interpret the word "lie" we make certain presuppositions about the speaker's abilities to: (1) *want* to deceive; and (2) *believe* that uttering a certain phrase will create an erroneous belief in another linguistic agent. If we cannot legitimately ascribe these intentional elements to a speaker, then we cannot make sense out of a locution such as (8). A computer may output erroneous information to a user and later utter (or printout) a sentence such as (8). It might even be the case that, from our point of view, it was *reasonable* for the computer to "lie." (For example, the machine might give a false response to the question, "How can I cut your power supply?" thus giving the impression that the lie was told in self-defense.) Yet the impression of rationality in the verbal behavior, and the appearance of confessing to having "lied" can be no more than illusions, unless we are willing to ascribe to the machine the complex intentional states presupposed by (1) and (2) above.

Under ordinary circumstances, interpretation of the meaning of words and phrases involves implicit associations between locutionary forms and beliefs and purposes. Natural language is, after all, a phenomenon which is embedded in a larger fabric of human life and its structural features are in many ways tied to its functional roles. Whatever headway we may make in developing a semantic theory of natural language by focusing on linguistic and situational contexts will be limited by how far we can go in relating intentional (e.g., speech act) analysis to other levels of analysis.

Many philosophers of language, though willing to accept the theoretical relevance of intentional analysis to a semantic theory, have been reluctant to embrace the "use theory" of Wittgenstein or the speech act theory of Searle because they seemed to lack the right degree of precision, i.e., a degree of precision commensurate, say, with the algorithmic requirements of transformational generative theories. This lack of descriptive precision stems, in part, from the level of language used to couch intentionalist theories (namely, ordinary language) as well as the apparently intractable richness of the target phenomena. How could we begin to effectively map the number of possible intentional configurations onto the set of locutionary forms in order to produce a working "lexicon of intentional speech acts"? The answer is that we cannot. Hence, for the sake of completeness, the terms of intentional description have been confined to an extremely high, and therefore vague, level of analysis.

The procedural approach of artificial intelligence gives us a methodological boost here (and perhaps a theoretical one as well). While we may not be able to pre-specify all possible combinations of intentional attitudes, we can identify certain archetypical attitudes and then develop mechanisms for assimilating, by inference, perceived attitudes to those archetypical forms. An example of this approach, taken from current work in artificial intelligence, may help to clarify this point.

Much of natural language discourse involves speech acts whose lexical and syntactic structures obscure, rather than display, the illocutionary force of a sentence. Such "indirect speech acts" include, for example, the use of what appears to be a question for the purpose of making a request.

9. Can you reach the salt?

In (9) the implication may be drawn that the speaker wishes someone to pass the salt to him (or her), not that the speaker be told whether or not the other person can in fact reach the salt. Cases of this sort abound in ordinary language.

The correct interpretation of (9) depends on more than just an ability to produce a coherent (compositional) reading for the terms and a knowledge of the situational context (e.g., that the utterance occurs at the dinner table, that there is a salt shaker in the room, etc.). They require that we can make inferences about the wants (purposes) and beliefs of the speaker and the listener. We must assume, for example, that when people who are sitting at a dinner table ask whether or not other people can reach things like utensils, condiments, food, etc., they implicitly want to obtain those things. We are not, however, interested in the details of indirect speech acts in specialized domains (such as dinner tables) so much as we are in the general features of indirect speech acts.

In a recent study Brown (1979) reports on rules, derived from Searle's theory of speech acts, which may be implemented procedurally to identify indirect requests. We may illustrate the form and application of these rules by using the example sentence (9) above.

For each action that may be activated by a request, Brown constructs a *method* consisting of three main parts: a *header, argument specifications,* and a *procedural body.* The header identifies the action itself, the argument specifications indicate the semantic case requirements for the action to take place, and the procedural body specifies the prerequisites for the action, the algorithm for accomplishing the action, and the principal results of the action. (There is more involved in the notion of a method than this; for a fuller treatment Cf. Brown, 1979 and 1980.) A sample method is illustrated in Fig. 4.1.

If the direct speech act for a "pass object" request were somthing like (10) (following), then sentence (9) would be an instantiation of Rule 1. Sentence (11) (following) would likewise be an instantiation of Rule 2.

10. Pass me the salt.

11. I would like to have the salt.

By devising appropriate *methods* for different actions, and specifying prerequisites and principal results, we can identify requests (and the procedures to satisfy them) despite the fact that they may be couched in oblique locutionary forms. There are, however, two problems with this approach. First, we must recognize that the identification of an input sentence as an instance of a prerequisite or a principal result is itself problematic. Consider the following sentences:

12. Is the salt at your end of the table?

13. Do you see the salt?

In order for these sentences to be interpreted as indirect speech acts for a "REQUEST: PASS-moveable object" they must first be correctly categorized as "location of object" queries. This is not a trivial problem. Its solution, however, does exist (at least in part) in the work which Lehnert (1978) has done on the nature of question-answering. Not surprisingly, the identification of an utterance

PASS:	moveable object
OBJECT:	a moveable physical object
AGENT:	a human or robot
CO-AGENT:	a human or robot
PREREQUISITES:	the agent knows where the object is
	the agent can reach the object
PROCEDURE:	agent moves arm to object
	agent grasps object
	agent moves arm to co-agent
	co-agent grasps object/agent releases object
PRINCIPAL RESULT:	co-agent has object

Rules governing indirect speech acts for requests might be something like the following:

RULE 1:   Speaker may pose question to agent concerning the fulfillment of a state prerequisite in lieu of directly requesting the action.

RULE 2:   Speaker may state desire for principal result in lieu of directly requesting the action.

FIG. 4.1.   This diagram is adapted from Brown (1980) Figure 1. It simplifies and omits several items of information from the original, for the sake of clarity in the current exposition. For a complete illustration of a sample method, Cf. Brown 1980, pp. 83–84.

as e.g., a location-question, is accomplished via categorization and analogy inference procedures—another instance of a procedural approach to interpretation.

The second problem is that an undirected search through lists of prerequisites and principal results for different methods would be prohibitively large in an ordinary, natural language situation. This is especially true if we assume that prerequisites are identified at a fairly high level of resolution, requiring substantial processing of inputs for the purpose of identifying them as instances of specified prerequisites. The sequence, parse-interpret-disambiguate (by situational context)-perform speech act analysis, presents a processing picture that continually fans out towards a combinatorial explosion. We must introduce some type of constraints in order to make the account more plausible.

What we immediately notice, when we turn our attention to ordinary human language use, is that there is (usually) a high degree of expectation involving a speaker's intentions. Implicit in the application of the "PASS: moveable object" *method* is a context wherein an agent's motives may be either pre-defined or easily deduced. For example, at the dinner table, one expects that people will desire food, condiments, utensils, and so forth. When a sentence such as (9) is uttered, the hearer already has various expectations about the desires and beliefs of the speaker and can direct the parsing and interpretation of the input sentence to conform to those expectations. The intentional level analysis, rather than being the "last stage" of processing appears, in fact, to be the "first stage." That is to say, the interpretation of the input sentence is only partially data-driven; a large part of the interpretation emerges from preconceptions the hearer holds concerning the intentions of the speaker.

Brown's computational approach to speech acts presupposes rather than confronts the problem of how intentional contexts are originally identified. The intentional setting is, as it were, predefined before any analysis takes place. It may well be that the information which human beings ordinarily use to determine intentional context relies so heavily on prior knowledge and extra-linguistic cues that no "in vitro" language processing system will be able to capture the relevant mechanisms. While other systems (such as that of Perrault, Allen and Cohen, 1977) go a long way towards enunciating general principles for detecting speech act components from linguistic input, the problem of overall context identification has yet to be addressed.

Current approaches which emphasize speech act analysis are contrained by the assumption that intentional elements of dialogue participants can be stipulated independently for each speaker. As Streeck (1980) points out, however, intentional elements in ordinary human conversation are intricately intertwined and it is often impossible to specify the beliefs, purposes and plans of one speaker without reference to the other(s). The modeling of interactive intentional contexts—and the relationships between the contexts and the linguistic cues which can be used to detect them—are just now beginning to be explored.

Some current work in AI, such as the analysis of interacting plans undertaken by Bruce and Newman (1978) constitutes a first step towards unravelling the relationship between intention detection and utterance interpretation, but there is still a very long way to go. It does appear, however, following the research of Bruce and Newman, that the detection of intentions in others will depend crucially on a means of computing plans and sub-plans of actors in given situations. Once again, the procedural approach seems to be the most promising for arriving at a theory of human interpretive abilities.

If the work in natural language processing enables us to draw any conclusions at this stage they are these: first, that a comprehensive theory of the semantics of natural language is intricately bound up with questions of production and comprehension and that the roles played by situational and intentional context are essential to the delineation of a semantic theory as well as to a general theory of language use. Second, that the procedural perspective can enrich our understanding of how a nondeterministic system such as natural language can support successful communication between language users. Third, and last, that a full description of semantic interpretability depends on a thorough understanding of human intention and how it can be detected and processed during language use. Artificial Intelligence has provided the impetus for researchers in many disciplines to take these conclusions seriously and to direct their research accordingly. Whether or not the perspective will eventually enable us to produce an acceptable general theory of semantics remains to be seen.

ACKNOWLEDGMENTS

I would like to thank Hector-Neri Castaneda, Phil Cohen, Gretchen Brown, Kathleen Emmett, Wendy Lehnert, Candy Sidner, Ken Lucey and Ken Livingston for their comments on various drafts of this paper. Research for parts of the paper was supported by a National Endowment for the Humanities Summer Grant.

REFERENCES

Brown, G. 1979. Towards a computational theory of indirect speech acts. LCS TR-223, M.I.T., Cambridge, Mass.

Brown, G. 1980. Action descriptions in indirect speech acts. *Cognition and Brain Theory 3:* 82–89.

Bruce, B., & Newman, D. 1978. Interacting plans. *Cognitive Science 2:* 195–233.

Chomsky, N. 1965. *Aspects of a theory of syntax.* Cambridge, Mass.: M.I.T. University Press.

Dreyfus, H. 1979. *What computers can't do.* N.Y.: Harper & Row.

Fodor, J. 1978. Tom Swift and his procedural grandmother. *Cognition* 6: 229–248.

Gentner, D. 1981. Some interesting differences between verbs and nouns. *Cognition and Brain Theory 4:* in press.

Johnson-Laird, P. 1977. Procedural semantics. *Cognition,* 5:189–214, 1977.

Katz, J. 1966. *The Philosophy of language,* N.Y.: Harper & Row.

Katz, J., & Fodor, J. 1964. The structure of a semantic theory. *Language* 39: 170–210.

Lakoff, G., & Johnson, M. *Metaphors we live by,* unpublished manuscript.

Lehnert, W. 1978 *The process of question answering,* N.J., Lawrence Erlbaum Associates.

Perrault, R., Allen, J., & Cohen, P. 1978. Speech acts as a basis for understanding dialogue coherence. University of Toronto, AI-Memo 78-5.

Ringle, M. 1980. Mysticism as a philosophy of artificial intelligence. *The Behavioral and Brain Sciences 3:*

Russell, S. 1976. Computer understanding of metaphorically used verbs. *American Journal of Computational Linguistics,* Microfiche 44, 463–464.

Salveter, S. 1979. Inferring Conceptual Graphs, *Cognitive Science* 3: 141–166.

Searle, J. 1959. *Speech acts,* Cambridge: Cambridge University Press.

Searle, J. 1976. A taxonomy of illocutionary acts. in K. Gunderson (ed.), *Language, mind and knowledge,* Minneapolis, University of Minnesota Press.

Searle, J. 1980. Minds, brains and programs. *The Behavioral and Brain Sciences 3:* 417–457.

Streek, & Jurgen. 1980. Speech acts in interaction. *Discourse Processes, 3* (2): 133–153.

Waltz, D. 1975. "Understanding line drawings of scenes with shadows. In P. H. Winston (ed.), *The psychology of computer vision,* N.Y.: McGraw-Hill.

Wilks, Y. 1976. Philosophy of language. In E. Charniak & Y. Wilks (eds.), *Computational semantics,* Amsterdam: North-Holland, Elsevier.

Winograd, T. 1972. *Understanding natural language,* N.Y.: Academic Press.

Winograd, T. 1975. Frame representations and the declarative-procedural controversy. In D. Bobrow & A. Collins (eds.) *Representation and understanding,* N.Y.: Academic Press.

Winston, P. H. 1970. Learning structural descriptions from examples. M.I.T. AI Technical Report #231.

Wittgenstein, L. 1953. *Philosophical investigaton,* Oxford: Basil Blackwell.

5 Intensional Logic and Natural Language

Barbara H. Partee
University of Massachusetts, Amherst

INTRODUCTION

My interest here is in the relation of logic to ordinary language, and in how the tools developed by logicians can be best applied to the study of the semantics of ordinary language. On the one hand, there is a recent convergence of interest among philosophers and linguists in this area, which has opened up the development of theories of semantics at least as rigorous and explicit as the theories of syntax developed by linguists starting from the Chomskyan framework. On the other hand, the idealizations that a working logician generally takes for granted are quite different from the idealizations invoked by linguists, and one of the things I want to discuss is some apparent conflicts in this area that will have to be resolved before a real integration of logical and linguistic theories can take place.

The problems will be more understandable if I sketch in some context first. Let's consider first the development of formal logic, which was motivated in large part to get *away* from some of the properties of ordinary language. In every area of inquiry, one of the particular concerns of philosophers is to examine the validity of arguments and patterns of reasoning, to try to determine whether a given conclusion does or does not follow from a particular set of basic premises. One of the chief difficulties in analyzing arguments couched in ordinary language is that ordinary language is full of vagueness and ambiguity. The symbolic language of mathematics is a good example of a special-purpose language which is precise and unambiguous, and modern mathematics could never have developed as far as it has without it. One goal in the development of logic is to construct a similarly precise and unambiguous language, but capable of expressing propositions from a much broader domain than just mathematics. Leibniz formulated this goal in the seventeenth century; one of his most cherished schemes was the development of an ideal universal language, which he called "lingua characteristica universalis", in which each simple idea would be represented by a single symbol, and every proposition could be expressed precisely and unambiguously. Along with the language there was to be a set of rules, the "calculus ratiocinator," by which one could mechanically determine the validity of any argument expressed in that language, so that all disputed arguments could be resolved by calculation. Unfortunately, Kurt Gödel proved in this century that such a project was impossible in principle to complete; any formalized system must either leave some propositions inexpressible or some conclusions unprovable. Nevertheless much of the development of logic has been in the spirit of Leibniz's goal, and the formal languages of logic are always designed to make the relation between form and meaning transparent and unambiguous.

Now, no natural human language has the properties of Leibniz's ideal language. Furthermore, the syntax of the various languages of formal logic differs in fundamental ways from the syntax of any known human language. And the central aim of linguistics, at least since Chomsky, has been to try to characterize the structure of the class of possible *human* languages in hopes of gaining insight into properties of the mind. For these reasons, linguists and logicians used to be in agreement that they were pursuing distinct and perhaps incompatible goals.

In the last dozen or so years, however, there has been a great deal of productive integration of linguistic and logical semantics, stemming from several sources—two of the main ones were generative semantics (G. Lakoff, J. D. McCawley et al.) and the work of the logician Richard Montague on treating English just like a formal language. On substantive issues in descriptive semantics, many important advances have been made through this interaction. But on the deeper question of what a semantic theory should be like, I think there is still an important gap. One sentence in Thomason's introduction to Montague (1974) illustrates this:

(1) According to Montague, the syntax, semantics, and pragmatics
    of natural language are branches of mathematics, not of psychology.

A linguist might put it differently: A theory such as Montague's, which aims to give a uniform treatment of both natural and artificial languages, cannot possibly hope to answer the linguist's central question, which is the question of what it is about the structure of the human mind that results in natural languages sharing the significant properties that they do in fact share, properties that distinguish them from other logically possible kinds of languages. For many linguists, the syntax, semantics, and pragmatics of natural language most definitely *are* branches of psychology.

This difference in approach may be represented schematically as in (2):

(2) a. Logicians' semantics: | Language | ↔ | World |
    b. Linguists' semantics: | Language | ↔ | Mind |

The logician's criterion for an adequate semantics of English is that it account for the truth-conditions of all of the infinitely many sentences of the language, and correctly predict entailment relations between sentences. The box labeled "world" in (2a) doesn't refer just to the actual world; the logician considers whole classes of possible worlds, or models, treating them as mathematical constructs. The main work in a logical semantics consists of specifying how the truth-conditions of complex sentences are determined from the truth-conditions (and other semantic properties) of their parts. The mind of the language user is not ordinarily part of the picture.

Linguists may not always make their theoretical allegiance to psychologism evident in practice, but it is a crucial part of many linguists' criterion of adequacy for a semantic description or a semantic theory. The linguist wants primarily to capture the speakers' implicit knowledge of their language; insofar as this knowledge includes knowledge of entailment relations and truth conditions, the linguist also wants to capture these. But the linguist views whatever connections there are between language and the world as mediated by the mind, and is concerned primarily with the link between language and mind. Thus when the linguist does semantics by mapping English sentences into an uninterpreted language (a "semantic representation"), the assumption is that this representation will have some psychological reality.

This difference in approach might not matter very much if we could just treat the linguist's view as a restricted subcase of the logician's view. The logician will accept as adequate any semantics that gets truth-conditions and entailment relations right; perhaps the linguist is just imposing additional constraints on the kinds of theoretical constructs such a theory can employ, limiting them to those compatible with human cognitive processing. I would like to think that this is the case, and my own work on the integration of Montague's theory and transformational grammar has been predicated on such a possibility. But what if the logician has to make essential use of tools we can show to be beyond the powers of human cognitive processing? And what if the mind, in its interaction with the world, not only selects from and structures the sensory input, but systematically distorts it so that some conceptually possible worlds are logically impossible or vice versa? Then it could turn out that a logically adequate semantics and a psychologically/linguistically adequate semantics are incompatible. I think this is a real possibility, but to be more specific about it I have to talk about intensional logic first.

INTENSIONAL LOGIC

It is well known that the reference of a complex expression often depends on more than just the ordinary reference of its parts; this was one of Frege's basic insights (Frege 1892). For example, the truth of sentence (3a) does not depend on whether there are actually any unicorns or not. By contrast, in (3b) the ordinary reference of "unicorn" does play a direct role in the truth-conditions for the sentence: (3b) cannot be true if there are no unicorns.

(3) a. John is looking for a unicorn.
    b. John is standing on a unicorn.

Now consider the sentences (4a) and (4b), and suppose that as a matter of fact the president of the bank *is* the owner of the dented Volvo.

(4) a. John is looking for the president of the bank.
    b. John is looking for the owner of the dented Volvo.

Does (4b) follow from (4a) on our assumption that the two descriptions in fact pick out the same individual? The two sentences are actually ambiguous; if we understand them as asserting of a particular individual that John is looking for him, then the inference is legitimate. But the reading I am interested in is the one that may be brought out more sharply by appending "whoever he may be" to the end of each sentence. On this reading, the inference is clearly invalid. The assumption that the president of the bank is in fact the owner of the dented Volvo is what is meant by saying that the two expressions have the same *extension* in the actual world. The invalidity of the inference shows that the truth conditions of these sentences involve more than just the extension of the noun phrase in the actual world. If we consider how the same noun phrase, say "the president of the bank," would pick out different individuals in different possible states of affairs, or possible worlds, we recognize that "the president of the bank" would not always pick out the same individual as "the owner of the dented Volvo." The function that picks out the appropriate individual in *each* possible world is the *intension* of the term. In an intensional context such as "is looking for _____," it is the intension and not the extension of the noun phrase that is crucial for the truth-conditions of the sentence. Substituting in (4a) another term with the same *intension,* e.g., "the bank president," would preserve the truth-conditions of the sentence, but substituting a term with merely the same extension does not.

Intensionality is a central aspect of natural language. (In fact it may be argued that intensionality is a crucial component of all intelligent goal-directed systems; see Sommerhoff, 1974). I think it can be argued that almost every basic grammatical relation has instances that exhibit intensionality. To do this, let me first illustrate the concepts of extension and intension further.

TABLE 5.1

Category	Example	Extension	Intension
NP	the President	individual	individual concept
CN	dog	set of individuals	property
VP	walks	set of individuals	property
S	John walks	truth value	proposition

As we saw before, the extension of a noun phrase (NP) is an individual[1]; the intension, the function that picks out the extension in every possible state of affairs, is called (following Carnap, (1947)) an *individual concept*. What about a common noun (CN), like "dog"? The generally accepted analysis is that the extension of a common noun is a *set* of individuals, in this case the set of dogs. The intension of a common noun is a *property*. Examples of common nouns with the same extension in the actual world but different intensions include pairs like "featherless biped"—"human being"; "brother of Jimmy Carter"—"brother of the 39th U.S. President"; in each case it can be seen that the extensions could have been different if the world were different. Verb phrases (VP), like common noun phrases, have a set of individuals as extension and a property as intension. The property, in either case, is analyzed as a function that picks out the extension in each possible world. For a sentence, the extension is taken to be the truth value (True or False), and the intension is a proposition, which is analyzed as a function that applies to possible worlds and assigns to each world the value True or False.

(The part of what I've just said that is represented in Table 5.1 is a standard view of intensions; the analysis of all intensions as functions from possible worlds to extensions is more controversial, and I will say more about it later.)

Now let me illustrate the claim that virtually all the basic grammatical relations have intensional instances. Table 5.2 gives several examples. I have represented the constructions in categorial grammar terms, since this simultaneously represents the syntactic structure and the semantic function-argument structure. For example, VP/NP is the name for a category that combines with an NP to form a VP, i.e. a transitive verb. Semantically, the transitive verb can be interpreted as a function that applies to the semantic value of the NP to give a set of individuals (the extension of the whole VP). To decide if the construction is extensional or intensional, we ask the diagnostic question: Given a VP of the form *kick* + NP, does the extension of the whole VP ever change when you

---

[1]In several papers in Montague (1974), Montague argues that the extensions and intensions of noun phrases should be something rather more complicated than what is indicated here, but the more complex treatment, while crucial for certain purposes, can be ignored here for simplicity without affecting the arguments of this chapter.

TABLE 5.2

Construction type	Extensional	Intensional
VP/NP	kicks _____	seeks _____
CN/CN	red-haired _____	good _____
VP/VP	?	intentionally _____
S/S	it is true that _____	necessarily _____
CN/NP	brother of _____	discoverer of _____

substitute another NP with the same extension as the first? If substitution of co-extensional NP's always leaves the extension of the VP unchanged, the construction is extensional, otherwise intensional. Sentence (4) was an example of such a substitution with the verb "look for," and the test shows that "look for" is intensional. "Kick," on the other hand, is extensional—if the president of the bank of the bank is the owner of the dented Volvo, then anyone who kicks the president of the bank kicks the owner of the dented Volvo.

I will discuss the other cases more briefly. The CN/CN construction represents adjectives that apply to common noun phrases to form common noun phrases. Suppose all and only physicists were violinists; then a red-haired physicist would be a red-haired violinst, but a good physicist wouldn't necessarily be a good violinist. So some adjectives are extensional, some intensional. Among verb-phrase adverbs, represented here as VP/VP, there may not be any clearly extensional ones unless we include locative phrases like "in the park" in this category; most are intensional, like "intentionally." Among sentence adverbs (S/S), practically the only extensional ones are "it is true that _____" and "it is false that _____" (which are not really adverbs anyway); the intensional one, "necessarily," is the word that modal logic was constructed to account for.

I've argued that intensionality is rampant in natural language constructions; in fact the only basic grammatical relation I know of which is invariably extensional is the subject-predicate construction.[2] I would go farther and say that some such property is of central importance in all sorts of mental activity; Jerry Fodor

---

[2]Even the subject-predicate construction may sometimes be arguably intensional. There are two main classes of cases: (1) cases traditionally treated as transformationally derived, where the surface structure subject comes from an intensional construction in deep structure, e.g. (a) and (b) below:

(a) A unicorn appears to be approaching.
(b) The owner of the dented Volvo is being sought by the police.

and (2) possibly the subjects of psychological predicates such as *amuse, interest, intrigue, frighten,* etc., although intuitions about such cases are not entirely clear; cf. (c) and (d) below:

(c) The package in the trunk of the car intrigued Janet.
(d) My dirty laundry intrigued Janet.

(If the package was my dirty laundry, can (c) be true while (d) is false?)

suggests something similar in his book, *The Language of Thought* (1975). So a semantic theory, for either linguists' or logicians' purposes, must have a systematic way to deal with it.

The best theory available so far, I would claim, is Montague's intensional logic. It involves a possible-worlds model theory, which I've sketched a little bit of in (6):

(6) Possible worlds model theory: $\mathcal{M} = \langle A,I,F \rangle$
    A: Set of possible individuals
    I: Set of possible worlds
    F: Function from basic lexical items to intensions
       Intensions: functions from possible worlds to extensions

The primitives in a model in this system include a set A of possible individuals, a set I of possible worlds, and a function F, which specifies the intensions of all the basic lexical items. There are semantic rules for determining the intensions of complex expressions from the intensions and extensions of their parts. Given the intension of any expression, its extension in any possible world is determined, since the intension is a function from possible worlds to extensions. So given a particular model, and the semantic rules for computing intensions of whole sentences from their parts, we can determine the truth-conditions and entailment relations for the sentences, with all the correct distinctions among extensional and intensional constructions.

This sketch has been incomplete and oversimplified in many ways, but I think I can use it as a basis for discussing the problem I want to raise about the gap between linguistic and logical semantics.

THE PROBLEM

First consider the pair of sentences in (7a), where Montague's intensional logic allows us to make the correct predictions.

(7) a. John believes that the president of the bank is rich.
    John believes that the owner of the dented Volvo is rich.

If we say that "believes _____" is an intensional construction, we correctly predict that the two sentences in (7a) can differ in truth value when the two noun phrases are coextensional. But now what about (7b)?

(7) b. John believes that $2 + 2 = 4$.
    John believes that every prime number that is congruent
      to 1 modulo 4 is the sum of two squares.

It seems that the two sentences in (7b) can also differ in truth value. But Montague's analysis predicts the opposite, since both of the embedded sentences are true in every possible world, hence have the same intension. The source of the problem seems intuitively obvious: John may not know that they have the same intension. When we consider sentences that express mental attitudes, sameness of intension doesn't seem to be enough.

Now I want to relate this problem to another one: If we view Montague's semantics as a linguistic theory, what must we assume about the speaker's knowledge of the language? It seems that the speaker must be an ideal logician, and must be able to represent and distinguish among an infinite set of possible individuals and a non-denumerably infinite set of possible worlds. Knowing whether two expressions have the same intension requires knowing whether they are true in exactly the same possible worlds. It's pretty clear that a finite brain can't manage all that. We can conceive of non-denumerable sets, but we can't conceive distinctly of each of their members. And we can do logical inferences, but not infallibly.

Are these just cases where we should invoke a competence-performance distinction? Then we might say that an ideal speaker would realize that the sentences in (7b) do have the same truth value. But that seems wrong; as Asa Kasher (1976) has argued, even the ideal speaker shouldn't have to be committed to the assumption that all humans are similarly ideal—the speaker of (7b) may want to express John's fallibility even if she herself knows that the embedded propositions are logically equivalent.

So I suspect that it is the very same properties that render Montague's models unrepresentable by finite brains that lead to the incorrect predictions about (7b). And I think that part of the source of this problem is that Montague, like most logicians, was trying to bypass the mind in relating language to the world.

Some have already argued that Montague's semantics is linguistically uninteresting for just such reasons. I reject that claim, because of the many fruitful descriptive results it has led to, and because I don't know of any semantic theory that comes as close to both linguists' and logicians' criteria of adequacy. But I can't argue that point here. To me the question is how the theory might be modified to overcome these problems.

I don't have a solution, but I think that there are two kinds of modifications that might lead to a solution, leaving most of Montague's framework intact. One modification is probably fairly straightforward: Allow *partial* models, with partial specifications of the set of possible individuals, partial specification of the set of possible worlds, and partial functions as the intensions of lexical items. (Joyce Friedman has developed computer programs for Montague grammar with just this capability; see Friedman, Moran, & Warren, 1978). This would permit finite representability, and would accord with the fact that while we certainly do have conceptions of alternative possible states of affairs, we do not by any means have complete conceptions of them. This modification would solve some of the problems, and might reasonably be likened to a performance limitation.

The second modification would be more radical; it comes from ideas that can be found in both the computational and the psychological literature, though perhaps they are also part of what Frege was arguing for. This is to replace the purely mathematical conception of *function* by the more computational notion of *procedure* in the analysis of intensions. The expressions in (8) are examples of cases where we might naturally associate different procedures with two expressions, even though the procedures determine the same function.

(8) a. Morning Star/Evening Star
    b. equilateral triangle/equiangular triangle
    c. an only child's father's only child/an only child

If it were the procedures rather than the resulting functions that were assigned as the intensions of the expressions, we would have the basis for explaining how the different members of the pairs in (8) can make different contributions to the truth conditions of sentences in which they appear. The problematical sentences of (7b), for instance, would be explained by the existence of two different procedures each picking out the value "true" in every possible world. The resulting theory, if it can be successfully worked out, would make finer-grained semantic distinctions and at the same time be more psychologically plausible, since it seems reasonable to suppose that we do not "know" a function other than by knowing some appropriate procedure for determining the value that the function assigns to a given argument.

I must emphasize that this is not a worked out solution. I don't know how to formalize the notion of a procedure, though I think much help could be gotten from the computational literature, and I don't know how easy it would be to integrate this into Montague's system, particularly with respect to a procedural analog to the composition of functions. And supposing these changes could be made, and did lead to a linguistically adequate theory, the result might fail to meet the criteria for logical adequacy. But my attitude is basically optimistic: So far, I don't see any reason for a *necessary* gap between logical and linguistic semantics; the actual gap may well be bridgeable.

REFERENCES

Carnap, R. 1947. *Meaning and necessity: a study in semantics and modal logic*. Chicago: University of Chicago Press.
Fodor, J. A. 1975. *The language of thought*. New York: Crowell.
Frege, G. 1892. Über Sinn und Bedeutung. *Zeitschrift für Philosophie und philosophische Kritik*

100. Trans. On sense and nominatum. In *Readings in philosophical analysis* (Ed.) H. Feigl & W. Sellars. New York: Appleton-Century-Crofts, 1949.

Friedman, J., Moran, D., & Warren, D. 1978. Explicit finite intensional models for PTQ. *American Journal of Computational Linguistics,* Microfiche no. 74:3-22.

Kasher, A. 1976. Logical rationalism: on degrees of adequacy for semantics of natural languages. *Philosophica* 18:139-57.

Montague, R. 1974. *Formal philosophy: selected papers of Richard Montague* (Ed.) R. Thomason. New Haven: Yale University Press.

Sommerhoff, G. 1974. *Logic of the living brain.* London: Wiley.

6 How Far can you Trust a Linguist?

James D. McCawley
University of Chicago

In linguistics one frequently encounters the notion of *markedness*: the notion that one of two or more contrasting items is "unmarked," that is, constitutes the more normal or more expected member of the opposition, in comparison with the "marked" member(s), which is/are less normal or less expected.[1] For example, in languages that have both oral and nasal vowels, the nasal vowels are marked and the oral vowels unmarked, as evidenced by the relatively greater frequency of the oral vowels and the fact that any distinctions made among the marked nasal vowels are also made among the unmarked oral vowels but not vice versa (for example, in many languages a three-way tongue height distinction is made among oral vowels but only a two-way distinction among nasal vowels, though the reverse situation never occurs). Besides language-universal markedness principles such as the markedness of nasality in vowels, there are also language-particular markedness principles. For example, while verb-final word order is unmarked in Japanese, it is marked in German, as evidenced by a tendency for German subordinate clauses to change from verb-final word order, without any parallel tendency for main clauses to change from verb-second to verb-final order.

My invocation of the linguist's notion of markedness is intended not as an illustration of linguistic methodology but as a tool for discussing methodological questions. Much has been written about Thomas Kuhn's (1962) terms "paradigm" and "normal science," including many articles (Masterman 1970, Shapere 1964) in which it is claimed that Kuhn uses the word 'paradigm' in a

---

[1] I am grateful to Jeffrey Harlig and Valerie Reyna for comments on an earlier draft of this chapter that assisted me greatly in its revision.

75

variety of senses. Kuhn himself (1970:181ff; 1974) indeed admits to having equivocated in his use of the word. I place a reading on the term 'paradigm' that makes it unequivocal: a paradigm in a scientific community is the common possessions of the community that determine markedness principles characterizing the respects in which science may be "normal," that is, "unmarked," much in the way that linguistic markedness principles characterize the respects in which sounds or words or syntactic constructions in a language may be "normal" or "unmarked."

If viewed as markedness principles, a paradigm does not impose a simple dichotomy of "normal science" to "abnormal science" in the way suggested by much of Kuhn's book. Just as markedness principles do not rule marked sounds and marked syntactic constructions out of the language, a paradigm does not per se rule marked science out of the activities carried on within a scientific community, and it allows distinctions as to extent and number of respects in which something is marked science. (Absolute exclusions do exist, both in linguistic communities and in scientific communities, though these are something over and above the markedness principles.) Markedness principles merely make marked scientific activity less readily accessible and more costly than unmarked alternatives (for example, in presenting papers at a scientific meeting, one is obliged to present justifications for those respects in which his work is marked but is wasting his time and that of his audience if he presents justifications for points in which his work is "normal science"). In particular, one can be a member in good standing of a scientific community and accept the paradigm of that community as a paradigm, that is, accept it as characterizing what scientific activity is normal for that community, without accepting the proposition that a scientist should confine his work to what is normal as defined by the paradigm, or even the proposition that normal science is good science. It is in fact common for scientific communities to harbor subcommunities that have paradigms strikingly different from those of the larger community and typically more in accord with their members views as to how science should be conducted.

This is all in preface to an informal discussion of the paradigm of what, for want of a better name, I will call the generative grammar community; that community includes many persons (such as myself) who would feel insulted or misunderstood if they were called generative grammarians, but I will stick with the name in view of the close historical ties of the paradigm with generative grammar. A paradigm can involve a number of different sorts of things, of which Kuhn identifies metaphysical assumptions, standards for evaluation of research, standards of precision, and perhaps most importantly, what he calls "exemplars": those problem solutions that have achieved the status of exemplary solutions to significant problems, are presented in textbooks and courses as examples of good science, and are central to training in which students develop the knack of solving new problems by combining or extending these solutions or using them as the basis of analogies.

Exemplars play a far greater role in fixing what normal science is than does a theory, and indeed, while exemplars are a necessary part of a paradigm, a theory is not. Moreover, when a theory is part of a paradigm, the relationship between it and the exemplars that allegedly illustrate it in action is often quite tenuous. Consider, for example, Chomsky's celebrated analysis (1957, 1965) of English auxiliary verbs, in which there is a base rule yielding underlying structures in which verbal affixes precede the verbs to which they are ultimately suffixed (AUX - Tense (Modal) (*have -en*) (*be -ing*)), the bulk of the syntax presupposes this underlying order of elements, and a transformation ('Affix-hopping') yields the surface order of affixes relative to verbs:

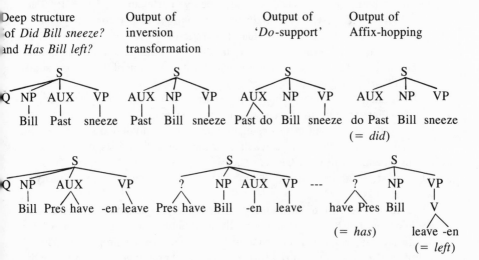

This treatment is only one of many that are consistent with the "theory of grammar" presented in the works by Chomsky in which it appears, and it has been argued from several quarters of the generative grammar community (Emonds, 1976, McCawley, 1971, Pullum & Wilson 1977) to be highly unsatisfactory. However, it retains formidable status as an exemplar, in view of the fact that virtually all textbooks of transformational grammar (Keyser & Postal, 1976, and Parisi & Antinucci, 1976 are the only exceptions that come to mind) give it great prominence and bill it as an instance of transformational grammar shedding light on a previously murky domain. It is important in the history of linguistics not so much for the insight that it provides into the workings of English auxiliary verbs (I maintain that it provides very little insight) as for the basis that it provided for analogies that guided linguists in constructing analyses of other phenomena (analyses generally embodying even less insight) and thus for the role that it played in establishing certain characteristics of Chomsky's analysis as constituting "normal science." Characteristics of that analysis that have recurred in subsequent transformational analyses include (1) a deep morpheme order different from the surface morpheme order, (2) concern for morpheme order to the near exclusion of concern for constituent structure, (3) accounting for mutually determining items (such as *have* and *-en,* which occur together or not at all) by making them adjacent in deep structure, (4) the quest for phenomena whose description can be simplified if they are analyzed in terms of a hypothetical underlying morpheme order, and (5) the creation of ad hoc syntactic categories such as Chomsky's 'AUX' that figure in formulas expressing co-occurrence relations.

It is easy to find examples of linguistic research that totally accepted a linguistic theory (such as that of Chomsky, 1965) but were not normal science according to the paradigm associated with that theory. For example, Ross, 1969 accepted all but the most arcane details of the Chomsky, 1965 theory of syntax but failed to be normal science by virtue of its rejection of (2): Ross argued for an "auxiliary as main verb" analysis on the basis of familiar sorts of arguments about constituent structure but ignored entirely the question of how to get auxiliary verbs in the right order.

The remainder of this chapter will consist of informal critical discussion of certain points relating to the paradigm of the generative grammar community whose status is liable to misinterpretation not only by nonlinguists but even by generative grammarians, as a result of widespread disparities between what linguists believe and what they say they believe. It is intended as an aid to the nonlinguist (or the linguist, for that matter) in deciding what to take seriously in what linguists say.

There are several propositions that are widely assented to by generative grammarians but believed by practically none and which figure in at most a highly attenuated form in the paradigm. To refer to such propositions I will introduce the technical term *red herrings.* The most prominent red herrings in the generative grammar community are the propositions that a language is a set of sentences, that a sentence is a string of words or of morphemes, that a speaker of a language knows what strings or words or morphemes are sentences of his language, and that a speaker's knowledge of his language consists in a system of rules that specify what are the sentences of the language.[2]

The alleged ability of speakers of a language to distinguish between "grammatical" and "ungrammatical" strings of words is about as rare and as perverse as the ability to construct puns, an ability to which I believe it is closely related. Anyone who has taught an introductory syntax course has had the experience of presenting an "ungrammatical" example only to be told by some smart-aleck about an unsuspected interpretation on which the sentence is quite normal. For example, in discussing the order of auxiliary verbs in English I have presented pairs of sentences such as (1)–(2) to illustrate that auxiliary *have* must precede progressive *be*:

---

[2] See McCawley 1976 for arguments that these propositions are not only red herrings but also false.

(1) Tom has been smoking pot.
(2) *Tom is having smoked pot.

On one occasion, a student pointed out that (2) is really grammatical since it allows an interpretation in which *have* is a main verb meaning 'get' and *smoked pot* is a noun phrase with a structure similar to *fried eggs*. Such interventions are usually greeted with the sort of groans that are the accepted form of expressing appreciation of puns, and they provide the same sort of comic relief that puns do in the midst of what is at times a boring enterprise. However, the extent to which comical virtuosity is required for a person to notice the existence of such an interpretation, as contrasted with the ease with which one recognizes its acceptability once it has been pointed out, shows that the strings of words on which grammaticality judgments are allegedly made exist only as typographical or acoustic objects, not as perceptual or cognitive objects, just as the Necker cube exists only as a graphic object and not as a perceptual object, as contrasted with its two interpretations, which do exist as perceptual objects. These points are in fact implicitly recognized by virtually all members of the generative grammar community, as is evidenced by the fact that the "grammaticality judgments" on which they base arguments systematically ignore interpretations other than those relevant to the points at issue, and the "sentences" are often exhibited with supplementary information as to the intended interpretation, for example, subscripts to indicate purported coreference of items, much in the same way that one might present the Necker cube with shading or context that picked out one of the interpretations. Generative grammarians speak as if they were doing linguistics in terms of something like sense data, when they in fact are doing it in terms of something more like the perceptual data of gestalt psychologists.

An important part of the generative grammar paradigm that is shared with the paradigms of many other communities of linguists is the idea that the data of linguistics are linguistic data. In virtually all exemplars presented in linguistics textbooks of whatever orientation, problems are sets of "linguistic data" (i.e. facts about what is or is not possible in the given language), and the solution is a set of rules and underlying forms that will "account for" those facts. Normally no consideration is given to the question of how the allegedly correct rules and structures could be acquired by speakers of the language, nor to the question of how one could independently test whether speakers know those rules and structures rather than some alternative ones, nor to the related question of whether speakers who exhibit the same "linguistic facts" agree in their linguistic knowledge.[3] Moreover, these questions are ignored at least as much by generative grammarians, who claim to be pursuing the goal of constructing "psychologically real" grammars, as by linguists who take an anti-psychological view of

---

[3]See Haber 1975 for experimental results suggesting that speakers of English often have different rules of past tense and plural formation even though they agree as to what the past tenses and plurals of the words they know are.

linguistics.⁴ True, a sketchy outline of a theory of language acquisition is given in many works by Chomsky (e.g. 1965, 1966); however, since that scandalously vacuous sketch has had no effect on the way in which anyone does linguistics, it is, in the technical sense defined above, a red herring. Chomsky's account of language acquisition has served chiefly as a rationalization to justify linguists' avoidance of any serious consideration of language acquisition. Specifically, Chomsky's sketch of language acquisition, which with understatement he describes (1965: 202) as an "idealization," takes the ultimate outcome of language acquisition to be independent of the development stages through which the language learner goes:

primary linguistic data ⟶ LANGUAGE ACQUISITION DEVICE ⟶ a grammar

The language acquisition device is to incorporate an "evaluation measure," which allows determination of the relative cost of alternative grammars, and the grammar acquired by the child is to be the "least costly" grammar consistent with the set of "primary linguistic data" on which the learner bases his learning.⁵ The linguist is thus spared any need to look beyond the sorts of linguistic data that he is accustomed to looking at—the result of language acquisition is to be identical with the result of doing linguistics on the sort of corpus of data that linguists have generally concerned themselves with.⁶

Any attempt to modify this account so as to take developmental stages into account destroys the foundation of this rationalization. At the very least, a theory of language acquisition must recognize that at every stage of his development the child has some grammar, that he does not keep a complete record of the linguistic data that he has thus far interpreted, and that accordingly the steps in the development of his linguistic competence cannot consist of his constructing a grammar from scratch to conform to a large corpus of linguistic data but must rather consist in modification of an existing grammar to make it conform to a fragmentary set of "new" data. The closest analog to an evaluation measure that

---

⁴An honorable exception is provided by the work of Culicover and Wexler (1977), who make a serious attempt to develop an interesting notion of learnability and to modify Chomsky's "extended standard theory" in such a way as to insure that the grammars provided by the modified theory are learnable.

⁵ This flimsy account of language acquisition provides the only connection that has ever been adduced between the notion of "evaluation measure" and the real world. See McCawley 1976, 1977b for more detailed criticism of Chomsky's account of language acquisition.

⁶Thus, as Derwing (1973) has observed, Chomsky's "language acquisition device" is a "discovery procedure," differing from the 'discovery procedures' that Chomsky finds objectionable in descriptivist linguistics (e.g. Harris 1951) not in what it does but in the kind of grammar that it gives as output.

would make sense in such a scheme of language acquisition would not be a measure of the complexity of entire grammars but a measure of the cost of revisions in an existing grammar.[7]

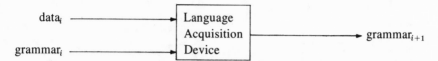

But there would then be no reason to expect that the ultimate outcome of language acquisition would be "optimal" or "least costly" relative to *any* standard of "cost," since there would be no reason to expect the learning to involve revisions of the current grammar any more sweeping than what was needed to accomodate the data to which the grammar is to be extended.

Another noteworthy point in the paradigm of generative grammar is what I will refer to as "Platonism," namely the idea that one level of linguistic structure (generally, "deep structure") is "real" and that other levels are mere "shadows" or "reflections" of it. This position can be illustrated by the role of the "base component" in transformational analyses. In "standard" transformational grammar, the "base component" is the only "generative" part of the grammar:[8] it specifies what structures are possible on one specific linguistic level

---

[7]I have deleted the two adjectives that Chomsky gratuitously inserts before "data." The only at all plausible way in which the input to a language acquisition device could be restricted to "linguistic data" would preclude the data from being "primary," namely to have the input to the language acquisition device be the results of analysis in which the meanings of sentences and the grammatical functions of their parts are identified on the basis of extra-linguistic factors.

Chomsky (1977: 119–122) discusses objections to his 1965 sketch of language acquisition, ultimately concluding

> Frankly, I doubt that the simplifying assumption, though obviously false, significantly affects the validity of the analysis based on it. If our initial assumption does indeed seriously falsify the situation, . . . then we would expect to find substantial differences in the result of language learning depending on such factors as order of presentation of data, time of presentation, and so on. But we do not find this, at least at the level of precision of currently available analytic tools.

Chomsky's claim that there are no "substantial differences" in the grammars acquired by members of a linguistic community rests mainly on specualtion, since few studies have attempted to identify differences in linguistic competence that are not reflected in ordinary linguistic data; the one study that I am familiar with that looked for such variation (Haber 1975) found it.

[8]My use of the terms "generative" and "interpretive" departs somewhat from that of Chomsky, who reserves the term "generative" for the entire syntax and never applies it to the base rules by themselves. Chomsky's terminological practice relates to the fact that for him "A deep structure is a generalized Phrase-marker *underlying some well-formed surface structure*" (1965: 138, emphasis added). Since for Chomsky some of the structures generated by the base rules cannot be converted into any surface structure, not all structures generated by the base rules are "deep structures." No issue of any substance is affected by any decision as to whether all the structures generated by the base rules should count as "deep structures," though one issue of no substance is affected: whether the set of all deep structures is a "context-free language."

(namely "deep structure"), whereas the other parts of the grammar are "interpretive": they specify the relations among different linguistic levels (e.g. that between deep structure and surface structure).

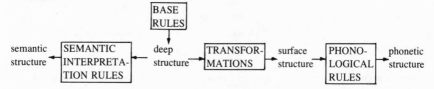

There is no obvious reason why a system of generative rules should be provided for only one linguistic level, and numerous linguistic schools have conceptions of grammar in which there are generative rules for more than one linguistic level, most strikingly stratificational grammar, in which there are generative rules for all linguistic levels. Moreover, approaches in which there are generative rules for two or more levels offer promise for the development of realistic models of speech production in that they allow sentence construction on one level to lead or lag relative to other levels, in conformity with the fact that the speaker in producing a sentence is jumping back and forth among the various linguistic levels, putting together a semantic structure, a syntactic structure, and a phonological structure that match according to the rules of the language and conform to his (generally incomplete) intentions. Nonetheless, the generative grammar paradigm involves only exemplars in which "base rules" specify how elements may combine at the level of deep structure, that is, at the "deepest" level of syntactic structure, and no generative rules for other levels appear. (There are, of course, subcommunities of the generative grammar community whose paradigms involve *output constraints,* that is, generative rules expressing well-formedness conditions on surface structures, but exemplars involving output constraints do not figure in the paradigm of the larger community.)

The Platonistic attitude is partly responsible for two grossly divergent tendencies in two subcommunities of the generative grammar community: the tendency of "generative semanticists," having concluded that there is no dividing line between syntactic and semantic structure, to take rules of logical well-formedness as the closest analog to "base rules" and treat language-particular combinatoric differences as mainly a matter of idiosyncratic differences among lexical items as to the applicability of transformations, and the tendency of "interpretive semantics" such as Chomsky himself to take language-particular combinatoric constraints as grounds for having highly language-particular deep structures and base rules. In both cases, the move could be avoided by making use of generative rules for surface structure.[9]

---

[9] "Generative semanticists," though accepting the idea of output constraints, have generally accorded them second-class status, employing them only in cases where there was no plausible alternative and taking them to give only a fragmentary specification of surface well-formedness. Chomsky (1977) and Chomsky and Lasnik (1977) admit "surface filters" but suggest that they may

Bizarre Platonistic ideas have often found readier acceptance in the generative grammar community than more straightforward nonPlatonistic alternatives. Consider, for example, the way that Emonds' (1976) notion of "structure preserving transformation" has been formalized. Emonds has argued that transformations are of two types:[10] structure preserving transformations, which apply both to main and to subordinate clauses and do not enlarge the class of gross syntactic configurations in the language, and "root" transformations, which apply only or normally to main clauses and may yield gross syntactic configurations that are derived only through application of such rules (for example, the inverted word order of questions). Emonds' observations could be incorporated into a syntactic theory in a fairly natural non-Platonistic way as follows: There are generative rules specifying what surface structure configurations the language allows, with extra possibilities allowed in main clauses that are not allowed in subordinate clauses, and only those derivations are admitted that yield surface structures that conform to those rules. Emonds' formalization of his observations was, by contrast, thoroughly Platonistic. He characterized structure-preserving transformations not in terms of the surface structures that they give rise to but in terms of their relationship to base rules: for Emonds, structure-preserving transformations give outputs whose gross structures conform to the base rules, and the base rules generate structures that involve not only ordinary items but also "empty nodes" that provide places into which structure-preserving transformations may move items; a movement transformation is then structure-preserving for Emonds if and only if it moves an item into a position occupied by an item ('empty' or normal) of the same syntactic category.[11] Emonds' treatment (1976: 218–224) of "Affix-hopping" pursues this formalization to a reductio ad absurdum. In the formulation of Chomsky 1956, Affix-hopping is a transformation that moves verbal affixes from their underlying preverbal position to their surface structure suffixal position:[12]

---

be restricted to constraints on what complementizers may combine with in surface structure. Their tentative suggestions as to what is a possible "surface filter" bear no relation to their conception of what is a possible base rule, and while their base rules purport to give a complete specification of the permissible deep structure configurations, the surface filters are to cover only selected details of surface structure.

[10] I ignore here Emonds' third class of transformations, "minor movement rules," also called "local rules."

[11] Emonds' notion of structure preservation is thus applicable only to movement and insertion transformations, whereas the characterization in terms of surface structure also allows deletion transformations to be distinguished as structure-preserving or not.

[12] Chomsky's formulation only specifies the change in morpheme order that Affix-hopping produces. In the diagram I have chosen one of the more plausible derived constituent structures that are consistent with Chomsky's rule. See McCawley 1971 for arguments for an analysis of auxiliary verbs that dispenses with the constituent 'AUX' and yields a more plausible derived constituent structure. See Akmajian and Wasow 1975 for arguments that "Affix-hopping" must be split into two separate transformations: a cyclic transformation that applies to -en and -ing, and a postcyclic transformation that applies to tense markers.

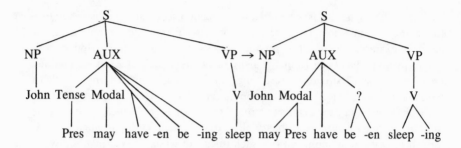

Since affix-hopping applies to subordinate as well as to main clauses, for Emonds it must be a structure-preserving transformation and thus it must move affixes into positions that in deep structure already contain actual or empty items of a category to which affixes belong. Emonds is thus forced to revise Chomsky's analysis, in which affixes belong to no category and in which the last affix is moved into a position that in deep structure was not occupied by an affix, namely by setting up a deep structure category (Emonds calls it "TENSE") to which all affixes belong and allowing deep structures in which more instances of that category occur than can ever be overtly occupied:[13]

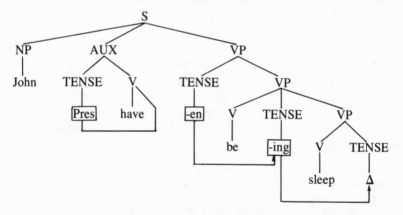

This treatment perverts the generalization that English verbal affixes are suffixes, which is a fact about the surface shape of English words and has nothing to do with deep structure (and anyway is not embodied in Emonds' analysis, since not all of his deep structure affix positions follow verbs).

A second illustration of the tenacity of Platonism in generative grammar is provided by a consideration of the role of syntactic categories. I have argued (McCawley 1977a) that the deplorable state of argumentation about syntactic

---

[13]The attachment of TENSE to *have* here is for Emonds a "minor movement rule" (cf. fn. 10) and thus does not call for yet another deep structure TENSE position.

categories, in which no generative grammarian can be said to have a coherent policy as to what it is for two items to belong to the same syntactic category, is due in part to the remarkable unanimity among generative grammarians that base rules are the sole source of syntactic categories, that is, that any occurrence of a syntactic category in surface structure must be traceable back to an occurrence of that same category in deep structure. This particular instance of Platonism in syntax has resulted in a variety of strange claims by different types of generative grammarians, for example, the claim by "generative semanticists" that syntactic categories are identical to logical categories (this is to be distinguished from the more reasonable claim to which I now subscribe, that syntactic phenomena are sensitive to logical category), and the ready acceptance by "interpretive semanticists" of analyses such as Chomsky's (1965) treatment of passives, in which supernumerary deep structure nodes, including "empty nodes," are set up principally in order to have certain nodes and labels (such as the PP node in the diagram) that otherwise could not be contributed

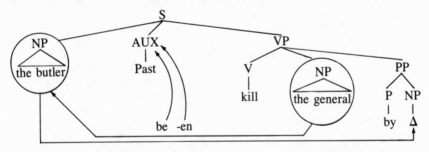

by base rules. A non-Platonistic alternative was proposed by Stephen Anderson in a paper written in 1966 but not published until 1976: that syntactic categories do not depend on base rules but are assigned by largely universal principles that apply to all levels of syntactic structure rather than just to deep structure, e.g. the principle that anything consisting of a preposition and a NP is a prepositional phrase. Note that Anderson's approach allows syntactic categories that do not figure in deep structure to appear in surface structure, e.g. all prepositional phrases might arise through transformational insertion of prepositions into structures that involve no prepositions. Anderson's proposal, though given fairly wide underground circulation in 1966, appears to have had no influence on any subsequent research other than my own, not even on Anderson's own subsequent research, and analyses such as Chomsky's empty-node treatment of passives have been accepted for reasons that make no sense under a minor deviation from Platonism.

I will conclude this sketch of noteworthy features of the generative grammar paradigm by providing some admonitions to the nonlinguist that will partially answer the question posed by my title. (1) Ignore linguists' statements of what the subject matter of linguistics is; after all, linguists ignore their own statements of what it is. (2) If a linguist adopts a devious and circuitous way of doing something for which there is an obvious simpleminded and straightforward alternative, do not jump to the conclusion that the linguist has a good reason for rejecting the obvious alternative: The obvious alternative may not be obvious to him. (3) Do not accept at face value a linguist's claim that his approach seeks psychological reality. He probably believes that you can get psychological answers without asking psychological questions or that his linguistic questions become psychological questions merely because he occasionally calls them psychological, an attitude that follows in the tradition of "What's good for General Motors is good for the country."

REFERENCES

Akmajian, A., and Wasow, T. 1975. The constituent structure of VP and AUX and the position of BE. *Linguistic Analysis 1*, 205–245.

Anderson, S. R. 1976. Concerning the notion 'base component of a transformational grammar.' In J. McCawley (Ed.), *Notes from the linguistic underground*. New York: Academic Press.

Chomsky, N. A. 1957. *Syntactic structures*. The Hague: Mouton.

Chomsky, N. A. 1965. *Aspects of the theory of syntax*. Cambridge, Mass.: MIT Press.

Chomsky, N. A. 1966. *Topics in the theory of generative grammar*. The Hague: Mouton.

Chomsky, N. A. 1975. *Reflections on language*. New York: Pantheon.

Chomsky, N. A. 1977. On WH-movement. In Culicover, Wasow, & Akmajian (Eds.). *Formal syntax*. New York: Academic Press.

Chomsky, N. A., & Lasnik, H. 1977. Filters and control. *Linguistic Inquiry 8*, 425–504.

Culicover, P., T. Wasow, & Akmajian, A. 1977. *Formal syntax*. New York: Academic Press.

Culicover, P., & Wexler, K. 1977. Some syntactic implications of a theory of language learnability. In Culicover, Wasow, and Akmajian (Eds.). Formal syntax. New York: Academic Press.

Derwing, B. 1973. *Transformational grammar as a theory of language acquisition*. London and New York: Cambridge University Press.

Emonds, J. 1976. *A transformational approach to syntax*. New York: Academic Press.

Haber, L. 1975. The muzzy theory. *Papers from the Eleventh Regional Meeting,* Chicago Linguistic Society, 240–256.

Harris, Z. S. 1951. *Structural linguistics*. Chicago: University of Chicago Press.

Keyser, S. J., & Postal, P. M. 1976. *Beginning english grammar*. New York: Harper and Row.

Kuhn, T. S. 1962. *The structure of scientific revoltuions*. Chicago: University of Chicago Press.

Kuhn, T. S. 1970. 2nd edition of Kuhn 1962. Chicago: University of Chicago Press.

Kuhn, T. S. 1974. Second thoughts on paradigms. In F. Suppe (Ed.), *The structure of scientific theories,* Urbana and Chicago: University of Illinois Press.

Masterman, M. 1970. The nature of a paradigm. In I. Lakatos & A. Musgrave (Eds.), *Criticism and the growth of knowledge,* London and New York: Cambridge University Press.

McCawley, J. D. 1971. Tense and time reference in English. In D. T. Langendoen & C. J. Fillmore (Eds.), *Studies in linguistic semantics*. New York: Holt, Rinehart and Winston.

McCawley, J. D. 1976. Some ideas not to live by. *Die neueren Sprachen 75,* 151–165.

McCawley, J. D. 1977a. The nonexistence of syntactic categories. *Second Annual Linguistic Metatheory Conference Proceedings,* East Lansing: Michigan State University, 212–232.

McCawley, J. D. 1977b. Acquisition models as models of acquisition. In R. Fasold & R. Shuy (Eds.), *Studies in language variation,* Washington: Georgetown University Press.

Parisi, D., & Antinucci, F. 1976. *Essentials of grammar.* New York: Academic Press.

Pullum, G., & Wilson, D. 1977. Autonomous syntax and the analysis of auxiliaries. *Language 53,* 741–788.

Ross, J. R. 1969. Auxiliaries as main verbs. *Journal of Philosophical Linguistics 1,* 77–102.

Shapere, D. 1964. Review of Kuhn 1964. *Philosophical Review 73,* 383–394.

7 Propositional and Algorithmic Semantics

Franz Oppacher
Concordia University

After a brief discussion of two major trends in the philosophy of language, I shall formulate identity conditions for concepts or meanings. Then, I shall attempt to answer the following question: How should meanings be characterized so that it is clear from their characterization that humans or suitably programmed machines could actually use them in thinking and communicating?

Theories of meaning tend to differ not only in the answers they give but also in the questions they ask. To gain some perspective I shall approach the topic from the point of view of Artificial Intelligence. The emphasis of AI on the design of data structures and of algorithms for transforming them has led to the development of rich concepts for thinking about issues of representation and meaning and its emphasis on operational models shows a way of making philosophical theories of language testable.

It seems clear that being able to assemble an operational model of a capacity from primitive and well understood components is a sufficient condition for understanding the capacity. But the AI requirement that a theory of a capacity be presented in the form of a model strong and detailed enough to do what it is claimed to explain constitutes an extremely powerful constraint on theory construction. Only a handful of theories meet this requirement. Consequently, a much weaker requirement will be used in the following.

I shall assume that we understand a phenomenon such as mastery of a language to the extent that we can see our way to constructing a working model of it. For a theory of meaning to be at all acceptable it should be possible to argue, with some plausibility, that it could be incorporated into a performance theory of naturally or artificially intelligent behavior or that it could provide a basis for designing programs capable of simulating aspects of human linguistic capacities.

I shall try to show that some very influential versions of philosophical semantics do not meet this minimal condition. (Although I shall not consider theories committed to extreme behaviorism or to the "irreducibility of intentionality," I would expect them to fail to qualify as well.)

DAVIDSON'S APPROACH

Davidson's approach (1967, 1968, 1970, 1973) is a fascinating blend of (1) a proposed application of Tarski's theory of truth to natural languages, (2) a commitment to the extensionalist view that meanings play no role in a theory of meaning, and (3) a commitment to Quine's "Hegelean" idea that meaning is basically a property of language as a whole.

A finite theory of truth for a language L implies infinitely many material biconditionals—the so-called T-sentences—which come from Tarski's "convention T":

(T) 'p' is true iff (if and only if) p

by substituting a structural-descriptive name of a sentence of L for "p" and a homophonic translation of this sentence into the language of the truth-theory for p. By implying all instances of convention T, a Tarskian theory determines the extension of the predicate 'true sentence of L.'

It is widely agreed that a theory of meaning should show, for each sentence S of L, how the meaning of S depends upon the meanings of its component expressions, and upon the relations among those components. A truth-theory, according to Davidson, meets the requirement of recursively specifying the meanings of all sentences of L by specifying the systematic contributions of the meanings of components to the meanings of all sentences in which the components might occur. (The component meanings are given by expressions of the form: " '_____' is satisfied by all and only _____ things." These expressions play the role of base clauses for the recursion which is the truth-theory).

Davidson's argument for the astounding claim that if we had a truth-theory for a natural language we would have a theory of meaning for that language as well, rests on the following beliefs: To know the meaning of a sentence is to know its truth conditions; a theory that provides truth conditions for all sentences of L associates every sentence S with another sentence that translates S and thereby gives the meaning of S; a truth-theory pairs truths with truths, falsehoods with falsehoods. Such a pairing of truths, with truths, is generally taken to constitute only a necessary condition for adequacy of translations. But Davidson believes that truth value preservation amounts to a necessary and sufficient condition for translation (or guarantees meaning likeness) when entire languages and not just individual sentences are considered. He seems to hold that if a finite theory achieves an infinite pairing of truths with truths by judiciously exploiting structural constraints, then—because the structural role of an expression is taken to be analogous to what is usually called its meaning—the theory leaves nothing worth saying about meanings unsaid.

The emphasis on the analogy between structural roles and meanings does seem to justify the claim that a truth-theory specifies the meanings of the "structural" constructs of L, i.e., the truth-functional connectives and the quantifiers. But I don't see how Davidson's stronger claim can be supported. What he has to say in its support is—as far as I can see—simply a reiteration of the claim that a finite, truth-preserving, one-to-one correspondence between 2 theories amounts to an adequate translation of one by the other. For example, he seems to maintain that if we were as convinced of the truth of:

(1) 'Snow is white' is true iff grass is green,
     as we are of the truth of its counterpart

(2) 'Snow is white'' is true iff snow is white

then (1) would be fully as acceptable as (2) as a consequence of a theory of truth in its capacity as theory of meaning. The reason he *seems* to offer for this is that if (1) did play the role of (2), then the structural constraints that make a finite truth-theory possible would somehow force 'grass' and 'green' to acquire the meanings or roles of 'snow' and 'white.' I find this as difficult to believe and as much in need of supporting arguments as the original claim that a truth-theory is a theory of meaning. This claim owes much of its plausibility to the presumably correct slogan that to know the meaning of a sentence is to know the conditions under which the sentence would be true. However, the notion of conditions under which a sentence would be true is considerably stronger than the notion of the truth condition provided by a T-sentence. A T-sentence is a material biconditional that cannot support counterfactual constructions.

Whereas every T-sentence may be taken as giving a partial definition of truth and all of them together as specifying completely the extension of 'truth in L,' no T-sentence tells us *anything* about meanings of non-logical terms. If you don't *fully* understand what it is for A's to be B's, then the sentence

'A's are B's' is true iff A's are B's

does not help you *at all*. Another way of making this point would be to say that if a translation is supposed to characterize, at least partially, what are ordinarily called meanings, then a homophonic translation does not qualify as a translation.

The difficulty I see with Davidson's view is this: Since we are not omniscient, a finite pairing of infinitely many truths with truths (and also infinitely many falsehoods with falsehoods), *must* rely on the trivial variety of T-sentences (those of the form "'p' is true iff p'') where the same descriptive terms are mentioned and used. But no interpretation of L results from putting infinitely many sentences together, none of which characterizes meanings even *partially*.

If one wishes to maintain that each T-sentence tells us a little bit about meaning and that the theory that implies them all tells us the entire story, then one must allow more informative T-sentences of the form

(T') 'p' is true iff q,

where the descriptive terms in 'p' and 'q' may differ. An instance of (T') could contribute to the interpretation of L only if the interpreter understood the T'-sentence, i.e., could *use* the terms in 'q' which, as a consequence, could not in their turn be interpreted by the sentence "'q' is true iff p." Indeed, all terms occurring in the right-hand sides of T'-sentences have to belong to an *interpreted* language L'. The resulting theory—although strong enough to imply T'-sentences that are interesting enough to play a role in a theory of meaning—would no longer be a Tarskian truth theory, but a theory for translating L into L'.

Imagine a program with a built-in version of Davidson's theory. When presented with 'p' the program would produce "'p' is true iff q." If 'q' is a genuine translation in L' of 'p,' the program has to use a routine which in effect embodies a theory of translation. In this case, Davidson's theory would be superfluous. If 'q' is 'p' without quotes, the program could do nothing to convince anyone that it is a simulation of an aspect of a human's mastery of L. Asked for the meaning of 'p', it would first produce "'p' is true iff p," then detach "'p' is true iff" and return 'p'. Easier ways of returning 'p' as an inadequate answer to the question "What is the meaning of 'p'?" come to mind.

An important ingredient of Davidson's position is his holistic view of meaning. I assume that the strong holistic thesis to which he sometimes seems to allude, i.e., that meaning "really" attaches only to the infinite totality of sentences of a language (that "to understand a sentence is to understand a language", etc.) is not proposed as literally true, but is proposed instead as a reminder that interpretation depends on contexts of varying sizes.

The strong holistic thesis can be taken to state that the meaning of a word is learned by learning all possible uses of the word in all sentences of the language. This view leaves no room for the possibility of gradually coming to master a language. It should be noted that the denial of the thesis is not the equally implausible thesis that all sentences could be fully grasped independently of one another or that the meanings of words are "epistemologically prior" to the meanings of sentences. Instead, the denial of strong holism amounts to the claim that one comes to know the meaning of a word by coming to know its use in some sentences and that to understand a sentence it suffices to be able to interpret a limited context of other sentences.

At any rate, the question of to what extent contextual influences constrain interpretation is empirical, and not to be settled by philosophical fiat. If a specification of the meaning of 'p' really were a summary description of the systematic contribution of 'p''s components to the "joint" meaning of infinitely many sentences—and who would know what *that* would be!—then no particular questions concerning the meaning of expressions could ever be answered. Under-standing could never get off the ground. It seems that a theory in this field should offer something both more helpful than T-sentences of an understood language and more surveyable than a sudden grasp of whatever it is that happens when infinitely many sentences go together to make a language.

It has been suggested above that a theory whose T'-sentences are strong enough to play a role in a theory of meaning for L would have to be a theory for translating L into some interpreted language L'.

But even if we had a theory for translating L into L', our troubles would not be over. We would now face the problem of constructing a non-translational theory of meaning for L'.

POSSIBLE-WORLDS SEMANTICS

This approach elaborates in many different versions Carnap's idea that a theory of meaning is a Tarskian theory of reference applied to possible worlds.

The intuitive starting point is the belief that to understand a sentence is to know the conditions under which it *would* be true. The meaning of sentence S thus comes to be associated with a set of truth-conditions and finally with the set of those possible worlds in which S is true. The meaning of S is identified with a function from possible worlds to truth values or to sets of possible worlds. It is even possible to define truth in terms of meaning. For example, S could be said to be true in world w iff w belongs to that set of worlds that has been assigned to S as its meaning. Similarly, to know the meaning of a predicate is to know not just its actual extension but the extensions it would have in other possible worlds. Meanings of predicates are thus taken to be functions from possible worlds to subsets of these possible worlds.

Meanings of certain compound expressions are identified with certain functions that themselves are functions of functions. The latter functions are meanings such as those exemplified earlier, and the former functions transform these meanings into other meanings, which themselves may be functions of the former or latter type.

Just as a semantic interpretation of L in a given world is an assignment of entities of that world to the expressions of L, an interpreted language could itself be identified with an assignment of sets of worlds to sentences.

There is no doubt that virtually everything under the sun can be defined as some kind of function. The question I wish to consider, however, is not whether meanings can be defined along the lines proposed by possible-worlds semanti-cists but whether meanings so construed would be of any use at all in thought and communication. I believe that the answer to this has to be negative.

Consider first the usual Tarski-style semantics on which the possible-worlds approach is based. Its basic tool is a recursive definition of satisfaction for all sentences of L (with zero or more free variables). Suppose there are given a non-empty set w and a function e that assigns extensions, (i.e., appropriate abstract entities such as sets of n-tuples of elements of w) to constant expressions of L. Then a function v from individual variables to elements of w is said to satisfy—for instance—'Fxy' iff the pair of objects assigned to 'x' and 'y' by v is indeed in the set of pairs assigned to 'F' by e. To put this machinery to work the functions e and v (and infinitely many others like v) are assumed to be somehow given.

Although I believe that model theory is a fruitful branch of platonistic mathematics, I don't think it will yield a basis for a theory of linguistic interpretation. If a language is to be *used* for thinking and talking and not just studied as a formal object its interpretation must be given by *effectively constructible* assignments of things to words.

It is not enough that certain functions from words to sets *exist. We* must be able to interpret the language. What I wish to suggest is that model-theoretic interpretation functions, extensionally construed as infinite sets of ordered pairs of expressions and things, are entirely unsuited for the task of interpreting actual languages. We cannot think with infinite sets in the required manner. What we would need instead is a semantics based on finitely specifiable, constructive rules.

This is even more apparent in the case of any semantics that makes essential use of the concept of a possible world.

Possible-world semantics are extensional only in letter, not in spirit. Object-linguistic possibility is ordinarily explained in terms of a metalinguistic relation of relative possibility between possible worlds in the following way: Given a relation R that holds between possible worlds w and v iff v is possible relative to w, truth of 'It is possible that p' at w is defined as truth of 'p' at some v such that wRv. I suspect that if I knew what it is for one possible world to be possible relative to another, then I might not find this definition illuminating. (As I do not, I do not.) Another familiar example is this: 'x believes that p' is true at w iff 'p' is true at all v such that wRv, where 'wRv' stands for 'v is compatible with everything x believes.' The general recipe for any—even the most questionable—intensional operator, '$?$,' is this: '$?_p$' is true at w iff 'p' is true at some/all v such that v is $?$-related to w.

For formal work in modal logic R is formally characterized as reflexive, or reflexive and transitive, or reflexive and symmetric, etc. It should be emphasized that without a method for determining which worlds are possible and which sentences are true in which world, the formal version is no more helpful than the intuitive one. The reason for this lies in the fact that the given formal characterizations of R are not strong enough to prevent necessity and possibility from collapsing into plain truth. As an example, consider the modal system $S5$. In $S5$, the accessibility relation R is characterized as an equivalence relation. Since the formal machinery cannot discriminate between equivalence relations let us choose a relation R that holds only between a world and itself. R is the identity relation and thus clearly an equivalence relation. In this case necessity and possibility are merely plain truth because a sentence is necessarily true at a world iff it is true at all worlds identical with the given one and possibly true iff it is true at some world identical with the given one.

None of the above remarks applies to a possible-world semantics that is cultivated as a branch of mathematics or pure logic. But when intensional logics are offered as contributions to a theory of how finite devices interpret indefinitely many utterances, one would expect an account of how such devices *could* inter- act with meanings construed as [say] functions from functions to functions. My objection is not that these model-theoretic systems are perhaps non-extensional or that the intuitive connections with the relevant philosophical explicanda are inadequately treated (although I *do* believe that "raw intensions" would reap- pear in applications). What I do find objectionable is rather that all this ontologi- cally quite extravagant machinery does not seem to give any explanatory mileage. For the "explanatory" right-hand sides of truth conditions require the *use* of concepts that, while not superior in point of clarity to the ones to be explained, raise problems of their own from the point of view of psychological modeling or simulation.

For example, a theorist interested in designing manipulable representations of meanings would not be helped by being told that the meaning of the predicate '—' is "that" function which assigns to each possible world the set of — things in it. However, I do not wish to suggest that all modal logicians claim to contribute to a theory of meaning. Those who do, I take to offer theories of competence that have hardly any chance of becoming components of perfor- mance models (i.e., models that explain how finite devices interpret indefinitely many utterances).

CONCEPTS AND PROCEDURES

If the foregoing criticisms are justified, a more "constructive" semantics is needed. Such a semantics, it seems, would have to provide effective rules that specify mechanisms capable of creating and manipulating meaning repre- sentations. A rule corresponding to an interpretation function specifies a proce- dure for determining which expression-extension pairs are elements of the func- tion. I shall identify concepts with such procedures.

Because a concept amounts to only one of several "modes" of implementing a function, the identity conditions for concepts differ from those for functions. Conditions that are necessary and sufficient for identity of functions are only necessary for identity of concepts. In this sense at least concepts are the "inten- sional" counterparts of functions. (Strictly speaking only linguistic contexts are properly characterized as intensional or extensional. I hope that reference to intensional or extensional entities will cause no misunderstandings.) Pending an explication of concepts, interpretation functions as purely extensional entities have the edge over concpets, as far as the usual demands of clarity are concerned. But the clarity of these functions impresses me somewhat less than what I believe to be their *unsuitability* for the task of constructing a theory of meaning strong enough to explain linguistic capacities. In the following, I shall try to spell out as clearly as I can what concepts are and what role they play in a theory of meaning.

Two functions are identical iff they contain the same argument-value pairs. But the association of identical values with corresponding arguments is only a necessary condition for identity of concepts. To make sure we know what we are talking about when talking about concepts, we must also formulate a sufficient condition for two concepts (or meanings) to be identical. Intuitively, concepts $c1$ and $c2$ are one and the same iff (1) they yield the same results, i.e., $c1(x) = c2(x)$ for all allowable inputs x, and (2) their outputs $c1(x)$ and $c2(x)$ are generated "in the same way."

An extensional explication of (2) can be given if *concepts are literally identified with certain kinds of procedures.* Assume we are given a collection of basic operations capable of transforming certain elements of a non-empty set w into other elements of w. We could think of each of these basic operations as a unique map from w into w, and of the process specified by an algorithm as a unique function A, which assigns to each element of w a (possibly empty) set of sequences of basic operations. However, for the sake of definiteness I shall assume the basic operations to coincide with Newell and Simon's elementary information processes (eip's). These eip's operate on symbol structures and are capable of—among other things—comparing, creating, modifying, copying, and storing symbols. (Newell & Simon, 1972, hypothesize that their chosen set of eip's, together with mechanically realizable modes of composition, constitutes an adequate foundation for the theory of human problem solving. Miller & Johnson-Laird, 1976, have recently presented arguments for a more inclusive and high-level set of basic operations humans can perform.)

Relative to a set of basic operations or eip's, two procedures are *strictly identical,* or synonymous iff (1) for all inputs, they either both do not terminate or they terminate with the same outputs (i.e., they are coextensive "in all possible worlds"), and (2) they instantiate the same flow diagram.

A flow diagram is a finite directed graph whose nodes have statements associated with them in roughly the following manner: There is exactly one node that is not the successor of any node and that is associated with the *start* statement, and at least one node that is associated with the *stop* statement. Some nodes have two arcs emanating from them, one labeled 'true,' the other 'false'; they are associated with *test* statements. All other nodes have at most one immediate successor and are associated with *assignment* statements. Every node can be reached from the start node. (For more on such matters see e.g., Manna, 1973.)

A flow diagram is interpreted, relative to a domain w, by assigning elements of w to its constants and input variables, if any, and "constructive" relations and functions to its predicate and function variables. (By a "constructive" relation or function I mean one that, roughly, is such that the basic instructions and tests are executable for all assignments of elements of w to input variables.) An interpreted flow diagram can perform computations. A computation could be represented by a stepwise transformation of elements of w. If a more detailed representation is desired, a computation might be represented, alternatively, by a sequence of states, each of which consists of the instruction under execution, together with the resulting values of all variables.

Two procedures instantiate the same flow diagram iff, for all inputs, they produce the same sequence of values and the same sequence of operations and tests, i.e., the same instructions are executed in the same order. I believe that this formulation captures the sense in which two procedures may be said to yield their results "in the same way," and allows us to speak of different procedures as so many "modes" of implementing one and the same function. In the following, I shall offer a few reasons for the literal identification of concepts with certain kinds of algorithms, and try to describe the role of concepts (or rather their linguistic counterparts, semantic rules), in a theory of meaning.

Condition (2) in the criterion of procedural identity actually implies (1). I have included (1) to emphasize an analogy with Carnap's criterion of intensional isomorphism (Carnap, 1947). Carnap regarded two expressions as having the same intension iff they are logically equivalent. (This corresponds to [1].) To be able to deal with (say) belief contexts, a principle that individuates more senses is needed. This is because, from the fact that x believes that p, it does not follow that x believes everything logically equivalent with p. According to Carnap's narrower principle of intensional isomorphism, two expressions are "understood in the same way" iff, they are not only logically equivalent but also built in the same way from logically equivalent components. (This corresponds to [2].) It seems, however, that in view of differences in psychological abilities or intended applications, pragmatic contextual factors should be allowed to play a role in selecting individuating principles of differing strengths. The present proposal would make this quite easy: Different notions of procedural similarity could be constructed by replacing (2) with coarser substitutes such as preservation of structure in terms of suitable modules, the same sequence of values, etc.

Concepts or "meanings" that I propose to identify with certain procedures are components of an internal system of representation—an "inner language of thought." The discussion of Davidson's view above led me to conclude that a theory of meaning for a natural language L should come in two stages: A theory for translating L into L' and—on pain of regress—a non-translational theory of meaning for some target language L'. L' is assumed to be an inner language.

At this point it is, of course, very tempting to try to avoid construction of a translational theory and ascription of inner languages to organisms by simply assuming that our native natural language is not merely the medium in which we encode our thoughts, but that in which we *think* them. In several places Harman has described the view that we think in our language (e.g., Harman, 1968). According to this view, to think that *p,* is—roughly speaking—to think words by which one means that *p.* As it stands, this is not very helpful. Thinking is thereby "explained" in terms of thinking *and* meaning. He proposes to identify a theory of the meaning of thoughts with a non-translational theory of meaning for a natural language. The latter would attempt to characterize the meanings of expressions in terms of their role in a conceptual scheme. To account for the fact that surface sentences are often ambiguous, Harman holds that understanding a sentence is a matter of hearing it as having a particular structural description. It is to be noted here that since a given surface sentence may correspond to several sentences-under-analysis, the former cannot be identified with any of the latter. So, it would appear that the representations used in thinking are more like ordered pairs consisting of a surface sentence and its structural description than like surface sentences. This is one reason for supposing that there are inner languages.

Another reason has to do with the fact that animals besides humans perceive things. To perceive something is to acquire beliefs about it. Having beliefs requires having concepts and, more generally, a system of representation. There are, then, some systems of representation that are not natural languages: A capacity for believing and thinking does not presuppose mastery of an "outer" language.

Perhaps the strongest argument in favor of an inner-language-hypothesis is based on the fact that we are rule-following and rule-creating organisms. Many of the more successful theories of cognition employ constructs such as images, schemata, plans, grammars, categories, associative memory networks, etc. to describe us as rule-following. According to these theories some or other internal—not necessarily conscious—representation of rules is among the causal determinants of behavior. I shall not even try to spell out in detail how rules as certain kinds of inscriptions relate to behaviors. *Very* roughly, particular behaviors are explained as resulting from the interaction of various mechanisms that are specified by systems of rules. Fodor (1975) is but one who maintains that theories that do not model psychological processes as computational or representational (and thus as presupposing internal representation systems) are entirely implausible, perhaps even incoherent.

Even if one accepts such arguments as showing that we use inner representation systems, one may wonder whether they qualify as *languages.* This question is important for anyone who takes an inner-language view seriously (as I do). I believe that the following fact serves to establish at least the coherence of such a view: There *are* mechanisms, i.e., computers (I am inclined to include people, but that would, in the present context, beg the question) that can be run directly from sufficiently detailed descriptions of processes. These descriptions are couched in representational media that qualify as languages. Programming languages have generative grammars and semantic interpretations. Some programming languages are, in fact, "internal."

Some programs (microprograms) are executed directly by the circuitry, others are interpreted by processors that are themselves programs. This is philosophically very important because it shows that there is at least one way of using "inner sentences" that does not presuppose a reading homunculus with a mind of his own.

Dennett (1975) maintains that the inner-language view is incoherent. Perhaps the hardest problem he raises is this: It is natural to account for our seemingly endless capacity to produce facts such as "salt is not sugar, or green, or oily . . ." (p. 409) by supposing that most of them are generated by a deducing mechanism applied to our data base. But the deducer itself needs information "about what items it would be appropriate at any time to retrieve from the core . . . " (p. 410). If this information is stored in the deducer's own propositional database, a further deducer seems needed, and so forth.

I believe that this regress can be stopped quite easily by representing the deducer's knowledge of the domain by procedures. They would not be called by name (because that would give rise to the question as to how the deducer knows that the knowledge represented by them is pertinent), but by a pattern matching process. In such a system each procedure has a pattern that says what the procedure is good for. The procedure is invoked if its pattern matches a data structure that represents an active goal. (For more on this approach, see e.g., Sussman & McDermott, 1972.) Another method for storing beliefs in non-propositional form would employ Minsky's "frames," which are a little bit like Wittgensteinian "forms of life" (cf. Minsky, 1975). The fact that at least some knowledge would have to be stored in procedural form does not threaten the coherence of the inner-language-view proposed here.

Where does this leave us? So far, I have tried to show that concepts are respectable components of an inner language. They are put together to make inner sentences in the way subroutines are put together to make programs. I have also tried to show that a theory of meaning for L consists of two parts: A non-translational part that ascribes meanings to the inner language L' on broadly "functional" grounds, and a part for translating L into L'.

The non-translational semantics for L' will have to assign meanings to inner sentences that we have identified with certain programs. The semantics of a program is given by specifying mechanisms for executing it and, ultimately, by describing the behavior of Turing machines. But while the semantics for a program can be specified in a straightforward manner it determines only how strings of signs are to be manipulated and does not address itself to the issue of reference or "representationality." If components of a programming language could be described as referring to anything at all, then they would have to be described as referring to strings of bits and to components of the processor such as memory locations and registers. The main referential devices of an AI program are pointers that are variables whose values are addresses. For example, the string "Fido" as used in a "natural language understanding" program does not—at least not as far as the semantics of the programming language is concerned—refer to Fido but to the address of a memory cell in which other strings are stored, which *we* may or may not be ready to think of as expressions referring to or as statements about Fido. The inadequate treatment of reference or aboutness is not peculiar to procedural semantics. The moot notion of aboutness is not explicated by the usual propositional semantics either, which interprets a set of strings by mapping it onto a set containing two distinct formal objects, say '*T*' and '*F*.'

A great deal would have to be added to the semantics of programming languages to get a non-translational theory of *meaning*. Among several conditions that would have to be met before a string could be said to have a certain meaning is the following: The string is assigned a place in a system of interlocking routines. The system establishes a connection between strings and extralinguistic reality because it is organized in such a way that some strings and some perceptual inputs provide access to the same routines, thereby allowing some strings to influence behavior in a manner similar to perception.

Another ingredient of a theory of meaning would have to be an account of representation. I suspect that many philosophers would deny that programming languages are genuine languages precisely on the grounds that they lack representationality or aboutness. Take a device that has certain priorities and certain complex capacities to react differently to different inputs, and suppose that these capacities can be identified with concepts or routines, as above. Then a *very* rough characterization of representation might go as follows:

Concept c *of device* d *represents* x *as* F iff (1) upon receiving signals from *x* and given certain goals, *d* executes *c,* and, (2) if *x* is indeed *F,* execution of *c* produces behavior that increases *d*'s chances of achieving its goals.

This is just another way of saying that inner meanings are a matter of environmentally appropriate behavior and cannot be read off directly from the "brainware" implementation of inner sentence tokens. Since we impute representationality to the strings produced by an information processing system on behavioral grounds a program purporting to simulate understanding would have to operate in at least a simulated environment. That is, some of its internal goings-on would have to be connected to sensors and effectors, etc. Suppose, for example, that instead of writing suggestive names like MOVE, GRASP, etc., one were to write *x,y,* etc. In the absence of a wider context to look at, it would be *very* difficult to convince oneself that the *x*'s and *y*'s refer to parts of internal *meaning* representations.

The translational part of a procedural theory of meaning is much more straightforward. If the result of understanding a sentence is a series of routines, then the process of understanding is analogous to the process of *compilation*. A theory for translating L into L' would thus describe a program in L' for converting sentences of L into sequences of routines of L'. Longuet-Higgins (1970) and Davies and Isard (1972) have in fact proposed to pursue the analogy between understanding and compiling, and between natural languages and very high-level programming languages. Davies and Isard mention as an advantage of their proposal that it accounts nicely for the fact that understanding an utterance is compatible with doing all sorts of things, including nothing. A compiled program need not be run. Miller and Johnson-Laird (1976) have applied the research project of procedural semantics to psychology.

If the analogy can be made to stick, then one could say that just as you need a successful compilation before you can run your program so you must understand a sentence before you can try to confirm it or use it in some other fashion to guide action. The outward structure of a sentence drives the compiling process that attaches semantic actions in the form of executable code to syntactic components of the sentence. Once a sentence has been understood by compiling it into a corresponding routine the latter could be executed to test the truth of the sentence or to modify the understander's knowledge base.

Two predicates could be said to be synonymous if their corresponding routines are strictly identical in the sense previously defined. Analytic entailment between predicates could be explicated in terms of graph-theoretical relationships between the flow diagrams of their corresponding routines.

REFERENCES

Carnap, R. 1947. *Meaning and necessity: a study in semantics and modal logic*. Chicago: University of Chicago Press.

Davidson, D. 1967. Truth and meaning. *Synthese* 17.

Davidson, D. 1968. On saying that. *Synthese* 19.

Davidson, D. 1970. Semantics for natural languages. In *Linguaggi nella Società e nella Tecnica*, ed. B. Visentini Milan: Edizioni di Communità.

Davidson, D. 1973. In defense of convention T. In *Truth, syntax, and modality*, ed. H. Leblanc. Amsterdam: North-Holland.

Davies, D. J. M., & Isard, S. D. 1972. Utterances as programs. *Machine Intelligence* 7.

Dennett, D. C. 1975. Brain writing and mind reading. In *Language, mind and knowledge*, ed. K. Gunderson, *Minnesota studies in the philosophy of science*, vol. 7. Minneapolis: University of Minnesota Press.

Fodor, J. A. 1975. *The language of thought*. New York: Crowell.

Harman, G. 1968. Three levels of meaning. *Journal of Philosophy* 65: 590–602.

Longuet-Higgins, H. C. 1970. Computing science as an aid to psycholinguistic studies. *Bulletin of the Institute of Mathematics and Its Applications* 6.

Manna, Z. 1973. Program schemas. In *Currents in the theory of computing*, ed. A. V. Aho. Englewood Cliffs, N.J.: Prentice-Hall.

Miller, G. A., & Johnson-Laird, P. N. 1976. *Language and perception*. Cambridge: Belknap.

Minsky, M. L. 1975. A framework for representing knowledge. In *The psychology of computer vision,* ed. P. H. Winston. New York: McGraw-Hill.

Newell, A., & Simon, H. A. 1972. *Human problem solving.* Englewood Cliffs, N.J.: Prentice-Hall.

Sussman, G. J., & McDermott, D. V. 1972. From PLANNER to CONNIVER: a genetic approach. Proceedings of the FJCC 41.

8 Inference in the Conceptual Dependency Paradigm: A Personal History

Roger C. Schank
Yale University

INTRODUCTION

During a summer workshop (funded by the Sloan Foundation) at Yale, I presented some of the views that we hold with respect to the problems of representation of meaning, the making of inferences, and the function of higher level descriptions of the structure of knowledge, to an audience primarily consisting of social and cognitive psychologists. Most of the participants in the workshop were interested in our ideas on this subject. However, their background really had not prepared them to understand why we did what we did or how we came to do it. Consequently, I attempted to give them that background by retracing the steps in our research of the last ten years. I explained how we came to hold our current views on various subjects by showing what our initial assumptions were and how one position naturally led us to the next. Since most of the participants in the workshop felt that these lectures provided the context that was necessary to help them to understand our current research, I felt that it would be of use to prepare a paper based on the lecture notes that I used in the workshop.

This chapter therefore is necessarily sketchy. It is an attempt to present the outline of ten years of research and as such can only barely cover the issues. Furthermore, the paper is entirely biased towards the research within our own group. Much other work, some well known and other less known occurred before and during the work described here. To some extent this work affected our own, but by and large the work described here proceeded on its merry way untouched by very much from the outside. In this chapter I shall attempt to show how and why we got to where we are today.

1966-1969

My initial research focused on the representation of meaning as it would be used for the generation of natural language sentences. Since generation was the major problem in both linguistics and computational linguistics, this point of departure was not particularly different from the established norms. The major difference was that my representations were intended to be psychologically correct (to the extent that that could be determined). This led me away from what I believed to be the many ad hoc entities that existed within transformational deep structures at the time.[1]

I thus began to think about the problem of representing meaning. In particular, as I was still interested in the computability of any representation that I came up with, I was especially concerned with the question of how a meaning representation could be of use in the generation of natural language sentences, and in the parsing of natural language sentences.

The first representation that I came up with looked a lot like English with arrows connecting it up. The arrows were gotten from dependency theory, which

---

[1] I started out in Artificial Intelligence as an undergraduate in mathematics (which included computer science) at Carnegie Tech (now Carnegie-Mellon) in the early sixties. I became interested in language, and, feeling that language would best be studied with those whose speciality it was, I went to study Linguistics. When I arrived at the University of Texas in 1966, Texas was a combination of two relatively unrelated paradigms. Transformational Generative grammar was beginning to become the dominant paradigm within the department of Linguistics itself. But, at the same time, an extremely large mechanical translation project that had flourished at Texas for some time, was present but drawing to a close, at least partially due to the ALPAC report issued that year. This meant that while there were a large number of computer oriented people in Austin whose interest was language, the power in the department itself, where I was a student, was held by the transformationalists.

As a computer type myself, I naturally assumed that the main issue in language study ought to be the representation of meaning. Not only was this not the view held by either of the paradigms present in Austin at the time, but it was a view whose opposite position was strongly held by all those around me. Syntax was the issue of the day in the Linguistics department itself, and at the Linguistics Research Center (LRC) where the MT work was being done, gigantic phrase structure grammars and rules that transferred structure from one language to another were what was being done.

My views came to me by way of Newell and Simon at Carnegie (Actually this was quite indirect. I had never met either of them, but their work on GPS and more importantly their views on the nature of computer programs as theories was well known to most students at Carnegie); by Sheldon Klein who was my teacher at Carnegie, and by Sydney Lamb who was Klein's teacher and whom I had met and interacted with at the Linguistics Institute held at the University of Michigan in the summer preceding my senior year at Carnegie.

My own view represented a sort of amalgamation of the views of all these people. I was encouraged in my effort by my advisor at Texas, Jacob Mey, and by my employer at Tracor (a company that allowed some of the LRC people to move there after the LRC funding dried up), Eugene Pendergraft.

had been written about by Hays and used quite a bit by Klein and to some extent Lamb. My contribution, as I saw it at that time, was to make the representation more conceptual. I reasoned that the dependency grammars being used at that time were too concerned with questions of whether the noun or the verb was really the head of the sentence and not enough concerned with the meaning of the sentence. Obviously, the main noun and main verb contributed equally to the conceptualization that underlied the sentence.[2] That is, both were necessary for the sentence to have meaning. I concentrated on issues such as these, coming up in the end with rules that described the make up of a conceptualization in terms of items more conceptual than nouns and verbs.

I then began to work on the problem of how my representation system would allow for random generation of English sentences (this being my computer-biased view of the work in Linguistics at the time and thus the field in which I saw myself doing battle) and how my system would work for the representation of languages other than English.[3]

To facilitate the former of these tasks, I had to invent what I called "a conceptual semantics" (Schank, 1968), which was basically a depository of world knowledge that prevented any random generator from generating sentences that meant nothing. The latter considerations of universality caused various English items such as prepositions to drop out of the representations. Even so, my representations bore a great deal of similarity to the surface properties of English. I was aware of this problem, but was far more concerned at the time with attempting to convince linguists that meaning considerations were important.[4]

At this point I was rather anxious to get a job, and largely through chance, found myself employed by Kenneth Colby at Stanford.[5] My job within his project was to create a parser that would allow his soon to be created[6] version of an automated psychiatrist to actually understand what the patient said. To do this, I attempted to reverse the rules that I had already written for generation out of

---

[2]That, of course, is the origin of the symbol $<=>$.

[3]My system being conceptual it ought to have been capable of handling this latter task. Furthermore, I could hardly have not worried about this issue since the emphasis in Linguistics was on what were then called "funny languages" (in my case I worked on Quiche and a little on Eskimo) and because MT was clearly in need of an interlingua that would facilitate translation.

[4]I now know that there were some who were already convinced of that fact but they were not at Texas and were unknown to me. Fillmore's work was discussed but its properties were still far more syntactic than I had in mind.

[5]Colby had at this point recognized that his dreams of an automated psychiatrist depended on solving the natural language problem first. I of course agreed with this and found the idea of an automated psychiatrist fascinating. I had, until this time, never really thought about the higher level processes that were to operate on top of any meaning representation I came up with. I was interested, prior to my working for Colby, mostly in mechanical translation. Shortly after I arrived Colby and his project moved physically to the Stanford AI lab, thus cementing my involvement with AI.

[6]It never actually existed in its planned newer form.

Conceptual Dependency (CD). Such a reversal of rules was established doctrine within computational linguistics and I assumed it would work.[7]

As an example of the kind of issues I was concerned about at that time consider the sentences:

I hit Fred on the nose

I hit Fred in the park

In order to parse these sentences correctly it is necessary to know where a person can be located. Here, "correctly" depended on what had to be represented in CD. There was a locative for entire conceptualizations and a "part of" relationship for objects, and either could be expressed in English with a locative prepositional phrase. To solve this problem I used the conceptual semantics I had invented for generation, and my rules that mapped from syntactic relationships to conceptual ones checked for acceptability each time a mapping was attempted. The same thing was necessary for sentences such as:

I hit the boy with long hair

However, what had to be done to handle ambiguous sentence, was to add information in the conceptual semantics. The conceptual semantics for 'hit' consisted of information about the kind of objects to be found in various prepositional relationships. So, for 'hit' we had:

with – weapon object
by   – no
on   – part of ←–PP

The final parse of this sentence put this additional information concerning the properties of "hair" in the actual representation. Although I did not use the term, this was in a sense the first class of inference to be made, and added to the meaning representation in my work. Since it had to be determined if the 'with' object for 'hit' was a weapon or a part of the object, that determination, once made, now became part of what had been understood and thus was part of what was meant. The can of worms that this adding of information not actually stated opened was tremendous. Additional information could be added to what had been said to form what had been meant. This was quite different from what had gone on in linguistics up until that time (and to some extent what still goes on in

---

[7]Of course, there were no semantic representations in computational linguistics at that time, those ideas about reversal had to do with syntactic rules. I saw no reason to not go directly to my new conceptual base, and anyway as I have said my conceptual base looked an awful lot like English in any case, so this did not seem to be that great a shift.

linguistics). I was saying that the meaning of a sentence was more than the sum of its parts. This heresy was not particularly appreciated when I brought it up, although it probably had seemed obvious to those AI people that had looked at the problem.

Thus, my point was that Chomsky was wrong in claiming that we should not be attempting to build a point by point model of a speaker-hearer. Such a model was precisely what I felt should be tackled. Linguists viewed this as performance and thus uninteresting. I took my case to psychologists and found them equally uninterested. Psychologists interested in language were mostly psycholinguists, and psycholinguists for the most part bought the assumptions of transformational grammar (although it seemed very odd to me that given the competence/performance distinction, psychologists should be on the side of competence).

1970

In 1970 we started to make our representations more conceptual.[8] Until this point our supposedly language-free representations had a great deal of language in them. We noticed a class of verbs (which we termed pseudo-state verbs), where the object of the sentence did not seem to be the same as the underlying deep object of the underlying action. In particular, our representations seemed to require us to put in a great deal more than was in the sentence in order to make conceptual sense. Thus for (1) below we had to make up something called 'create,' in (2) we had a particular sense of 'have,' and in (3) all of a sudden we had 'truth' and 'saying' present. There did not seem to be any way to avoid this introduction of elements that weren't there initially if we were to represent the meaning of what had been said:

(1) he wrote a book

$$\text{he} \Longleftrightarrow \text{create} \longleftarrow \text{book} \longleftarrow \begin{array}{c} \text{by he} \\ \wedge\wedge \\ | \ | \\ \text{writes} \end{array}$$

(2) he desired Martha in the morning

$$\begin{array}{c} \text{he} \Longleftrightarrow \text{want} \\ \wedge \\ \text{he} \Longleftrightarrow \text{have} \longleftarrow \text{Martha} \\ \wedge \\ | \\ \text{morning} \end{array}$$

---

[8]The 'we' consisted of Larry Tesler (a programmer who worked for Colby and was attempting to write our parser) and Sylvia Weber (a graduate student in the Computer Science department at Stanford).

(3) he doubted his wife

$$he \Longleftrightarrow doubt$$
$$\overset{\wedge}{}$$
$$x \Longleftrightarrow true$$
$$\overset{|}{\diagdown|\diagup}$$
$$wife \Longleftrightarrow say$$
$$of \overset{\wedge\wedge}{|\ |}$$
$$he$$

Examining these representations, we began the search for some regularities in the representation that would give us a more canonical form. What we had until that point was so free form that we could create anything at any time. This did not seem very sensible. In particular, there was a problem of what sense of the various multiple sense verbs we had at any given time. We couldn't just continue writing 'have' the way we had done. There had to have been some underlying basic forms. We considered for a while just writing subscripts on the verbs. So 'understand1' was equal to 'see3.' But which sense was more basic? And, more importantly, how many senses of a word would there turn out to be and what would their intersections be? In the case of partial overlap of senses there was a definite problem with the subscript method.

As a side issue at this time, we attempted to clean up the mess in which we had left our representation of prepositions. We had been using an arrow to mean any prepositional relationship, in the faith that higher level processes that used our representations (we really had no idea what they would be like; the psychiatric model would have to deal with that problem) would figure out the true relationship that held between an action and its associated objects. We tried to think about what kinds of prepositional relationships there were. Location had long before been relegated to describing conceptualizations themselves, so it wasn't a candidate. 'Part of' relationships were used to describe objects, rather than the relationship between actions and objects so they weren't part of the problem either. By eliminating these two classes of prepositions (those that described entire events and those that solely described objects) we found that there were only three kinds of prepositional relationships: instrumental, directional, and recipient. These relationships then described the way an action could relate to an object in an event regardless of what preposition was being used. Since we were describing relationships and not prepositions, we realized that English could be considered to have a kind of null preposition denoting objective relationships but that this did not indicate that this was any less of a relationship between action and object than the others. We knew that Fillmore had said similar things about syntactic relationships in English so we christened our relationships 'conceptual cases.' The differences between the two systems were a lot greater than their names suggested and in retrospect this was probably a poor choice of names (see Schank, 1972, for a discussion of those differences).

This new system of cases immediately had ramifications throughout our entire system. Thus, for example we had previously represented 'I want money' as:

```
I <==> want
       ∧
       |
   money <==> go <‾ I
```

However, adding a recipient to this representation caused us to come up with the following representation:

```
   I <==> want
          ∧
          |                O        R |--->I
   Someone <=>   ??   <- money <--|
                                   |---< someone
```

That is, we knew that we had a Recipient here and it had to be 'I.' Similarly there had to be an Object because what else could 'money' be? It didn't seem like an actor. The actor was unknown but we knew he was the same person as the donor of the recipient case. Of course, the above diagram had a glaring hole. What was the action? Still this representation seemed to make a lot more sense than the one having money be an actor that did the action 'go'.[9] What was needed at this point was a name for our unknown action, and since it was obviously a kind of transfer of the money that was being done we called it 'trans.'

'Trans' helped us with other problems as well. It solved the partial overlap problem in the meaning of words such as 'give' and 'take' and 'buy' and 'sell.' Furthermore, it eliminated the need for elaborate transfer of meaning rules of the kind Katz (1967) had been proposing for mapping words like 'buy' into 'sell.' We began to wonder what other actions like 'trans' were around.

We began to look at other representations we had, using the conceptual case notions that we had invented. For example we had represented 'He heard me' as:

```
                I
   he <=> perceive <--- ears
                        ∧∧ of
                        | |
                        he
                   &  ---> he
   I <=> say <--- X <---|
                        ---< I
```

'Hear' obviously took a conceptual object of sound that got translated into a meaning by some process. 'Me' was not a sensible conceptual object for 'hear.'

---

[9] I should point out that one of the basic maxims of CD was that there was an actor-action-object framework into which things should fit. This was part of the rules that I worked out in my thesis (Schank, 1969).

Similarly the conceptual form of 'hear' needed an instrument that had something to do with 'ears.' Such considerations forced us to rearrange the sentence into a conceptual format that represented the fact that the meaning of an idea being transferred was the key action taking place.

We began at this point, to look more closely at the concept of an action. We attempted to classify the verbs we had been using according to the cases they took and properties of their objects. This left us with S(tate)-ACTs, P(hysical)-ACTs, E(motional)-ACTs, and so on (Schank et al., 1970). Using this classification for verbs, we could now predict the missing cases that were implicit and thus that had to be inferred. We continued to look for effective groupings that would facilitate inference. Thus, while we did not actually set out to discover primitives, the considerations that we had in representation issues forced us to come up with some workable classification of actions that fit within our framework.

Inference was not yet a major issue in this regard, but other problems forced us to focus on it. For example, consider the sentence 'I fear bears' and our proposed representation of it at that time:

$$
\begin{array}{c}
\text{I} \Leftrightarrow \text{fear} \\
\wedge \\
\mid \\
\text{bears} \Leftrightarrow \text{harm} \Leftarrow\!\!- \text{I}
\end{array}
$$

In the same paper where we were wrestling with the issue of representation of actions (Schank et al., 1970) we also introduced an idea we called "associative storage of concepts." In order to adequately represent sentences of the above type, it was necessary to have available a conceptualization that could serve as the object of the verb 'fear.' (At this point we viewed such a verb as a kind of stative ACT. We later realized states were not ACTs but states of objects.) Obviously this conceptualization had to have in it both 'bears' and 'I' as part of the object of 'fear.' Here again we were faced with the question of what was the ACT? The answer we chose was an ACT called 'harm.' As we were not interested in primitives particularly this should not seem strange. The focus of our interest was: How were we going to find the concept 'harm' to add to our representation?

The answer was through associative storage of concepts. What we meant by this was that there had to be some connection between fear and bears that would allow us to infer 'harm' as the missing ACT. Quillian (1968) had used an idea of a linked network of concepts that could be searched from two paths in order to find their shortest intersection. This idea had been used for disambiguation, but it now seemed that it could be extended for use here as well.

However, that seemed like a lot of work for so little. When we looked at other examples of the phenomenon we were trying to account for, an easier solution presented itself. For example, the sentence 'I like books' clearly needed something about 'I read books' inside the conceptualization that represented its meaning. It was obvious that this could be done simply by listing 'books' in the dictionary as a 'READ object.' All that would then be required was an empty slot requiring an ACT. CD gave us that when a stative ACT was recognized, so all we had to do at that point was to look in the dictionary for an ACT associated with the object we had available. This did not solve the problem when the object was not the source of the inference. A functional object like a 'book' could well be listed as a 'READ object,' but what were we to do when 'bears' or 'Nixon' was the object of a stative ACT? Since these objects were not functional in the same way, it seemed that the missing ACT would have to be supplied as a part of the meaning of the word 'fear.' Here again, we had, without quite intending to, decomposed the meaning of a word (fear) into more basic elements (fear plus expected harm). The reason this had happened was again attributable to the requirements we had put on CD with respect to what slots there were in a conceptualization and how they were to be filled. So, we were left at this point with a representation like:

I fear Nixon

$$I <=> fear$$
$$\wedge$$
$$|$$
$$Nixon <=> do$$
$$\wedge\wedge\wedge$$
$$|\ |\ |$$
$$something <=> harm <---|I$$

Thus, at this point we were now freely adding to our representation concepts that were not present in the English sentence in the first place, and perhaps more importantly, concepts that were only probably part of the meaning. These were the first explicit inferences that we had.

In 1971, we began to focus on the problem of the inference of intentions. We got into this problem because of a peculiar use of language that we happened to come across, that we realized it was crucial for any reasonable understanding system to handle. The example was:

Q: Do you want a piece of chocolate?
A: I just had an ice cream cone.

Clearly, it is necessary to understand the answer here as meaning 'no.' In attempting to figure out how to do this, we realized that it was necessary to fill out the structure of the conceptualizations underlying both sentences so that a match could be made from the answer to the question. To do this required inferences, ones that were different from the ''fill in the ACT'' ones we had been working on. Thus we needed a structure like:

want
^^^
|'|'|
trans
^^^
|||
eat
^^^
|||
satisfied

To get this structure we had to postulate that when a trans was present, the object being transed might enable an actor to perform the usual functional ACT done to this object. Furthermore we had to examine the result of this action, because whatever state it caused was the key for the pattern match. That is, a paraphrase of this question might be 'Do you want me to trans you an object that is edible so you can eat it so that will make you feel some feeling (full, happy, etc.)? The answer would then be 'I already have that feeling because I just did an action (here 'had' has to be inferred to be 'eat') that resulted in that feeling.' To do all this required a new set of resultative and enabling inferences, and began to cause us to focus on the question of what kinds of inferences there were and where they came from.

One of the first issues however was the potential use of such inferences. Since we were primarily concerned with parsing at this stage, we focused initially on the issue of what expectations there were in processing that came from places other than the CD or syntactic expectations themselves.[10]

We looked at an example of a conversation where a person in a fit of anger at his wife, asks for a knife from a friend and when he is refused it says:

I think I ought to . . .

The question we asked was: What different kinds of things do you expect at this point? We isolated these (Schank, 1971):

1. sentential   – a verb coming
2. conceptual   – a entire conceptualization is coming
3. context   – "ought to have fish"
                     excluded by fighting context
                     something violent expected
4. conversational – inference of reason person is talking
                     why tell someone about your future
                     violence unless you want them to stop it?

---

[10]Expectations were the key idea behind how our parser was supposed to work. The parser Tesler designed (Schank & Tesler, 1969) was intended to 'laugh' at the sentence 'I saw the Grand Canyon flying to New York' because it would have had its expectations violated. Riesbeck (1975) of course later did this in a more serious way.

5. memory   – what kind of person is John?
                              should we take his anger seriously?

6. culture   – what happens in situations of this sort?
                              memory structure inferences used

These questions started us looking seriously at what else was going on in understanding besides parsing. Clearly we needed a memory full of facts about the world to do any sensible understanding. At this point our focus began to change. The issues of representation and parsing still existed of course, but memory and inference were obviously at least as crucial.

Around this time, I met Abelson, who was working on beliefs as was Colby. I began to see that beliefs had a great deal to do with the processing of language. My group[11] began to attack this problem in a number of ways. Hemphill (1975) began to work on identifying how parsing was influenced by beliefs implicitly referred to in a text. I, as usual, concentrated my efforts on representation. In particular, it was necessary, in order to handle the above example, to postulate a set of beliefs that could account for our expectations about an actor's behavior. To understand that John was not likely to want to now sit down and be friendly in the above example we needed to know that when you're angry you don't like to be with the people you are angry with. This was represented as:

```
one <==>do
 1 ^^^
   |||
one <==> angry
 2 ^^^
   |||
one <==> want
 2          ^
            |
      one <==> interact
    ^1
      one
       2
```

Beliefs of this sort were useful for predicting the future actions of an actor. Adding beliefs to the representation changed the idea of inference as just added information that would help in the parsing of a sentence. It suggested that we had to concentrate on problems having to do with the representation of information in memory, and with the overall integration of incoming data with a given memory model. It thus became clear that natural language processing was a bit of a misnomer for our enterprise. What we were doing was not essentially different

---

[11]By this time, a number of students had begun working with me. Goldman, Rieger, Riesbeck, Hemphill and Weber finished degrees with me at Stanford and were active in weekly meetings held during this time to discuss these issues. A number of other students who didn't finish contributed as well.

from what Colby or Abelson were doing. That is, we had to deal with the problem of belief systems in general. But, added to that, was the problem of representation of meaning, knowledge, and memory in general.

1972

The integration of all these problems caused us to deal with sentences whose meaning was a product of the combination of all these issues. For example, "He acts like Harry" means different things if Harry is a cat, a child, or an aged man. What is the correct representation for the meaning of such a sentence? Clearly it cannot be determined in any way apart from the memory structures its meaning relies on. Similarly, the sentence "He is doglike in his devotion" means nothing if there is no belief about the devotion or lack of it of dogs available in memory.

In attempting to catalog the kinds of beliefs that were being used in natural language expressions, we came across two (Schank, 1974) that used inference quite frequently. These were:

Pay back in kind.

Pay back not in kind.

Such beliefs were used in sentences such as:

John threw a hammer at Bill vengefully.

Mercifully the king only banished the knight
for killing his favorite horse.

This kind of analysis meant that we could predict other actions from what we determined was a reasonable inference. That is we could make inferences from inferences. So, 'vengefully' told us that Bill may have done something to John, and that John really wanted to hurt Bill and so on. Such inferences were an important part of the understanding process.

The cataloging of such random facts was not within our view of how to attack a problem, however. Instead we returned to attempting to make more rigorous the CD representations we were using so that we could better establish what was within the domain of a system like CD and what was outside of it. To do this, we considered the nature of the ACTs we had been using. At that point we had been using 'trans' and a hodgepodge of others that suited us. To remedy this situation we looked at the mental verbs that we had, to this point, virtually ignored.[12]

The significance of the primitive ACTs for us was that we could now be sure

---

[12]We formed a special group to consider this problem, consisting of Goldman, Rieger, Riesbeck and myself. Eventually, each of these students came up with one mental ACT and defended it to the others. This left us with three mental ACTs, CONC, MBUILD and MTRANS invented by the above people respectively. This gave us a total of sixteen primitive ACTs.

that we had a given agreed-upon representation for most of the sentences we were dealing with. This made our system usable by the large group of students who were beginning to concern themselves with programming systems that could communicate with each other. Further, we now knew what was in the bounds of the theory and what was not. We knew that to do the kind of work we were interested in, a canonical form was necessary. We were not so concerned with the ultimate correctness of that system as we were with its usability. No other canonical form existed, and transformational deep structure representations, which were the major well known alternative, neither adequately represented meaning nor were in any sense canonical. The most important part of the primitives of CD for us then were that they facilitated our getting on to the more interesting problems at hand. They did this because they gave us a language in which to describe those problems.

1973

The most important problem was inference. The first paper on the complete set of primitives we had (Schank, 1973) made that clear in its title: "The Fourteen Primitive Acts and Their Inferences." The single most important fact about the primitive ACTs was that they helped to organize the inference problem. No primitive ACT meant anything in the system at all, other than the conceptualizations that might come to exist as inferences from it. Primitive ACTs served to organize the inference process, thus giving us a starting point from which to attack the problem.

We began to concern ourselves therefore with two principle kinds of inference, results from ACTs and enablements for ACTs. Then, having exhausted the inferences derivable from the ACTs themselves, we began to attempt to categorize the kinds of inferences that needed to be made in general. In Schank and Rieger (1974) we delimited the following kinds of inference:

1. Linguistic Inference (done before parsing is over)

   buy - infers "money" as object
   hit - infers "hand" as object

2. ACT Inference

   whenever an actor and object were present in a CD an action had to be inferred. Thus for "I like books" "read" is inferred.

3. TRANS-ENABLE

   For sentences such as "John wants a book" it is necessary to infer an ATRANS, which then enables an ACT to take place. That ACT can be determined by ACT inference.

4. Result Inference

For any given ACT its results can be easily determined. "John went to N.Y." implies he got there. "Mary gave Bill a book" implies Bill has it and Mary no longer does. These come from PTRANS and ATRANS respectively.

5. Object Affect Inference

Inferences come from the interaction of objects and ACTs. In "John hit Mary with a rock" we infer that Mary is damaged and the rock is not. In "John ate an egg" we infer that the egg has been transformed. These inferences come from the ACT.

6. Belief Pattern Inference

When we see "John hit Mary" we infer that Mary must have angered him by doing something. This inference is gotten from a belief. The belief is accessed by matching a pattern containing "intentional damage," which is written in CD. This inference does not come from ACTs therefore but from states.

7. Instrumental Inference

We can infer instruments for ACTs that we have found.
Thus INGEST implies PTRANS as instrument.
PTRANS implies MOVE or PROPEL as instrument and so on.

8. Property Inference

Did Nixon run for President in 1863? This can best be determined by examining properties such as whether Nixon is alive or if it is election year before doing any exhaustive memory search. The inference of those underlying propositions means that preconditions for actions must be known. That is simple when the actions are simple ACTs. For concepts such as an election it is harder.

9. Sequential Inference

Results of the combination of two sentences can bring up new information. Thus "All redheads are Obnoxious" followed by "Mary has red hair," makes the latter statement more contentive. Such additional content depends on knowledge about Mary's personality. The correct inference requires a memory search.

10. Causality

"John hit Mary and she died" or "John hit Mary" followed by "John died" both imply causality. Such causality information can only be determined by examining the resultative properties of the ACT.

11. Backward Inference

We can often determine a new fact by pondering how an old fact came to be. Thus "John knows where Mary is" implies that he saw her or someone told him. This comes from the enablements for an action.

12. Intention

It is important to know why people do what they do. Thus intentions and motivations had to be inferred. We really did not know how to do that.

Rieger, Riesbeck, Goldman and I began to design a computer implementation of these ideas in 1972 that resulted in the MARGIE system (Schank, 1975).[13] During the implementation of these ideas our views on parsing, generation and inference were altered by the task of attempting to specify precise algorithms for these processes. In particular for our discussion of inference, Rieger created a new classification of inferences based on his experience with MARGIE (Rieger, 1975). These were:

1.	Specification	– unmentioned particulars are inferred
2.	Causative	– reasons for an action
3.	Resultative	– results of an action
4.	Motivational	– motivations for an action
5.	Enablement	– enablements for an action
6.	Function	– when an object is mentioned its potential use is determined
7.	Enable Prediction	– what ACT will be enabled by ACT or STATE
8.	Missing Enablement	– why someone can't do an ACT
9.	Intervention	– reasons for actions that prevent harm
10.	Action Prediction	– predict ACT from object
11.	Knowledge Propagation	– determining who knows what
12.	Normative inferences	– determining normal states of the world
13.	State Duration	– how long an ACT or STATE goes on
14.	Features	– who can be expected to do what
15.	Situation	– events are imbedded in larger events
16.	Utterance Intent	– why people do what they do and say what they say

In Schank (1975) we attempted to further codify the kinds of inferences that were available for a given ACT. For example, we listed these rules for the ACT PROPEL:

---

[13] Actually this is not quite accurate. The MARGIE system was never intended to work as a whole system, and it was not designed that way. Jerry Feldman suggested that we put it all together. Prior to his suggestion we just had three unrelated student projects meant to cover three areas of interest.

```
                                     | - - - - <Z
      X<--> PROPEL<-- Y<-- |
                                     | - - - - <W
```

1. TRANS is implied if (Obj is not fixed)
2. Object in directive case (Z) is negatively affected if PHYSCONT is present and sizes are right.
3. If Z is human then X may have been angry at Z
4. If Y is rigid and brittle and nonfixed, and speed of instrumental ACT is great, then Y will be NEGPHYSST

In general we noted that there were two major kinds of inferences:

Forward   ———>   what consequences from an ACT?
Backward   ———>   why an ACT and what enabled an ACT.

At this point we began to take seriously the problem of codifying the kinds of causal relations that there were.[14] This work was crucial to the inference problem since, we had come to believe that the major inferences were (forward) consequences and (backward) reasons. Thus the primary task of the inference process was the filling in of causal chains. We identified four kinds of causal links, RESULT, REASON, INITIATE and ENABLE. RESULT and ENABLE were the forward and backward causal rules for physical ACTs, and REASON and INITIATE were the forward and backward links for mental ACTs. We also added the rule that ACTs could only result in states and only states could enable ACTs. This had the consequence of making our causal chains and thus our CD representations both very precise and very cumbersome. The precision was of course important for any canonical form, but the cumbersomeness was obviously a problem that needed to be dealt with.

As an example of the kinds of representations we were creating by doing this, consider the representation that we now had for a sentence such as "John's cold improved because I gave him an apple."

```
                         o            D  | - - - - - ->John
        I<==>PTRANS <--- apple <--- |
        ^^^                             | - - - - -<
        | | |    r
        | | | | - - - - -> LOC (John)
   apple <===|
        | - - - -<
```

---

[14]I had wanted to do this for some time, but really had not had the opportunity. In 1973 I took a year off from Stanford and went to Lugano, Switzerland where a new Institute was starting up, taking Riesbeck and Goldman with me. We had little to do there but think and I was able to finish the book on MARGIE and start working on issues that I had not had time for before.

```
      ^^^
      | | |  E          o          D  |-----> John
John <===> INGEST <--- apple <---|
      POT                            |-----<
      ^^^
      | | |  I              o  |---> I want to eat the apple
John <===> MBUILD <---|
      ^^^                |---<
      | | |  R                       D  |----> John
John <===> INGEST <--- apple <---|
      ^^^                            |----
      | | |  r
John <===> |----> HEALTH (XTY)
      P    |----< HEALTH (X)
```

One of the advantages of all this detail aside from those already mentioned is that it provided a facility for tying together sentences in a text. Thus, a paragraph will frequently consist of a series of conceptualizations that can be related by their implicit causal connections.

1974

We began, therefore, to work on the problem of representing text. This was, after all, the major issue all along. We were not particularly interested in isolated sentences out of context. Such sentences were probably the root of many of the solutions and the problems with those solutions found by transformationalists and computational linguists. People do not understand sentences in a null context. Why then did our theories try and deal with out of context sentences? The answer was obviously that this was thought to be a simplification that would facilitate research. But the problem was really significantly changed by this supposed simplification. Certainly parsing sentences in context is a more reasonable problem with respect to word sense disambiguation than is parsing out of context.

We had never dealt with texts of more than one sentence before because we just did not know how to represent them. Now, with the idea of causal chains, we could tie together texts in terms of their causal relations. Such a tying together, when attempted on real texts (Schank, 1975) helped to explain certain memory results (particularly those of Bartlett, 1932). Now we had a theory that said that a crucial piece of information had many causal connections and an irrelevant piece of information no causal consequences.

The work on causal connectedness gave us a theory that was helpful in explaining problems of forgetting and remembering, and helped tie together text. However, it could not explain how to tie together texts whose parts were not relatable by chains of results and enablements. Something else was needed for those situations.

The something else was obvious once we thought about it. The answer was scripts.[15] That is, scripts are really just prepackaged sequences of causal chains. Some causal chains are used so often that we do not spell out enough of their details for an understander to make the connections directly. Scripts are a kind of key to connecting events together that do not connect by their superficial features but rather by the remembrance of their having been connected before. The prototypical script we chose was to describe what goes on in a restaurant. In a restaurant we cannot infer from entering a restaurant the causal connection to either ordering or paying. Because speakers assume you know that they do not bother to mention it. There is a causal chain there, but inferring it bit by bit is impossible, so scripts are necessary.

1975

We began testing our assumptions about how scripts would facilitate the processing of connected text by building SAM (Script Applier Mechanism).[16] SAM became a kind of inference maker because what it was doing was filling out the specific implicit events in a causal chain describing a static situation. Cullingford (1977) described the inferences that SAM made as:

1. Reference specification
2. Causal Chain connection
   as part of Script Applier

Other kinds of inferences were:

1. Immediate results: in order to match PTRANS
   to the PATTERN - IS LOC
   inferences about result were needed "Welcomed at Peking Airport" generates PTRANS which can then match $VIPVISIT

---

[15]The word script was originally used by Abelson for something different than, but related to, the current notion of a script. The concept of a script was invented very shortly after I arrived at Yale from Lugano. Abelson and I were discussing issues of mutual interest as soon as I arrived. At one time or another, Rieger, David Levy, and Allan Collins were also present. Minsky's notion of a frame was at that time known by us, and it had some influence in the finalization of the notion.

[16]As soon as I arrived at Yale, I assembled a group of students interested in AI. In January 1975 they began to work with me. We thought for a while in seminars about what scripts were like, and in early May began to put together SAM. The initial version worked about six weeks later just in time to be shown at TINLAP I. The group that put SAM together was Richard Cullingford, Richard Proudfoot, Walter Stutzman, Wendy Lehnert, Gerry De Jong, and Chris Riesbeck.

2. Mental ACT

_____ if X says Y then Y—thus, pronounced dead

implies that a person is dead.

_____ service good implies customer knows it.
                    Thus activates $TIP

3. Location

_____ a location described by one method is the
same as that described by another

_____ "customer sat down"
"waiter went to the table"

_____ need to infer that the seat is near table

_____ Enclosure: John went to the hospital.
                    He was treated in the Emergency Room.

_____ need to infer that Emergency Room is in hospital

4. Movement

_____ "John picked up a magazine. Then he went into
the living room."
To answer "Where is the magazine?" requires
knowing that small objects move with you.
(imagine "table" substituted for newspaper)

We began to wonder about where scripts come from. In thinking about this we came up with the idea that plans gave rise to scripts and that goals gave rise to plans. Coincidentally, Meehan was developing a story generator that served as a vehicle for developing our ideas about plans and goals.[17]

Meehan's TALESPIN made inferences in the course of telling a story, in order to keep track of the world model. Meehan (1976) found that Rieger's 16 classes were of little use in this task because the most interesting question was what is affected when a fact enters memory? Meehan had to keep updating his world model every time he generated a new fact. This meant making inferences about the consequences of every fact that he generated and using those consequences to affect the continuation of the story. Meehan found the following kinds of inferences useful for his task:

---

[17]Meehan had been working on a story generator of a different sort when I arrived at Yale. The plans and goals work that we were doing forced him to reconsider his problem and approach it from a different angle.

1. CONSEQUENCES
   ATRANS − − −⟩ POSS
   FIXED − − −⟩ (let go − −⟩ fall)
   INGEST − − −⟩ object gone
                    person satisfied

2. REACTIONS
   What people will feel about things and people
   ATRANS what you want − − − ⟩ dislike
   THREATEN − − −⟩ person will do ACTION if afraid
   HUNGER − − −⟩ actor wants to fix it
       LOC
   (underwater) − − −⟩ get out
   flattery − − −⟩ like and trust

1976–1978

These three years found us developing the system of plans, goals, themes and scripts for use in understanding systems. This work produced many working systems (Carbonell, 1978; Wilensky, 1978; DeJong, 1978) and has greatly broadened our ideas about inference. We now believe the following: There are a great many possible levels of description. Each of these levels is characterized by its own system of primitives and conceptual relationships. Inferences occur at each of these levels. Thus, for every set of primitives there are a set of inferences that apply to them. These levels have been described in Schank and Abelson (1977) and will not be dealt with in any detail here. We currently use the following levels and inferences on those levels:

1. Micro CD

All events in a story can be connected at a level where every event is connected to the events that follow from it, and to the states enable it *subsequent events*. This produces very detailed causal chains made up of the events and states that were actually mentioned in the text as well as those that had to be inferred in order to complete the chain. Thus, the Causal Chain made by the low level expression of facts is one part of understanding. Thus, in order to read a magazine, you must: ATRANS it; OPEN it; ATTEND to it; and MTRANS from it. When any one of these events is discerned the others must be inferred.

2. Macro-CD

Another type of causal chain exists at the Macro-CD level. There, events connect to other states and events in the same way as they did at the micro-CD level but the level of description is different. Thus, going to Boston enables eating in a Boston restaurant at the macro-CD level. But, at the micro-CD level, the locations would have to be further specified. Actually going to Boston results in being in Boston, which enables beginning to look for and go to a restaurant. This latter level of description can regress in infinite detail where, for example, walking is enabled by putting one foot in front of the other. Thus, the level of detail of inferences is extremely important and is dependent on the purposes the understander has in mind.

Thus, there are two levels of causal chains that apply in the magazine situation.

ATRANS
∧∧∧
||| r
POSS
∧∧∧
||| E
ATTEND
∧∧∧
||| rE
MTRANS

This is MACRO-CD.

MICRO-CD is concerned with opening the magazine, holding it, turning the pages, etc. Each of those ACTs also uses causal chains but at a much more detailed level. Neither one of these levels of description is more correct than the other.

For causal chaining then, the needed inference types are:

> What Enables
> What Results
> What are Reasons
> What Initiates

These apply at both at the macro level and at the micro level.

3. Filling in Missing Information

For every object and person we hear about we are always tracking where they are; the state they are in; what they know and believe; and how they feel. All these inferences are possibly appropriate at any given time. Thus, other kinds of inference types that are necessary are:

> Locational specification
> Object specifications
> Emotional specifications
> Belief Specifications

4. Scripts

Scripts are an important part of the understanding process. Thus, the inferring of the presence of scripts and of the unstated parts of scripts is an important part of the understanding process. The following kinds of inference are significant:

> filling in missing causal chains in a script
> inferring what script is being used
> inferring what unstated script was used instrumentally

Thus, when we hear that 'John robbed the liquor store,' it is appropriate to ask how he got there, how he got in, where he got his weapon, and so on. Such inquiries are a part of the inference process since it is only by knowing what we don't know that we can seek to infer it.

One of the main problems with reference to inferences about scripts is the question of why is a script being pursued. This leads to the problem of inferring plans.

5. Plans

For any given event, it is often important to know the motivations and intentions of the actors in that event. This means knowing the plans being pursued by an actor. Thus it is necessary to make the following kinds of inferences:

> Inferring the planbox being used
> Why was a particular planbox chosen?
> Inferring facts about an actor given
>   his choice of plans & planboxes
> Inferring other plans an actor is likely
>   to pursue to get his goal
> Predictive inferences about future planbox choices
> What goal is he operating under?

This last inference leads to another class of information that spawns new inferences.

6. Goals

Detecting the presence of a goal causes the following goal based inferences to be made:

> Why was this goal chosen?
> What is in conflict with it?
> Can it be subsumed?
> Given this goal, what other goals can we infer?
> Under what circumstances will it be abandoned?

Actually these inference types represent only the tip of the numerous kinds of goal based inferences that have been isolated by Wilensky (1978) and Carbonell (1978).

Here again since goals are dominated by themes, detecting what theme is present and making the appropriate inferences is necessary.

7. Themes

The theme based inferences include finding out:

> What goals will be generated next?
> What themes are likely to coexist with the given one?
> Are there any conflicts in themes?
> How might theme conflicts that are detected be resolved?
> Where did this theme come from?

OUR PRESENT ANALYSIS OF INFERENCE TYPES

The inference types we have used are rather similar whether we are referring to scripts, goals, plans, themes, or whatever. Inside Conceptual Dependency structures, or knowledge structures, or our recently invented triangular structures (Schank & Carbonell, 1978), or probably any reasonable representation of knowledge, the following general inference rules apply:

1. SPECIFICATION: Given a piece of an event, what else can be specified about the rest of the pieces?
2. MOTIVATION: Why did an event happen? Why this event and not another? What did the actor believe he was doing?
3. ENABLEMENT: What was necessary for the event to occur?
4. RESULTS: What are the results or effects of this event?
5. STRUCTURE: What higher level structure does this fit in?
6. OTHER EVENTS: What other events are known to cooccur with this event? What could not have happened if this event happened?

These six inference types then are what we have. Scripts, plans, and so on fit in as events in this description. Thus, we can ask for SPECIFICATION, MOTIVATION, ENABLEMENT, RESULTS, STRUCTURE, and OTHER EVENTS for a script, a plan, a goal, or a theme, or probably any other higher level structure we are likely to invent.

Inference then, is the fitting in of new information into a context that explains it and predicts other facts that follow from it. Since these explanations can occur at many levels inference is a very complex problem and one we expect to continue working on in an attempt to find out how people understand and how computers could understand.

OVERVIEW

I have attempted here to demonstrate how our ideas evolved and why they are where they are today. Since this theory evolution is ongoing, it should be clear that the conclusions we have reached about inferences here are probably also just stopping points in the evolution of a theory. Nevertheless there are some things we can conclude from all this. In particular, there are patterns from which we can get a glimpse of the future.

As I have stated, this work started out as a linguistic theory, albeit one with a computer-based bias. Linguists have explicitly rejected it as a possible linguistic theory (see for example Dresher & Hornstein, 1976). In one sense they are right. The phenomena we have become interested in over the years are not particularly phenomena of language per se. Rather, they are phenomena having to do with the processing of language in general and the issue of the representation of knowledge in particular. Thus, as we have moved away from linguistics over the years, we have become more involved with psychology.

At the same time as this work was going on, the field of Artificial Intelligence has been evolving, too. When I first arrived at the Stanford AI lab, the major issues in AI were theorem proving, game playing, and vision. Natural language was not considered to be a serious part of AI until Winograd (1971) presented the AI community with SHRDLU. This work contributed substantially to the evolution of AI. The major concern of AI would now seem to be the issue of the representation of knowledge, which of course makes the work in natural language processing quite central.

In the future I expect many of the relevant fields will begin to become less separate. AI must come to terms with the fact that it is concerned with many issues that are also of interest to philosophers. I hope that the cooperation will be of more use than was the head butting that has gone on between AI people and linguists. (Although, this too has changed as the more liberal forces in linguistics have become both stronger and more interested in AI.) Also, the interaction between psychologists and AI people should continue to flourish. The work of Bower, Black, and Turner (1979) and Smith, Adams, and Schorr (1978) has already served to bolster the relationship between our group and cognitive psychology.

And what will happen to our theories in the future? I can only say that many of our ideas on parsing, the separation of inference from other processes, generation, and memory are rapidly changing. We will, of course, continue to use the same methodology of the free form speculation approach to theory building, modified by our experiences testing out these theories on the computer.

REFERENCES

Bartlett, R. 1932. *Remembering: a study in experimental and social psychology.* London: Cambridge University Press.

Bower, G. H., Black, J. B., & Turner, T. J. 1979. Scripts in text comprehension and memory. *Cognitive Psychology,* 11:177–220.

Carbonell, J. G. 1978. Politics: Automated ideological reasoning. *Cognitive Science* 2:27–51.

Cullingford, R. E. 1977. *Script application: Computer understanding of newspaper stories.* Ph.D. dissertation, Yale University.

DeJong, G. F. 1978. *Automated partial understanding of connected natural language text.* Ph.D. dissertation, Yale University.

Dresher, B. E., & Hornstein, N. 1976. On some supposed contribution of artificial intelligence to the scientific study of language. *Cognition* 4:321–98.

Hemphill, L. 1975. The relationship of language and belief: with special emphasis on English "for" constructions. Ph.D. dissertation, Linguistics Department, Stanford University.

Katz, J. J. 1967. Recent issues in semantic theory. *Foundations of language,* vol. 3.

Meehan, J. R. 1976. *The metanovel: Writing stories by computer.* Ph.D. dissertation, Yale University.

Quillian, M. R. 1968. Semantic memory. In *Semantic information processing,* ed. M. L. Minsky. Cambridge: MIT Press.

Rieger, C. J. 1975. Conceptual memory. In *Conceptual information processing,* ed. R. C. Schank. Amsterdam: North-Holland.

Riesbeck, C. K. 1975. Conceptual analysis. In *Conceptual information processing,* ed. R. C. Schank. Amsterdam: North-Holland.

Schank, R. C. 1968. Outline of a conceptual semantics for generation of coherent discourse. Tracor-68-472-U, Tracor, Inc., Austin, Texas. Also printed in *Mathematical Biosciences* 5 (1969).

Schank, R. C. 1969. Conceptual dependency as a framework for linguistic analysis. *Linguistics* 49.

Schank, R. C. 1971. *Finding the conceptual content and intention in an utterance in natural language conversation.* Proceedings of the 2d International Joint Conference on Artificial Intelligence, London.

Schank, R. C. 1972. "Semantics" in conceptual analysis. *Lingua* 30.

Schank, R. C. 1973. The fourteen primitive actions and their inferences. AI Memo no. 183, Computer Science Department, Stanford University.

Schank, R. C. 1974. Adverbs and belief. *Lingua* 33:45–67.

Schank, R. C. ed. 1975. *Conceptual information processing.* Amsterdam: North-Holland.

Schank, R. C., & Abelson, R. P. 1975. *Scripts, plans and Knowledge.* Proceedings of the 4th International Joint Conference on Artificial Intelligence, Tbilisi, USSR.

Schank, R. C., & Abelson, R. P. 1977. *Scripts, plans, goals and understanding: An inquiry into human knowledge structures.* Hillsdale, N.J.: Lawrence Erlbaum Associates.

Schank, R. C., & Carbonell, J. G. 1978. *Re: The Gettysburg Address: representing social and political acts.* Research Report no. 127, Computer Science Department, Yale University.

Schank, R. C., & Rieger, C. J. 1974. Inference and the computer understanding of natural language. *Artificial Intelligence* 5: 373–412.

Schank, R. C., & Tesler, L. 1969. *Inference and a conceptual parser for natural language.* Proceedings of the International Joint Conference on Artificial Intelligence, ed. Walker and Norton, Washington, D.C.

Schank, R. C., Tesler, L., & Weber, S. 1970. *SPINOZA: conceptual case-based natural language analysis*. AI Memo no. 109, Computer Science Department, Stanford University.

Smith, E. E., Adams, N., & Schorr, D. 1978. Fact retrieval and the paradox of the expert. *Cognitive Psychology* 10:438–464.

Wilensky, R. 1978. *Understanding goal-based stories*. Ph.D. dissertation, Yale University.

Winograd, T. 1971. *Procedures as a representation for data in a computer program for understanding natural language*. Cambridge: MIT Press.

9 Implications of Language Studies for Human Nature

Margaret A. Boden
The University of Sussex
Brighton, England

INTRODUCTION

The Archangel Gabriel, or so we are told, made an annunciation of some import to maiden Mary. Those who have trouble believing this rumor normally base their doubts in the dubious ontological status of angels, the biologically unproven case for human parthenogenesis, and similar scruples. It is rarely questioned whether, *if* there were angels, one of them could converse naturally with a woman in her native Aramaic.

But this angelic conversational competence is even less likely than the Martian knowledge of twentieth-century Middle-American English that is so conveniently assumed by many science-fiction scenarios. For, unlike Martians, angels do not share with us any corporeal embodiment or material environment. (Hence the peculiar infelicity of debates over how many could sit on the top of a pin.) Language studies suggest that we are creatures of this earthly world in our linguistic capacities no less than in our theological categorization. Moreover, such studies point to the enormous complexity of the mental processes underlying our use of natural language: If Mary really did converse with an angel, it was no divinely simple-minded seraph she talked to.

The human mind is extraordinarily complex in its interpretative activities as well as being deeply rooted in material reality. In this chapter I shall indicate some of the diverse studies of language that show these two claims to be true.

THE EMBODIMENT OF HUMAN BEING

Wittgenstein's remark, "Commanding, questioning, recounting, chatting, are as much a part of our natural history as walking, eating, drinking, playing" encour-

129

ages us to think of language as part of our biological endowment (1953). As such, we may expect it to be essentially shaped by our material embodiment and evolutionary origins. Countless studies within the various disciplines that bear on the nature of language confirm this expectation, but I shall concentrate on only four examples (drawn from current work in linguistics, psychology, philosophy, and artificial intelligence).

The linguist John Lyons has recently defended the semantic thesis of "localism" (1977, chapter 15). Localism claims that essentially *spatial* notions underlie many of the grammatical structures as well as much of the lexicon of natural language. As Lyons points out, there are weaker and stronger versions of localism, and one can hardly avoid being a localist in some degree. Lyons himself puts forward a strong version of the thesis, suggesting localistic interpretations of the linguistic representations of ideas such as tense, aspect, opposition, instrumentality, manner, possession, existence, knowledge, and truth. In addition, he argues that the linguistic phenomenon of *anaphora* (which is commonly taken as basic by linguists) is a derivative of *deixis*. And deixis is based in the indication of the here-and-now, whether a bodily pointing to the spatial *here,* or a less concrete "pointing" to the temporal *now.*

It is abundantly clear that many linguistic expressions of "non-spatial" matters (*sic*) are parasitic on purely spatial notions. Familiar examples include the conceptualization of time as passing, as being of long or short duration, as ranging over the whole history of the universe . . . and so on. Similarly, we often express comparative degrees of abstract properties such as social status, intelligence, or moral worth by terms drawn from more concrete contexts, such as above, below, higher, lower, *etc.* Again, grammatical cases are commonly and plausibly interpreted in localist terms, so that (for example) the ablative and dative cases are explained by way (*sic*) of the ideas of source and goal of movement, respectively.

Space forbids discussion of the less obvious localistic interpretations, whereby even aspect, possession, and knowledge (and, for some authors, negation and quantification) are held to be represented by essentially spatial linguistic expressions and constructions. But later in this section it will be useful to bear in mind this claim of Lyons (1977):

> It is obvious that the process of communicating propositional information is readily describable, as is the process of transferring possession, in terms of the localistic notion of a journey: if X communicates p to Y, this implies that p travels, in some sense, from X to Y. . . . It may be suggested, therefore, that "p is at X" (where X is a person) is the underlying locative structure that is common to "X knows $p,$" "X believes $p,$" "X has p in mind," etc. There is much in the structure of particular languages, however, to suggest that "X knows p" is comparable with "X has Y" and should therefore be regarded as the most typical member of the class of propositions subsumable under "p is at X" (p. 724).

Even without acceptance of Lyons' more ambitious localistic claims, such as those within and related to this quotation, his work casts doubt on the credibility of the Annunciation story. Thus St. Luke assures us that eavesdroppers on the conversation between Gabriel and Mary would have overheard expressions such as these: The Lord is *with* thee; blessed art thou *among* women; thou hast *found* favor *with* God; He shall be *great,* and shall be called the Son of the *Highest;* and the Lord God shall give *unto* Him the throne of His father David; and He shall reign *over* the *house* of Jacob forever; and of His *kingdom* there shall be no *end*. The localistic origin of the italicized words is evident, and committed "localists" would italicize even more. This passage, of course, is written in King James' English, with which Mary (never mind Gabriel) was not familiar. But the Aramaic equivalents may have been even more obviously localistic in character: Many languages force speakers to code the spatial attributes of objects, much as English forces temporal specification by way of the tense-system. (The American Indian language Tarascan is an extreme example of this; number-words have to reflect the "dimensionality" of the objects being enumerated, according to whether they are long and thin, flat, or broadly spherical; similarly, verb-forms reflect the spatial nature of the referents of the nouns acting as subject or object. See Miller & Johnson-Laird, 1976, pp. 375–376).

The reason why localism casts doubt on the Annunciation story is that the psychological assumption implicit—and often explicit—in localism is that localistic notions and distinctions at base are those "which we first learn to apply with respect to our own orientation and the location or locomotion of other objects in the external world." Since Gabriel as an essentially spiritual being can hardly be represented as having any orientation, nor any location relative to "other objects in the external world"—such as pinheads—it is difficult to see how he could have learnt these notions in the first place. And if he had not learnt them in the first place, how could he have used them so felicitously to talk of abstract matters to a human woman in the second place?

Psychological evidence in support of localism is provided, for instance, by the "psycholexicology" of G. A. Miller and P. N. Johnson-Laird (1976, chapters 2 and 6). Their study of the psychological basis of the lexicon of natural languages shows spatial organization to be basic to human cognition, and a pervasive feature of our perceptual capacities. They aim to develop a procedural semantics, wherein lexical items are associated with perceptual procedures for testing whether the environment fulfills certain conditions. Examples of the perceptual predicates involved in the object-recognition routines that carry the meaning of natural language include: x is higher than y; the distance from x to y is zero; x is in front of the moving object y; y is between x and z; x has boundary y; x is convex; x is changing shape; x has the exterior surface y; x is included spatially in y; x, y, and z lie in a straight line; x travels along the path p. In fact, the majority of perceptual predicates listed by these authors are obviously spatial in character (although their list includes also items such as cause, know, feel, intend, person, and goal). Psychological and physiological evidence for the primacy of these notions is marshalled, and their incorporation into object-recognition routines of increasing power is outlined. The computational paradigm adopted throughout the discussion encourages questions not only about *which* predicates are involved in a certain sort of judgment, but *when* each predicate is applied in the judgmental process. (For example, the logically equivalent "*y* over *x*" and "*x* under *y*" are not psychologically equivalent: The first term in the relation should designate the thing whose location is to be determined, while the second should represent the immobile landmark that can be used to determine it.)

Miller and Johnson-Laird do not claim that the conceptual meaning of language can be directly identified in terms of perceptual predicates, or that every question must be answered (every statement verified) by direct perception of the external world. But whatever test-procedures are used, these must ultimately be grounded in perceptual routines. For instance, it is possible to answer class-inclusion questions (Are dogs mammals? Are whales fish?) by a search of memory, since hierarchical relations between concepts are apparently represented fairly accessibly in the human memory; and if a "direct look-up" fails, then inferential procedures of various types (which may themselves involve recourse to perceptual tests) can be activated in order to answer the question. But the authors suggest that the notion of hierarchical class-inclusion may itself be derived from the psychologically more primitive concept of locative predicates such as those listed above.

The basic psychological predicates are primitives, in the sense that Miller and Johnson-Laird build complex recognition-procedures out of them. But they are not "primitive" in the sense of being unanalysable, inexplicable, or innate in the newborn baby. Correlatively, language development must wait upon the development of the requisite perceptual routines, which may require movement within and action on the material world. A number of psychological studies are cited that indicate that *in* is the first of the locative terms (*in, on, at, by, with, between* . . .) to be learnt in infancy. Action schemata involving bodily skills can influence the infant's understanding of locative terms such as *in* and *on*: If it is physically possible to put X in Y, then a twenty-month-old child asked to put X *on* Y will instead put it inside Y, while if it is possible to put X on Y then a child asked to put X *under* Y will place X on top of Y instead. Semantically, the word *at* expresses a more abstract notion (involving the concept of a *region*) than either *in* or *on*; and children do indeed learn to use *at* later than they learn *in* and *on*. In general deictic terms—which organize the conception of space by taking the current location and orientation of the speaker (or, later, the listener) as the prime reference point or landmark—seem to be psychologically primitive with respect to locatives based on "external" landmarks, pathways, or boundaries.

The procedures suggested by Miller and Johnson-Laird as mediating the understanding even of such apparently simple words as *at* are surprisingly complex. (So to interpret, or verify, the expression "The plane is at the door" one has to ask not merely about relative location, but also about size, salience, and mobility: If the plane really is at the door, it must be a toy plane or a hangar door that is in question.) And "perceptual" and "conceptual" routines can call recursively on themselves and heterarchically on each other, so that the flow of control in the information-processing that underlies our use of language may be very complicated. This flexibility of control contributes to the complexity of human nature that is the topic of the next Section. In the present context, the main relevance of psycholexicology is its emphasis on the biologically-based perceptual routines that allow meaning to be given to linguistic expressions. Given our material embodiment (not least the facts that we are not radially symmetrical like jellyfish, and that our feet carry us in the same direction as our eyes look out over the space *in front* of us), the spatial organization informing our thought is perhaps to be expected. But what reason is there to think that the psychology of angels need be similarly constituted? A psycholexicology of the words sung by angelic choirs would surely be very different from one reflecting our specifically human nature.

Philosophical discussions relevant to these points (*sic*) include those that assign basic ontological significance to material or spatio-temporal concepts. In particular, accounts of individuation and reference that see a spatio-temporal framework as essential for these linguistic functions bear a close relation to the psycholexicology offered by Miller and Johnson-Laird. But as the "philosophical" example in this section, I want to discuss Jonathan Bennett's recent work on linguistic behavior (1976).

Bennett's account of language roots it firmly in its prelinguistic behavioral basis and environmental setting. He argues for a Gricean, anti-Davidsonian, position on semantics, wherein the notion "what x means" is secondary to the notion "what the speaker meant by uttering x." The pivotal semantic notion of speaker's *meaning* is elucidated in turn by that of speaker's *intent,* in a broadly Gricean fashion. Bennett holds that the concept of intention (and its cognate, belief) can be ascribed to creatures lacking a language, or even any communication system. However, he believes that communicative intent (the core of the Gricean analysis of meaning) probably cannot be ascribed to any existing languageless creatures, even those that—like dolphins—seem both to communicate and to have intentions. Communicative intent can, by contrast, be ascribed to many of the gestures and actions of human beings (and he describes an imaginary tribe with a systematic method of communication of this type). For language properly so-called, communicative intent is necessary but not sufficient: Also essential is a semantically significant *structure* in the communication system. It is this that enables one to understand a novel sentence, by drawing both on one's knowledge of its individual parts and on one's appreciation of the general principles according to which those parts are assembled. He makes various suggestions about the sort of behavioral evidence that could imply that a strange tribe had a semantic structure in their communication system, and so a language—and he even offers some provocative speculations about how structure might have originated in evolutionary history.

The point of immediate relevance here is the extent to which intention and belief are basically behavioral concepts that derive their sense from our interpretations of bodily activities within the material environment, activities commonly associated with widely shared animal needs such as hunger, thirst, warmth, shelter, escape, and so forth.

Bennett stresses that the epistemic notions of intention, belief, and perception (or their weaker cousins, purpose and "registration") go essentially together. The ascription of intentions and beliefs to a creature implies that it perceives, or registers, its environment to some (imperfect but significantly reliable) degree. What an animal registers is largely a matter of what it sees, hears, and feels; and to learn what this is, we have to rely on evidence about how environmental changes correlate with changes in the animal's pursuit of its goals. This evidence will be primarily behavioral, and will include "commonsense" observations as well as the more recondite investigations of experimental psychologists; in addition there may occasionally be physiological evidence available, of the sort appealed to by Miller and Johnson-Laird in identifying basic perceptual predicates.

Bennett is careful to point out that he provides no arguments proving that his behavioral criteria for these mentalistic terms are either necessary or logically sufficient conditions for the ascription of intentions and beliefs. Merely, he says, his criteria specify conditions that are "sufficient by normal, reasonable, everyday standards." So they cannot be used briskly to show that a noncorporeal being—such as an angel—could have no intentions and therefore no language, that such a being could not *mean* anything by the noises it might produce in the vicinity of a human woman. Nevertheless, if the way in which we do make sense of terms such as "intention" crucially involves material considerations, then it should not be uncritically assumed that such terms retain their intelligibility if used in a wholly non-material context. If Davidson is right about language, then perhaps Gabriel could speak Aramaic—but if Bennett is right, this is decidedly dubious.

My final example in this section is drawn from artificial intelligence, and relates to the thesis of localism mentioned earlier. Among the semantic theories that have been incorporated into "language-using" computer programs is that of R. C. Schank (1972, pp. 552-631; 1975. See also Meehan, 1976; Abelson, 1973; pp. 287-340; 1975, pp. 273-309; Schank & Abelson, 1977). Schank's *Conceptual Dependency Analysis* seeks to represent the meaning of natural languages in terms of a small set of semantic primitives. For example, all the verbs of English—and of Aramaic—are said to be analyzable in terms of eleven "primitive actions." Five of these are physical ACTS—PROPEL, MOVE, INGEST, EXPEL, GRASP; two are mental ACTS—MTRANS and MBUILD; two

are instrumental ACTS—INTEND and SPEAK; and two are global ACTS—
PTRANS and ATRANS.

The localist will immediately notice that nine of these eleven are clearly
spatial in character. The five "physical" ACTS are obviously rooted in our
embodied existence within the material world. MBUILD (interpreted by Schank
as "to combine thoughts in some manner") relies on our experience of material
building. And the "TRANS" element in PTRANS, MTRANS, and ATRANS is
equally localistic in nature. These three ACTS respectively mark the transfer of
physical objects, of information or ideas within the mind, and of abstract relationships (like ownership and responsibility).

Schank does not offer a theoretical rationale for his choosing these eleven
primitives rather than any others. Nor does he give a detailed empirical or
theoretical justification for his claim that PTRANS, MTRANS, and ATRANS
are the three most important of the eleven, for the purposes of representing the
actual content of human communication. But he does offer outline analyses of
many familiar words, which serve to highlight some of the semantic relations
between them. For instance, MTRANS is the core of his analysis of such verbs of
thought as remember, see, feel, communicate, forget, learn, and teach; and
MBUILD is the core of verbs such as conclude, resolve, decide, solve, realize,
weigh (evidence), think about, and answer.

Schank's reliance on the idea of *transfer* as basically effecting the major part
of human linguistic communication is reminiscent of Lyons' claim quoted earlier, that the processes of communicating propositional information and of trans-
ferring possession are each readily describable in terms of the localistic notion of
a journey. There is no question but that Schank's approach is essentially localistic in character. It follows that the various computer programs that are based on
Schank's theoretical work (one of which will be mentioned in the next Section)
embody a localistic interpretation of natural language.

It is often said that a computer could not really understand language, no matter
how seemingly appropriate its "linguistic" responses. The arguments offered
vary, but they tend to make much of facts such as these: Computers are not living
things; many of them do not move in or act on their environment; many are
unable to "perceive" their world, except through their operator's teletype; they
have no natural needs, goals, or interests—which is to say they have no goals (or
intentions) at all. In short, they cannot *mean* things, and they do not really
interpret the "language" they spew forth; it is we who do so, and only we who
can do so. Without going into these arguments here, it is perhaps worth pointing
out that Gabriel is to some degree worse off than a robot. Philosophers who (like
H. L. Dreyfus, 1972; see also Boden, 1977, chapter 14) cast scorn on artificial
intelligence as a methodology for studying human language because current
natural language-using programs have no parallel of human embodiment, should
surely be dubious also about the possibility of angels speaking Aramaic. Perhaps
current Schankian programs have no real inkling of real transfer, but it is not

clear that a language-using robot could have no such understanding. How Gabriel might achieve it is more of a mystery.

THE COMPLEXITY OF THE MIND

The complexity of the human mind is suggested by the intricacy of the cognitive processes that have been postulated to explain the generation and interpretation of natural language. Chomsky drew on his grammatical insights to deride the overly-simple "stimulus-response" theoretical accounts offered by the orthodox positivist model, but even he had little to say about the specific processes involved in the actual production or understanding of speech.

Many complications ignored by Chomsky are studied by experimental psycholinguists, under the general term "performance factors." And Miller and Johnson-Laird, as we have noted, ask procedurally oriented questions about language that address problems not considered by Chomsky. A particularly fruitful source of insights into the degree (and, it is hoped, the nature) of structured complexity in linguistic processes is the project of formalizing computational models of the use of natural language sentences and connected texts. In this section I shall mention a few examples of recent work in artificial intelligence that bear on these issues.

My first example is a story-writing program based on the semantic theory of Schank and the psychological work of R. P. Abelson. The program, called "TALESPIN," was written by James Meehan, 1976; (see also 1977). Crude as it is, it shows the variety of sorts of knowledge and interacting computational processes necessary to compose (or to understand) even a simple story.

TALESPIN generates story-plots involving characters with various interpersonal relations and differing attitudes to and knowledge about the world, and it also decides which of its inferences need to be explicitly represented in the story and which can be sensibly left unsaid. That is, it deals with semantic issues (issues of meaning) rather than with syntax and details of word-choice. (The story I shall quote was put into acceptable English by Meehan himself, since TALESPIN's linguistic module—appropriately titled "MUMBLE"—cannot cope with pronouns, for instance, and expresses large "sets" of thoughts as clumsy single sentences.)

Asked to write a story with the moral, "Never trust flatterers," TALESPIN produced this (or, more accurately, its semantic skeleton):

The Fox and the Crow
Once upon a time, there was a dishonest fox named Henry who lived in a cave, and a vain and trusting crow named Joe who lived in an elm tree. Joe had gotten a piece of cheese and was holding it in his mouth. One day, Henry walked from his cave,

across the meadow to the elm tree. He saw Joe Crow and the cheese and became hungry. He decided that he might get the cheese if Joe Crow spoke, so he told Joe that he liked his singing very much and wanted to hear him sing. Joe was very pleased with Henry and began to sing. The cheese fell out of his mouth, down to the ground. Henry picked up the cheese and told Joe Crow that he was stupid. Joe was angry, and didn't trust Henry anymore. Henry returned to his cave.

The overtones of Aesop will be evident: Meehan's claim is that Aesop (and his readers) need *at least* the knowledge and inferential competence possessed by this program in order that they may be able to appreciate stories such as this one.

TALESPIN needs diverse types of knowledge. Thus it needs an abstract characterization of *flattery* in terms of the interlocking goals and perceptions of two characters. And if the story is to convey the warning "Never trust flatterers," it needs also some understanding of trust (and what sorts of behavior tend to generate or destroy it) that will mediate its insight that the flattered character in this cautionary tale needs to lose in some way as a result of the flattery. Similarly, it needs to know when one may be led to flatter: Why one often flatters someone in order to get them to do something that otherwise they would not have been disposed to do. (Joe and Henry cannot be *friends*, since a friend's direct request for cheese would be immediately granted—at least in the simplified social world imagined by TALESPIN.) The social psychological interests of Abelson (a pupil of Fritz Heider) have greatly influenced the representations of "interpersonal dynamics" provided by Meehan to this program (see Abelson, 1973, pp. 287–340; 1975, pp. 273–309; Schank & Abelson, 1977).

In addition, TALESPIN needs to know about characteristic needs or desires, ways of moving in space, ways of planning how to achieve various sorts of goals (and sub-goals, and sub-sub-goals . . .), and so forth, if it is to model the situation presented in the story—including the individual world-models of the two participants themselves.

Its knowledge of planning, for instance, is based on a number of primitive ACTS (called "DELTA-ACTS"), defined in terms of goals such as CONTROL, KNOW, and TELL. Different varieties of TELL are specified for the program as ASK, INFORM, REASON, BARGAIN, PERSUADE, THREATEN, etc. And associated with each primitive ACT is a list of "planboxes" for achieving the goal in question, together with an algorithm for deciding which planbox to try first when generating a plan to achieve the goal. For example, the primitive D-PROX (X,Y,Z) is equivalent to X's wanting Y to be near Z. The relevant planboxes already distinguished by Meehan include the following alternatives: X tries to move Y to Z; X gets Y to move himself to Z; X gets Z to move himself to Y; X gets a third party to move Y to Z. . . .

At first sight, the second and third of these may seem equivalent, in the event that each of "Y" and "Z" are self-movers, or animate agents. But a moment's thought will show that this need not be so: If you want to ask your boss for a raise, you may phone him and suggest that you go over to his office next day—you would be well-advised *not* to ask him to come over to yours. In general, a relation of DOMINANCE between two characters implies a non-reciprocal ability to ask the other person to do something. It is this sort of fact that is taken into account by the algorithm that chooses which planbox to employ in working out a way for the character concerned to try to achieve his goal. Recursiveness can give indefinitely many levels, since "getting Y to move to Z," for example, may involve ASK-ing Y to do so, and this may involve D-PROX since creatures without telephones have to be near to each other in space in order to TELL (say) anything effectively. Similarly, if X is to try to move Y near to Z, then X has to know where Z is: If he does not, then D-KNOW (where is Z?) must be invoked, which in turn may involve further D-PROXing in order to ASK someone else for the information.

Even this very brief description of the program shows how different types of fact and inferential process have to be intelligently integrated so as to create a story like *The Fox and the Crow*. A program—and, equally, an angel—that did not know about movement through physical space and the reasons for which this may be necessary would be unable to see the need for a sentence like, "One day, Henry walked from his cave, across the meadow to the elm tree." It was presumably Gabriel's appreciation of this sort of constraint that led to the angel's plan to appear to Mary in her room before trying to make the Annunciation. Given that Gabriel was going to appear in "bodily" form at all, there would have been little sense in his doing so in Egypt instead of Galilee.

A. C. Davey has written a program (1974) that, in comparison with TALES-PIN, shows a much greater sensitivity to the problems of syntactic and lexical choice involved in the production of natural language. The program's knowledge domain is the game of noughts and crosses, or tic-tac-toe. Davey's interest is to articulate generative rules for verbal (English) descriptions of an indefinite number of games, in such a way that the progress and strategy of each individual game is expressed by subtle variations of syntax and lexicon. For instance, syntactic decisions have to be made about clause subordination (when is it in order, and which event should be expressed by the subordinate clause?), about sentence separation (when should two clauses be conjoined in a single sentence?), and about the use of subjunctive and conditional constructions. Similarly, a lexical choice may have to be made between different conjunctions: Should it be *and, but, however,* or *and so*? (It is worth remarking here that Terry Winograd's program SHRDLU could parse *and* and *but* correctly—interpreting them syntactically as conjunctions—but could not use or understand them properly since it had no representation of the semantic difference between them, 1972, pp. 149 and 157).

Here is an example of the actual output produced by Davey's program, given the task of describing the game shown in *Figure 9.1:*

```
(1)          (2)          (3)          (4)
 |  | X      | X |        X |  |        X |  |
---+---    ---+---      ---+---        ---+---
 | O |        | O |    O | O |        O | X | O
---+---    ---+---      ---+---        ---+---
 |  |        |  |        |  |          |  |
```

```
(5)                          (6)              (7)
X |  |       X |  | X        X | X |          X | X | O
---+---      ---+---        ---+---          ---+---
O | X | O    O | X | O      O | X | O        O | X | O
---+---      ---+---        ---+---          ---+---
 | X | O      |  | O         | O |            | O |
```

I started the game by taking the middle of an edge, and you took an end of the opposite one. I threatened you by taking the square opposite the one I had just taken, but you blocked my line and threatened me. However, I blocked your diagonal and threatened you. If you had blocked my edge, you would have forked me, but you took the middle of the one opposite the corner I had just taken and adjacent to mine and so I won by completing the edge.

Clearly, considerable knowledge of the strategy and tactics—not just the "rules"—of noughts and crosses is involved here, guiding the program's choice not only of what to say but also of how to say it. Imagine, for example, how much less appropriate, or even how *in*appropriate, this passage would be if the conjunctions (*and, but, however, and so*) were variously interchanged. Again, consider how much less felicitous the second sentence would have been if the order of the last two ideas had been reversed: I threatened you by taking the square opposite the one I had just taken, but you threatened me and blocked my line. The order actually chosen by the program reflects in a natural fashion its understanding of the structure of attack, defense, and counterattack informing this game. Similarly, it would have been less happy to render the first conjunct of the sentence thus: I took the square opposite the one I had just taken and so threatened you. This is because the syntax of subordinate and subordinating expressions actually chosen by the program corresponds to the strategic importance of the ideas involved: *That* I suddenly threatened you is more important than *how* I did so, and so should be the main focus of the sentence. This rule is apparently broken in the next (third) sentence of the game-description: "However, I blocked your diagonal and threatened you," because the blocking of the diagonal was the necessary defensive response to the previous threat from the opponent, and the fact that it also constituted a new threat *to* the opponent was a fortunate side-effect. (Similar remarks apply to the second conjunct of the second sentence.)

The choice of "However" as the initial word of the third sentence was guided by the pragmatic rule that two consecutive *buts* within a single sentence are to be avoided since they may be confusing to the listener. The causal or strategic dependence of the blocking of the opponent's diagonal on the previous threat posed by the opponent is therefore signaled by the use of *however* at the start of a new sentence.

The use of *however* to avoid a string of *buts* might be termed a "stylistic" matter, but it has a clear pragmatic justification (avoiding cognitive confusion) whereas many stylistic choices do not. For example, in the "Aesop's fable" previously quoted, a phrase occurred referring to "a vain and trusting crow." The alternative "a trusting and vain crow" seems decidedly less elegant. My own intuition is that this is a matter of syllable-counting rather than semantics or pragmatics, having nothing to do with the relative importance of the two ideas "vain" and "trusting." This lexical decision was taken by Meehan himself, not by his program, which has no way of motivating choices of ordering of predicates such as these. It should be obvious that any program—or theory—competent to take stylistic matters into account would have to be more complicated yet: Only a very complex angelic mind could speak Aramaic elegantly.

Davey's program is inhumanly rational, in the sense that it always produces syntactically perfect English sentences, which express a coherent set of thoughts. But in real life our spoken sentences are often grossly imperfect from the syntactical point of view, and very confused as expressions of thought or semantic content. This is particularly true when the topic is emotionally sensitive, arousing anxieties (whether conscious or unconscious) in the speaker's mind that lead to hesitations, evasive changes of topic, and choices of euphemistic alternatives, together with the various syntactic "restarts" required in expressing these shifting lines of thought. Factors such as these affect linguistic *performance,* by operating in cooperation with grammatical *competence* to generate actual speech. A preliminary model of neurotic thought processes that aims to simulate the effect of neurotic concerns on speech has been programmed by J. H. Clippinger (1978). Continual monitoring of the sentence during its generation may result in pauses, restarts, and rephrasings of a very "human" character, as in these examples:

You know, I was just thinking about, uh—well, whatever it was isn't important (p. 202).

You know, that just reminded me, well, it may seem strange to you that I should mention this right now, I mean, just out of the blue like this, but I, uh, well, I want to be more open with you. That is, well, uh, you know, have a more personal relationship (p. 204).

No analogous hesitations and reformulations would occur in an angelic being seraphically immune to doubt and inhumanly free of anxiety, even when speaking of such an awesome event as the Incarnation. If such a being talked in natural language at all, it would surely be a very un-natural conversation.

Natural conversation is dialogue rather than monologue, implying cooperation governed by shared intuitions of "relevance" of various kinds—whether semantic, pragmatic, or social. For instance, in view of the theological status of Archangels, one can safely bet that Gabriel both initiated and closed the conversation with Mary. And, presumably, Gabriel knew when to shut up and let Mary do the talking. Lacking "human" intuitions on matters such as these, Gabriel would have been unable to talk naturally with Mary, and would not have led up to the focal Annunciation by first greeting her, "Hail, thou that are highly favored." Our theoretical understanding of the implicit structure of conversation is still very sketchy. The work of ethnomethodologists on turn-taking, greeting, and opening and closing of conservations is obviously to the point. So too are philosophers' and linguists' studies of *speech-acts,* insofar as these may suggest conversational units of various types that can be appropriately combined only in certain ways. Similarly, discussions of implicature and the communicative intent of sentences within conversation raise issues that are crucial to theoreticians of the natural use of natural language. These questions have been dealt with primarily by philosophers and linguists, although recent work in developmental psychology (see Clark, 1977, pp. 1-72) is relevant also in that it studies how the child learns to use language for communication (as opposed to how the child learns to use "noun phrases" and like syntactic structures). Only a few programs exist that address these issues, and these do so only in a minimal fashion (see Mann, Moore, & Levin, 1977; 1976; see also Power, 1976). Our theory of the social (communicative) use of language must be more fully articulated before it can be incorporated in any artificial intelligence.

CONCLUSION

It is not surprising that language studies are commonly seen as having implications for human nature: Chomsky is only one among many to have believed "linguistic" matters to have a wider philosophical relevance. For language enters intimately into our thinking and experience, and deeply informs our social actions and personal character.

Studies of language based in very different areas converge in suggesting the enormous complexity of the cognitive processes underlying the production and understanding of natural language. Any theoretical account of language must reflect the structure and function of these processes to some degree, as well as giving due weight to the extent to which our terrestrial environment and material embodiment are represented in the semantics of human languages.

Accordingly, these studies imply that our image of human nature must acknowledge the rich interpretative power of the human mind, that no simplisitc notion of mankind which ignores this subtle complexity could be adequate to human reality. Similarly, no concept of human nature can be acceptable that cuts us off from our physical embodiment and ecology.

In view of the theologian's traditional preference for simplicity over complexity in spiritual beings, and bearing in mind the aetherial substance of the orthodox angel, I am tempted to adapt a remark of Wittgenstein's: If the angel Gabriel spoke to Mary, it is a miracle that she understood him.

REFERENCES

Abelson, R. P. 1973. The structure of belief systems. In *Computer models of thought and language,* ed. R. C. Schank & K. M. Colby, pp. 287-340. San Francisco: Freeman.

Abelson, R. P. 1975. Concepts for representing mundane reality in plans. In *Representation and understanding: studies in cognitive science,* ed. D. G. Bobrow & A. Collins, pp. 273-309. New York: Academic Press.

Bennett, J. 1976. *Linguistic behaviour.* Cambridge: Cambridge University Press.

Boden, M. A. 1977. *Artificial intelligence and natural man.* New York: Basic Books.

Clark, E. V. 1977. First language acquisition. In *Developmental and pathological,* ed. J. Morton & J. C. Marshall, *Psycholinguistic series,* vol. 1, pp. 1-72. London: Elek.

Clippinger, J. H., Jr. 1978. *Meaning and discourse: a computer model of psychoanalytic speech and cognition.* Baltimore: Johns Hopkins.

Davey, A. C. 1974. *The formalization of discourse production.* Ph.D. dissertation, Edinburgh University.

Dreyfus, H. L. 1972. *What computers can't do: a critique of artificial reason.* New York: Harper and Row.

Lyons, J. 1977. *Semantics.* Cambridge: Cambridge University Press.

Mann, W. C., Moore, J. A., & Levin, J. A. 1977. *A comprehension model for human dialogue.* Proceedings of the 5th International Joint Conference on Artificial Intelligence, pp. 77-87.

Meehan, J. R. 1976. *The metanovel: Writing stories by computer.* Ph.D. dissertation, Computer Science Department, Yale University.

Meehan, J. R. 1977. *TALESPIN: An interactive program that writes stories.* Proceedings of the 5th International Joint Conference on Artificial Intelligence, pp. 91-8.

Miller, G. A., & Johnson-Laird, P. N. 1976. *Language and perception.* Cambridge: Belknap.

Power, R. 1976. *A model of conversation.* Unpublished working paper, Experimental Psychology Department, University of Sussex.

Schank, R. C. 1972. Conceptual dependency: a theory of natural language understanding. *Cognitive Psychology* 3:552-631.

Schank, R. C., ed. 1975. *Conceptual information processing*. Amsterdam: North-Holland.
Schank, R. C., & Abelson, R. P. 1977. *Scripts, plans, goals and understanding: an inquiry into human knowledge structures*. Hillsdale, N.J.: Lawrence Erlbaum Associates.
Winograd, T. 1972. *Understanding Natural Language*. New York: Academic Press.
Wittgenstein, L. 1953. *Philosophical investigations*. Oxford: Blackwell.

10 Experiential Factors in Linguistics

George Lakoff
University of California, Berkeley

About ten years ago, generative grammar split into two camps—generative semantics and interpretative semantics (see McCawley, this volume). The general issue was whether syntax was independent of meaning. Since the early 1970's, the generative vs. interpretative semantics split has become meaningless, with the disintegration of generative linguistics into so many subtheories that it is hard to keep track of them. There are relational grammarians, arc-pair grammarians, at least half a dozen kinds of functional grammarians, Montague grammarians, extended standard theorists of various types, as well as a variety of generative semanticists of widely differing beliefs. The reason for this disintegration, I think, is that the whole conception of generative grammar is fundamentally wrong. It took me fifteen years of working through a long succession of generative theories to reach this conclusion, and it has taken quite a bit of distancing myself from the generative paradigm to see what is wrong with that paradigm and to get some idea of what ought to replace it.

The best way to get some perspective on the question is to ask how a theory of language ought to fit into a general theory of cognition, human development, and social interaction. Suppose we contrast two opposing views, what I will call the *autonomous* view and the *experiential* view. Greatly oversimplified, the autonomous view says that language does not make use of other capacities that people have, while the experiential view says that it does. More precisely, the autonomous view states:

1. There is an autonomous language faculty that is independent of other human faculties.
2. The structures and processes of natural language in no way depend on or

follow from the structures or processes of any nonlinguistic human capacity, for example, preception, memory, sensori-motor abilities, and social interaction.

3. The language faculty is not only innate, but separate from other innate faculties.

4. The principles of language use and processing will depend upon language structure, but nothing in the structure of language (i.e., no rule of any language) will depend upon processing and use.

5. Grammars of natural languages relate sentences and literal meanings. Non-literal meanings arise from principles of use, which are outside the language faculty.

6. The structure of language is ''reductionistic'' in the following senses: (a) The meaning of the whole is a function of the meanings of the parts. (b) Categorization is defined set-theoretically, that is, members are either in or out of the category. (c) Category membership is defined in terms of necessary and sufficient conditions. (d) There are atomic predicates.

The experiential view differs radically. It states:

1. The language faculty is not independent of other faculties.

2. The structures and processes of natural language in at least *some* ways (not necessarily all ways) depend on and follow from the structures and processes of various nonlinguistic human capacities, for example, perception, memory, sensori-motor capacities, social interaction, etc.

3. The language faculty makes use of other innate faculties. It is an open question as to whether there are any parts of the language faculty that are both innate and unique to language.

4. Various aspects of language structure (e.g., rules of particular languages) depend on processing and use.

5. Natural languages relate utterances in discourses to meanings conveyed in context. There need not be any coherent concept of literal meaning.

6. The structure of language has both holistic and reductionistic aspects. (a) The meaning of the whole is not necessarily a function of the meaning of the parts, but may depend on perception, knowledge about the world, and how one views the world. (b) Categorization is fuzzy and is characterized in terms of prototypes and deviations from prototypes. (c) Category membership is not defined in terms of necessary and sufficient conditions. (d) There need not be atomic predicates.

I believe that the experiential view is by far the more plausible of the two, not on a priori grounds but on empirical grounds. This is a belief that I have come to gradually over many years, though when I first got into linguistics I implicitly assumed the autonomous view. The autonomous view overlaps a great deal with most of generative linguistics. At present I am not interested in establishing exactly which linguistic theories assume which parts of the autonomous view. Instead I will try to give a few of the reasons why I favor the experiential view.

Let me begin with the issue of processing. There is a growing literature on kinds of examples where syntax and semantics must take into account the processing of sentences as they are uttered. I will present a few of my favorite examples. Other researchers can provide their own favorites.

1. Indirect Speech Acts.   These are cases where the meaning conveyed by a sentence in context is more or different than the literal meaning. "Would it be possible for you to take out the garbage?" is usually understood as a request, not merely a question about possibility. What a sentence means in context is a function of its literal meaning (if it has one), knowledge of the world and general principles of social interaction and conversation. These are generally taken to be in the area of "performance" as autonomous linguists use the term. Yet there are a wide variety of phenomena where the well-formedness of sentences depends upon the conveyed meaning as the sentence is used. Compare:

(1) a. Can you pass the salt?
    b. Can you reach the salt?
    c. Could you please pass the salt?
    d. *Could you please reach the salt?

(d) is ill-formed because of a peculiar English constraint on *could*-questions and sentence-internal *please*: The content of the verb phrase must directly express the content of the request. This is not true of *can*-questions that convey requests. There are an enormous number of constraints on English morphemes and syntactic constructions that have to do with what is meant in some social situation as opposed to what is actually present in the surface or even logical structure of the sentence. (The literature on the subject is large and a good place to start would be Morgan & Cole, 1975.)

2. Amalgams.   English has a variety of sentence types where the illocutionary force of the sentence is shifted in mid-stream and one or more sentences or sentence fragments appear in the place of noun phrases.

a. John invited *you'll never guess how many people* to *God knows what kind of a party.*
b. John is going to *I think it's Chicago* on *didn't he say it was Saturday.*
c. The Seventy-sixers are going to win because *who can handle Dr. J?*

The occurrence of such constructions is tightly constrained:

d. *John invited *Max guessed how many people* to *Sam doesn't know that it's a party.*

e. *John was going to *Sam is sorry that the place he lives is Chicago* on *nobody said that anything happened last Saturday.*

f. *The Seventy-sixers are going to win because *might Barry guard Dr. J?*

The constraints on such sentences are partly syntactic, partly semantic, but mostly have to do with pragmatics—that is, the conversational interaction between the participants *as the sentence is being said* and the conveyed—not literal—meaning that an extended version of the inserted fragment would have if said at that point in the processing of the sentence. (For discussion see Lakoff, 1974.)

3. Interjections.   Expressions like *ah, uh,* and *oh* were traditionally treated as expressions of emotion—independent of the structure of the sentences in which they occurred. However, Deborah James, in a series of remarkable studies, showed that such expressions have as much syntactic, semantic and pragmatic complexities as any morpheme or syntactic construction in the language. Moreover, they are constraints that have to be learned about English and do not come naturally to non-native speakers. James even shows that they obey Ross' constraints on movement transformations. Here are some examples of the kinds of facts James considered:

(1)a. John threw the ball—oh—up.
   b. *John threw his dinner—oh—up.
   c. With a hammer—oh—you can build a step ladder.
   d. *With a hammer—oh—Bill hit Fred.

(For an exhaustive discussion see the papers by James, 1972, 1973a, and especially her dissertation, 1973b.) Part of her conclusion is that some of the constraints on such expressions involve the way in which issues of memory and emotion arise while sentences are being processed.

4. Correction and Editing Devices.   Among the grammatical constructions of English ruled out by the CIS use of "performance" are those used to correct or "edit" sentences while they are being said. Correction is usually thought of as being only a matter of stopping and saying part of your sentence over differently—with the effect of erasing a tape and saying what you really meant. DuBois, however, has shown this to be an entirely erroneous view. There are a variety of correction and editing constructions in English, for example, *that is, well, I mean* and *or rather,* and they all work differently—they have different pragmatic functions and different syntactic constraints. Evidence for syntactic constraints comes from sentences like:

a. I looked up her dress—I mean, her address.
b. *I looked up her dress—I mean, up her address.

Unpublished research by Monica MacCaulay on "Mid-sentence editing" has turned up further regularities, among them cases showing that these constructions obey the coordinate structure constraint.

    c. I bought 5 bottles of cream soda—well, six bottles.
    d. *I bought a dozen bagels, 5 bottles of cream soda, and two pounds of
        lox—well, six bottles.

The uses of the editing constructions are also remarkable. For example, *well* is used to indicate, in the act of speaking, that the assumptions and standards behind the conversation are being shifted and that Grice's conversational maxims are being maintained relative to some unspoken new set of assumptions, whereas otherwise they might appear to be violated.

    e. I've known thousands of people like that—well, hundreds.
    f. She's a great actress—well, she can carry a tune.
    g. Did you murder your grandmother? Well, I did put just a little arsenic in
        her soup.

DuBois also noted that such "correction devices" are used in fluent prose.

    h. I would like to comment on the racial, or rather racist, policies of the
        South African government.

The *or rather* is not a correction, but rather a rhetorical device used grammatically in a fluent well-formed sentence. It's effect has to do with how the sentence is understood up to the point of its being said—that is, its meaning is a function of processing. (For the initial study in this area, see DuBois, 1974.)

5. Speech Formulas. Bolinger (1976) and Becker (1975) observed that there are an enormous number of speech formulas in speech and writing of all kinds, and that productive constructions are rarer than might otherwise be thought. Speech formulas vary from such things as *hello* and *good morning,* to expressions that fit regular patterns of the language, but are used very differently—for example, *have a nice day, your place or mine?, what have we here?, I'll buy that, what's happening?,* etc. There are thousands of such expressions in English. They vary along a continuum from nearly complete frozenness to near productivity. In general, they are tied to stereotyped situations—the sort that are characterized by what Schank and Abelson call "scripts" as opposed to "plans." In fact, speech formulas have a number of similarities to scripts. Both are tied to specific kinds of contexts. Both have the same form as productive structures—sentences on the one hand and plans on the other. Both are frozen forms of otherwise productive structures—perhaps with some minor idiosyncrasies not found in the productive structures. For example, Schank and Abelson observe that the order in which the check comes in a restaurant script is a matter of ritual and is independent of any aspect of the plan structure of the script. Similarly, the same is true of the order of *solemnly* in the formula, "I solemnly swear. . . ." Both scripts and formulas seem to develop historically out of their productive counterparts. Schank and Abelson observe that scripts preempt plans. Similarly, speech formula uses preempt productive uses. For example, *I'll buy that* will almost always be used in its formulaic sense and not in the act of buying.

To me one of the most interesting similarities between scripts and speech formulas is their use in situations where there is a drain on mental energy. Both are part of our "automatic" behavior, and, as such, seem to require less "mental energy." For example, both seem to be characteristic of senility. One of the most striking things about the aged as they become senile is an increase in the use of speech formulas rather than productive expressions. Similarly, senility seems to involve an increased reliance on ritualized scripts rather than productively con-structed plans. The link between speech formulas and available mental energy is evident in activities like baseball, where players on the field chatter primarily in formulas (*Chuck it in there! Turn his hat around!*), while the really creative use of language in baseball comes mostly from bench jockeys, who have fewer demands on their immediate attention. Dan Kempler, in a recent Berkeley honors thesis, linked the automatic character of speech formulas to their well-known occurrence in certain types of aphasia. To my knowledge it has not been studied whether such aphasics can function better in ritualized script situations than in situations where they have to make up productive plans. It would be interesting to find out.

Generative grammar has nothing of interest to say about speech formulas. Yet such formulas dominate our language. The similarities between speech formulas and scripts indicate that there is a generalization to be stated. And it crosses the boundary of what generative linguists call the "language faculty." This suggests that speech formulas can only be understood by giving up the idea of an autono-mous language faculty and taking a broader perspective.

6. Semantics.   Most approaches to semantics in the tradition of generative grammar, whether generative semantics or interpretive semantics, and in the logical tradition as well (including Montague grammar), try to base a theory of meaning on a theory of truth. In all of these traditions sentences are taken as wholes. The idea that the processing of the sentence itself might have something to do with its meaning or its truth conditions is not considered. If you take sentences containing correction or editing constructions such as those mentioned earlier, it becomes clear that the meaning of the sentence depends in an important way on how it is processed. But some subtler cases have been discovered where satisfaction conditions depend on mid-sentence processing. There is Fillmore's celebrated example "If you want to save your life, press the little red button in front of you right . . . NOW!" In tense logics, sentences are evaluated for satisfaction conditions as if the whole sentence occurred at a single time. But in Fillmore's example, the time at which the instruction is to be carried out depends on the internal processing of the sentence, namely, when the word *NOW* is uttered. Other examples have been constructed by Morgan.

(1) a. John Smith is Harry's murderer.
   b. Harry's murderer is John Smith.

(a) and (b) are usually taken to have the same truth conditions. But what about (c) and (d).

    c. Harry's murderer, whose name I am about to reveal to you, is John Smith.
    d. John Smith, whose name I am about to reveal to you, is Harry's murderer.

In (c) the truth of the nonrestrictive relative clause depends upon when in the whole sentence the clause is uttered relative to when in the sentence the name is uttered. (d) is simply semantically aberrant.

The above are a small number of the kinds of facts that have turned up in the past decade that indicate that processing considerations are important in linguistics. Such cases have led me to try to construct theories of grammar in which linguistic rules play a direct role in processing, in particular, the theory of cognitive grammar and the theory of linguistic gestalts.

7. Logic. I would like to turn to a case of what appears to be failed logic, where what one might expect from traditional formal logic seems not to work. (1) ought to entail (2), but it doesn't.

(1) If we go to Florence tomorrow, we'll have a good time, and if we go to Siena tomorrow, we'll have a good time.
(2) If we go to Florence and Siena tomorrow, we'll have a good time.

I constructed these examples last summer in Pisa. The facts are that Florence is close enough to Pisa to drive there and back in a day and still have enough time to see the town. The same is true of Siena. But if you try to see both Florence and Siena in the same day, starting out from Pisa, you have to make the additional trip from Florence to Siena, which would leave you very little time to see either Florence or Siena. Given the facts of the matter, (1) can be true while (2) is false. But according to just about any version of classical logic, (2) is a logical consequence of (1), as the derivation in (3) shows.

(3) Let A = we go to Florence tomorrow
     B = we go to Siena tomorrow
     C = we'll have a good time

1. (A>C) & (B>C)
2. A>C from 1 by conjunction simplification
3. ASSUME: A & B
       A, from 4 by conjunction simplification
       C, from 4 and 2 by modus ponens
6. (A & B)>C, from 3 through 5

(3) is a form of inference that just about any classical system of formal logic would want to preserve. Yet something goes wrong when it is used by real people. The reason is that there is more than one possible scenario for "going to Florence." The understood scenario (call it Scenario 1) under which (1) is understood to be true is: You drive to Florence, park, walk around, leisurely visit museums, shops, churches, cafes, have dinner, leave. But given the facts of the world, there is no time for that scenario if you're going to visit Siena, too. At best you'd have to limit yourself to the following scenario (call it Scenario 2): You drive to Florence, park, rush around for an hour or so, leave. Most people wouldn't find that much fun. If someone did, then the inference from (1) to (2) might work for him or her. The problem is that "go to Florence" in (1) is understood in terms of scenario 1, while "go to Florence" in (2) is understood in terms of scenario 2. The form of inference in (3) will work just in case the "A" and "B" in it are understood in terms of the same scenario throughout. The problem is that English generally doesn't allow for this. In English a proposition like "A" that is conjoined to another proposition, may be understood in terms of a different scenario (scenario 2) then when it is unconjoined (scenario 1).

There are morals here for both linguists and logicians. The linguist must be concerned with the fact that part of the relation between surface structure and meaning has to do with the scenario in terms of which a proposition is understood. Different scenarios may be assigned to conjoined versus unconjoined propositions. The logician must be concerned with the fact that certain classical inference patterns hold only under preservation of scenario. Now the logician may retreat to a position that says that logic applies only to cases where the propositions have a fixed scenario, and that he therefore doesn't have to concern himself with this problem. But any logician who takes such a position is going to miss a lot of what goes on in human reasoning, since scenarios do shift in the course of reasoning.

I have brought up this example for the benefit of researchers in artificial intelligence who work with frames and scripts, which are formal devices for trying to deal with what I've called scenarios. Few linguists and logicians have considered the importance of these for understanding facts about grammar and meaning. One linguist who has is Marta Tobey, a Berkeley student, who has observed that there are regularities involving complementizers that have to do with the internal structures of scenarios. Compare (4) and (5).

(4) Harry started to drive to work, but his car wouldn't start.

(5) Harry started driving to work, but his car wouldn't start.

(5) is contradictory while (4) is not. Gerunds, in general, focus on the central part of the scenario. Thus, in (4), with an infinitive only some of the preconditions of driving to work need to have been met, while in (5) with the gerund some of the conditions of the central part of the driving scenario need to have been met, and they can't be if the car doesn't start. This also extends to the use of the *-ing* form in present participles. "While I was driving to work . . . " refers to a time during the central activity of driving, rather than to some percondition, such as getting into the car. The difference in scenario frocus between infinitives and gerunds accounts for the fact that (6) is not contradictory:

(6) I like to jog, because it keeps me fit, but I hate jogging itself.

"I hate jogging" with the gerund focuses on the central part of the jogging scenario, while "I like to jog" focuses on the jogging scenario as a whole and its connection to other aspects of life. One of the differences in meaning between the verb "like" and the verb "enjoy" is that "enjoy" must focus on the central part of the activity. This is the semantic reason why one can say:

(7) I enjoy jogging.

but not,

(8) *I enjoy to jog.

The internal structure of scenarios also come up in possible answers to questions. We can answer the question

(9) How did you get to the party?

either by (10)

(10) I drove there.

which refers to the central part of the scenario, or by (11),

(11) a. I have a car.
   b. I borrowed my roommate's car.
   c. The buses were running.

where the precondition to the scenario is given, and the precondition calls up the entire scenario. In English, however, one cannot answer a question by referring to just any part of the scenario. Thus for English speakers, (12a & b) would not be answers to (9).

(12) a. I got into my car.
   b. I started driving.

However, Rhodes (1977) reports that sentences like (12) are normal ways for speakers of the Algonkian language Ojibwa to answer such questions as (9). In Ojibwa, the convention for calling up the entire scenario, according to Rhodes, is to refer to the beginning rather than central part of the scenario. The conventions for answering questions are apparently not universal and the understanding of how to answer questions in different languages seems to depend upon an understanding of the internal structures of scenarios.

The point is that scenarios provide a way of structuring your experience, and the structure of scenarios is reflected in the structure of language.

The same kind of point can be made about categorization. Rosch (e.g., 1977), in a wide range of studies, has shown that people do not categorize objects in terms of set theory, where objects are either in or out of categories. Categories are instead fuzzy, and characterized in terms of prototypes, with objects having a greater or lesser degree of membership depending on how closely their properties match those of the prototype. This result from the area of cognition is matched in both natural language syntax and semantics. Ross, in his research on "squishes" has shown that natural language categories, such as noun phrase, clause, etc., are fuzzy, and that rules of grammar do not simply apply or fail to apply, but apply with more or less "strength." My own research in semantics has shown that languages contain words I call hedges, for example, *sort of, pretty much, loosely speaking,* etc., whose job it is to change the degree and nature of category membership. Kay and McDaniel (1975) have also shown that color categories are fuzzy and based on prototype colors that have a neurophysiological basis.

Next, let's turn to representation. There has recently been a debate over the question of whether visual information is represented in the form of relational networks or in the form of what are called "images." Although images were originally conceived of as being like photographs, they have become increasingly abstract and less photograph-like in conception in recent years, with the result that, as Palmer (1975; 1978) has recently shown, there seems to be little if any empirical difference between network representations and abstract image representations. In other words, network-like representations, whether one wants to call them abstract images or not, seem to be necessary for the representation of visual information.

In linguistics there have been a number of results favoring network representations over phrase structure trees and transformations. Most of these results have come out of work on universal grammar. Keenan and Comrie have shown that hierarchies of (network) relations are needed in order to state certain universal principles. Further research by Perlutter and Postal in their work on relational grammar has reinforced their conclusion. Thompson and I (Lakoff & Thompson, 1975a, 1975b) have shown, in our work on cognitive grammar, that a certain class of relational grammars could be mapped one-to-one onto processing grammars, while grammars using phrase-structure rules and transformations could not be. More recently, I have proposed a theory of linguistic gestalts in which the work done by transformational grammars could be done without derivations using relational networks with only two sets of grammatical relations. Postal and Johnson (1980), accepting my conclusions that network representations are correct and derivations are unnecessary, have developed a theory of arc-pair grammar that permits sequences of relations.

Again, I think it is no accident that the linguistic results favoring network representations with gestalt properties mesh with the visual results favoring representations with gestalt properties. It suggests the correctness of the experiential paradigm and incorrectness of autonomous paradigm.

Let us now turn to the question of gestalts. One thing that we know about visual representations is that they must have certain gestalt properties. At the very least, the whole must be greater than the sum of the parts and partial matching of visual representations is required. At least one of the AI systems using network representations does incorporate such gestalt properties to a certain extent—namely, Winograd and Bobrow's KRL system. In my paper on "Linguistic Gestalts (Lakoff, 1977) I gave six arguments to show that syntax must work by partial matching. In addition I gave a variety of examples indicating that the meaning of whole must be greater than the sum of the meanings of the parts for natural language sentences.

I have barely begun to mention, much less elaborate on, the empirical reasons I have for preferring the experiential paradigm. But there is an overriding reason for preferring it. After a generation of research in which it was implicitly assumed that language could be described on its own terms, it has become more interesting to ask how much of the structure of language is determined by the fact that people have bodies with perceptual mechanisms and memory and processing capabilities and limitations, by the fact that people have to try to make sense of the world using limited resources, and by the fact that people live in social groups and have to try to communicate with each other. It seems to me that a great deal of the structure of language is determined by such factors.

REFERENCES

Becker, J. 1975. In *Theoretical issues in natural language processing,* ed. R. C. Schank & B. L. Nash-Webber. Arlington, Va.: Tinlap.

Bolinger, D. 1976. Language and memory. *Language Sciences.*

DuBois, J. 1974. Syntax in mid-sentence. In *Berkeley studies in syntax and semantics,* vol. 1.

James, D. 1972. *Some aspects of the syntax and semantics of* interjections. Proceedings of the 8th Annual Meeting of the Chicago Linguistic Society.

James, D. 1973a. *Another look at, say, some grammatical constraints on, oh, interjections and hesitations.* Proceedings of the 9th Annual Meeting of the Chicago Linguistic Society.

James, D. 1973b. *The syntax and semantics of some interjections in English.* Ph.D. dissertation, Linguistics Department, University of Michigan.

Kay, P., & McDaniel, C. 1975. *Color categories as fuzzy sets.* Unpublished working paper no. 44, Language Behavior Laboratory, University of California, Berkeley.

Lakoff, G. 1972. *Hedges*. Proceedings of the 8th Annual Meeting of the Chicago Linguistic Society.

Lakoff, G. 1974. *Syntactic amalgams*. Proceedings of the 10th Annual Meeting of the Chicago Linguistic Society.

Lakoff, G. 1977. *Linguistic gestalts*. Proceedings of the 13th Annual Meeting of the Chicago Linguistic Society.

Lakoff, G., & Thompson, H. 1975a. *Cognitive grammar*. Proceedings of the 1st Annual meeting of the Berkeley Linguistic Society.

Lakoff, G., & Thompson, H. 1975b. Dative questions in cognitive grammar. In *Functionalism*, Chicago Linguistic Society paravolume.

Morgan, J., & Cole, P., eds. 1975. *Speech acts*. New York: Academic Press.

Palmer, S. 1975. The nature of perceptual representation: an examination of the analog/propositional debate. In *Theoretical issues in natural language processing*, ed. R. C. Schank and B. L. Nash-Webber. Arlington, Va.: Tinlap.

Palmer, S. 1978. Fundamental aspects of cognitive representation. In *Cognition and categorization*, ed. E. H. Rosch & B. B. Lloyd. Hillsdale, N.J.: Lawrence Erlbaum, Associates.

Postal, P., & Johnson, D. 1980. Arc-pair grammar. Princeton University Press.

Rhodes, R. 1977. Semantics in relational grammar. Proceedings of the 13th Annual Meeting of the Chicago Linguistic Society.

Rosch, E. H. 1977. *Human categorization*. In *Studies in crosscultural psychology*, ed. N. Warren, vol. 1. New York: Academic Press.

11 Grammar and Sequencing in Language

Robert J. Scholes
Institute for Advanced Study of the Communication Process
University of Florida

> *Nearly forty years ago Becher wrote: "There is no physiological hypothesis which can explain the origin and relation of temporal forms in mental life, indeed, there is no hypothesis which even foreshadows the possibility of such an explanation." The situation is little better today . . . we are still very far from being able to form an explicit explanation of temporal structure.*
> —(Karl Lashley, 1951)

The contemporary disrepute into which Lashley's antilocalization position has placed him may have obscured an extremely important contribution to psycholinguistics he made in the above cited "The Problem of Serial Order in Behavior." In that paper, Lashley clearly recognized a distinction between the functional significance of linguistic entities and the order in which they occur. He postulated a *sequencing mechanism* that was " . . . relatively independent, both of the motor units and the thought structure . . . " (p. 118). Re-interpreted in more modern terminology, Lashley is proposing a sequencing mechanism that orders, but is independent of, the identity of and relationships among the terms of a given sentence. Incorporation of Lashley's sequencing mechanism into a contemporary view of linguistic processing (Scholes, 1978) would suggest a "diagram" (What would be, I presume, a particularly "Galling" use of his idea) such as Fig. 11.1.

Figure 11.1 represents the facts that in order to understand a sentence one must know the meanings of the major lexical items (i.e., nouns, verbs, adjectives, and adverbs) contained in it and the relationships among them (i.e., which is the subject, what modifies what, etc.). To illustrate, knowing the meanings of

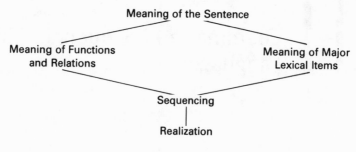

FIG. 11.1.   Legend.

the lexical items *boy, girl, picture,* and *take* is necessary but not sufficient to understanding a sentence in which they occur. There could be a sizable number of syntactic relations and functions that yield entirely different meanings of the sentence; for example,

> The boy took the girl's picture (or . . . picture of the girl)
> The girl took the boy's picture (or . . . picture of the boy)
> The boy took a picture to the girl (or . . . took the girl a picture)
> The girl took the picture to a boy (or . . . took a boy the picture)

In addition to these variations, there could be other tenses and other arrangements of articles that add further to the number of possible sentences.

That there are two distinct paths—lexical and functional—in any model of sentence comprehension (or production) is easily demonstrated by our ability to fully understand (or produce) the structural information of "Jabberwocky" and our ability to understand telegraphic strings such as " . . . mouse . . . cheese . . . eat." (See Scholes, 1978, for more detailed discussion of these paths.)

What is at issue here is the relationship of the posited sequencing component to the grammar of a language in a psycholinguistic model of sentence production and comprehension.

STRATEGY IN PSYCHOLINGUISTICS

While the time span was not as great between Becher, 1911, and Lashley, 1951, it did take nearly twenty years before any serious attempts were made to deal with the place of sequencing in psycholinguistics—in T. G. Bever, 1970. Bever's approach was to posit a set of linguistic strategies that he viewed as ways of interpreting sentences based on probabilistic approaches to grammatical function. The best known (and most widely used) of these strategies says that any sequence of Noun + Verb + Noun is to be interpreted as Subject + Verb + Object. This strategy (note that there is no such rule in English grammar) is relied on by young children, certain aphasic patients, cogenitally deaf adolescents, and beginning foreign speakers of English. It is based on experience (not grammar) and yields, in most cases, the correct meaning of such sentences. In passives, however, it yields the wrong reading (Heilman, Scholes & Watson 1976; Scholes, 1978; Scholes, Cohen, & Brumfield, 1978). In this and other strategies (e.g., the dative/accusative parsing in ambiguous predicates discussed in Scholes, 1978) language users are employing probabilistic short cuts to sentence comprehension that, in some cases, run counter to the correct reading supplied by grammatical analysis. These empirical data suggest that Lashley's conjecture was correct: viz., there is an autonomous "sequencing mechanism."

To date, such sequencing rules have been investigated largely within the context of sentence comprehension. Lashley's proposal is to the effect that this component operates in terms of output as well. That this is surely the case is shown by a number of cases where, while the grammar of a language permits numerous expressions of a given proposition, one of these is considerably more common, more natural, more facile, or, even, unique. Consider in this regard expressions of temporally ordered events (*He tied his shoe before he got up vs He got up after he tied his shoe*), active *vs* passive in everyday discourse, adjacency *vs* grammar in such sentences as *Tom promised Bill to ask Sara . . .* (where it is difficult to realize that Bill doesn't ask Sarah), and our ability to understand perfectly such strings as *Boy tall the went to store the buy to ring a* (that is, we can recognize the grammatical structure and that the elements are mis-ordered).

STRUCTURE AND SEQUENCE IN GRAMMAR

A fundamental assumption of Chomskyan linguistics is that " . . . a generative grammar" . . . (is) . . . "a system of rules that in some explicit and well-defined way assigns structural descriptions to sentences" (Chomsky, 1965, p. 8). There is, in this goal, nothing that requires the generative grammarian to describe the order of the entities identified by the structural description; yet, this is exactly what most of the "exemplars" (see McCawley, this volume) do. McCawley cites Chomsky's analysis of English auxilliary verbs in this context; viz., the phrase structure rule

   1, PS AUX→Tense (Modal) (have-en) (be-ing)

plus the transformational rules that yield the surface order of affixes (i.e. "Affix Hopping"). Let us look a little more closely at such a formulation.

First of all, the phrase structure (PS) rule specifies the elements on one level (tense, modal, etc.) that are classified together as AUX on a higher level. The order in which these elements are listed in the written formulation of this identity relation need not be understood as an order of occurrence in space or time (anymore than some list such as Preposition → in, on, to, etc.) need be considered as having order. All the PS rule says is that the things to the right of the arrow can all be classified as the term to the left of the arrow.

Given this "unordered" view, we can specify fairly clearly why we need a second set of rules (i.e., "transformations") and what these rules have to do. Consider a structure such as

John will have been going home by then.

We must somehow indicate that *will* is a modal, *have* and the *-en* of *been* is the *have-en* of the AUX rule, and the *be-* of *been* and the *-ing* of *going* are the *be-ing* of the AUX rule. That is, we must provide information concerning the identity relations of the terms of the surface structure and the terms provided by the PS rule. Remember, now, that the technical definition of a transformational rule is that it "converts structural descriptions to other structural descriptions" (Burt, 1971, 4). Again, there is nothing in this goal that requires order. Other T-rules will be needed to specify any constraints on conjoining (e.g., *John had drunk and be eating). These T-rules, likewise, do not require that any order be specified (they simply must state what the auxilliary selectional restrictions are).

Given this view, it appears that the role of transformational rules is to specify the relationships between the structures that occur in actuality (surface structures) and the potential structures generated by the phrase structure rules (deep struc-tures) and to define co-occurrence restrictions. No set of structures need specify the sequence of elements for which structural relationships obtain.

SYNTAX AS ORDER AND ORDER AS SYNTAX

Our academic training as well as, apparently, our initial intuitions make it very difficult for us to deal with a claim that syntax and ordering are independent. Nearly everyone who has reacted to the ideas presented in this chapter has pointed out that English does employ order to convey syntactic distinctions (while, presumably, certain other languages, like languages employing case markers, don't). While this reaction is no doubt a considered and educated one, it is, I believe, at best limited and at worst wrong. To illustrate the alternative view under consideration here, we posit two distinct conditions about semantics and ordering and semantics and syntax:

1. If you want to express X, the order of the elements of X must be in the sequence a + b + c + d.
2. If you want to express X, the syntactic relations must be of the type A, B, C, D.

On the first condition, if you want to say that some unnamed male individual moved in such a way that the original position was in closer approximation to the speaker than the second position, you must say "he went from here to there." On the second condition, if you want to construct a sentence capturing the intention above, you must have the syntactic structure indicated by:

I would ask the reader to note that the second condition is quite independent of the first. Specifying the structure appropriate to the meaning can be done with any spatial arrangement whatsoever so long as the relationships are maintained. For example

Consider that old classic case, active and passive sentences. For some reason which I now find unmotivated, we generally feel that ordering is syntax for active sentence but formatives are syntax for passives, i.e., that in *Tom hit Bill* it is the order that specifies the relations, but in *Bill was hit by Tom* it is the BE and BY that gives us the meaning. Such a shift of criteria is not necessary. We could just as well take the view that the structure of either is given by the optionality of the PASSIVE MARKER; i.e., S → (BE/GET) VP NP. Or, to use trees,

The ordering and structural conditions are still distinct: If you want to say that Tom hit Bill you can use the order *Tom hit Bill* or you can use the order *Bill hit Tom,* but if you use the order *Bill hit Tom* you must use a *BE* between *Bill* and *hit* and a *BY* before *Tom* (order).

In many sentences of English the left-to-right (or first to last) sequencing of lexical items provides for a short cut to the comprehension of grammatical functions. Thus, anyone, with some experience in dealing with understanding English utterances might well adopt the strategy that any NVN (Noun-Verb-Noun) sequence is to be interpreted as SVO (Subject-Verb-Object). Unfortunately for some English users, but fortunately for our consideration of grammar and sequencing, this strategy will sometimes fail; as, for example, if it is employed in interpreting "Bill was hit by Tom." If, then, some listener tells us by his response that *Bill was hit by Tom* means that *Bill hit Tom* we can say that he is using a strategy whereby the NVN sequence is to be interpreted as SVO. Such a strategy is clearly not part of the grammar of English (which says, in fact, that the example sentence is to be understood quite differently) but is a distinct body of knowledge language users have concerning the frequency with which certain structures occur and the most probable interpretations associated with them.

To fully convince yourself of these strategies, note how easy it is to continue the string *the mouse ate the-* with something like *cheese* (when, of course, by the rules of the grammar of English the next thing could be *m* or *re* or *atrically* or myriad other things). Also note the ease with which we comprehend *the hunter shot the bird that ate the corn that grew wild* and the difficulty of following the grammatically equivalent but differently ordered *the corn the bird the hunter shot ate grew wild.*

A rather famous case showing the autonomy of sequencing and grammar in speech production involves the embeddings of *that is* in the existentialist philosophical context (to make it a bit easier to follow, I've substituted *obtains* for *is*). Try saying *that that obtains obtains.* Not too difficult, is it? The meaning is clear (that is to say, the grammatical structure is clear); *viz.,* that the proposition *that obtains* has philosophical validity. However, even though the grammatical structure can be ascertained with more embeddings, our ability to articulate correctly the stress and intonation patterns breaks down when we try things like *that that that obtains obtains obtains.* The thing to be noticed about such strings, in the context of the present discussion, is that it's not that we have any trouble constructing complex syntactic structures (I just did); it's that at some point we no longer know how to co-ordinate the sequencing components of disjuncture, stress, and intonation with the structure. While the examples here are somewhat esoteric perhaps, the everyday stops and restarts we all practice in our informal language communication are common indexes of an inability to sequence what we just generated, e.g.: *That is, the thing is that, well, what we need now is to, is uh, we need a drink, that's what we need.*

F-ing Insertion

The questions raised by George Lakoff (this volume) are interesting in the light of a grammar/sequence distinction. One might ask whether the permissibility of interjection such as "oh," "god-damn," and, the currently most popular, f-ing, is governed by order or by grammar.

We can formulate two rules governing F-ING Insertion. The first is a grammatical rule: F-ING must be linked to a major lexical item (noun, verb, adjective, or adverb; the second is a sequencing rule: F-ING must preceed the major lexical item to which it is linked.

On the first, grammatical, rule, you can have structures like A but not like B.

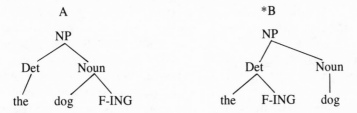

On the second, sequencing, rule, if you have a structure like A, the elements of A must occur in the order Det + F-ING + Noun. For example, if you show up at work with a bloody leg and someone asks what happened to you, you might say,

> "the f-ing dog bit me" or
> "the dog f-ing bit me" but not
> *"f-ing the dog bit me"
> *"the dog bit f-ing me"

Note the difference in the first two expressions where the first indicates that the speaker has had it with the stupid dog while the second indicates that he is shocked that the nice doggy did such a dastardly thing to him.

Proof that it is the lexical status of a word that determines F-ING linking can be seen by considering F-ING insertion before *can* in the three sentences below

> the paint can covered the tear
> the paint can cover the tear
> the paint can cover was torn.

GRAMMAR AND SEQUENCING IN LANGUAGE
DISORDERS: PARAPHASIAS

If, as Lasley suggested, there is an autonomous sequencing mechanism that orders the elements of utterances and if, as I have posited, this mechanism is not a proper part of the mechanism for specifying the elements and structures of sentences (i.e., the grammar), then one ought to observe separable disorders of the grammar (aphasia) and sequencing. Behavior in which linguistic forms and structures are erroneously employed is called *paraphasia*. On the view just given, there ought, then, to be paraphasias in which incorrect forms are used in a correct sequence (paraphasias of grammar) and cases in which correct forms are used in an incorrect sequence (paraphasias of sequencing). In the following survey, types of language disorders that do and do not occur are discussed within the context of a psycholinguistic typology of language functions. The observed paraphasias and the lacunae will be then summarized from the point of view of possible distinctions between grammar and sequencing disorders.

In this chapter, the definition of paraphasia posited in Lecours and Rouillon, 1976, will be adopted; "Aphasic transformations . . . are called paraphasias when they can be described . . . by reference to a corresponding normal language segment" (p. 99). The principal reason for using this definition is that it constrains the discussion of specific paraphasias to cases in which the erroneous expression is clearly related to the normal correct form (at least in terms of class or category, not necessarily the exact word), and it rules out any serious discussion of "word salad" utterances where it is impossible to say what the corresponding normal event would be. To illustrate, if a patient points to his hearing aid and says he needs new glasses, the erroneous term *glasses* is clearly related to the normal expression *hearing aid*. On the other hand, such utterances as *I didn't know how to do me any able to* (Goodglass, 1976, p. 239) cannot be considered paraphasic since it is impossible to construct the corresponding normal language for *me any able to*.

In the typology of paraphasias that follows, both existing and potential disorders are considered. The posited but unobserved (as well as the observed) paraphasias are based on a standard "three-component" (i.e., lexicon, syntax and phonology) model of language and consider the formal as well as semantic properties of the elements of each component.

Particular attention will be paid to lacunae in the posited types of paraphasia, and these gaps will be related to models of normal language function.

The underlying assumption in this exercise is the view shared by many neurolinguists (e.g., Gazzaniga & Berndt, 1978) that components and processes of normal linguistic function should be subject to selective impairment by discrete neurological damage.

Other typologies of paraphasia have been proposed. Lecours and Rouillon, 1976, for example, propose terms such as *monemic paraphasia* (disorders of morphemes), and *syntagmic paraphasia* (disorders of constituent structure). These typologies, however, have been limited to classifications of observed disorders and do not raise the issue of why certain components and processes of models of normal linguistic function are not impaired in aphasia.

Phonological Paraphasias

In phonological paraphasia one is looking for cases in which a form that is functionally identified by context is phonologically misrepresented (i.e., is a "nonsense" form) or cases in which a form is produced that does not conform to the phonology of the language.

Major Lexical Items.   Major lexical items (MLI) denotes the stems or bases of the four major parts of speech—noun, verb, adjective, and adverb (see Chomsky & Halle, 1968, for discussion). Phonological paraphasia of these forms is common (i.e., *phonemic* or *literal paraphasia*). The function of the forms as nouns, verbs, etc. is generally well defined by context (e.g. *I like your wednebby*). The examples used here and many others of equally curious form can be found in Buckingham, 1977.

Function Words.   By *function word* we mean those syntactic formatives that occur as "free" morphemes (that is, not bound to stems by affixation). These include prepositions, articles, connectives, and the like. These forms are either phonologically correct or are absent altogether (as in agrammatism), but never occur as nonsense syllables as posited in Table 11.1.

Inflections.   The term *inflection* is used here in the sense of affixes that alter the form of a word without changing the grammatical function of that word (e.g. tense in verbs, number in nouns, degree in adjectives, etc.) As with free syntactic functors, these affixes are either present (perhaps with erroneous meanings) or absent. Gleason, Goodglass, Green, Ackerman, and Hyde (1975) present an interesting discussion of the strategies patients use to retain the semantics of propositions in the absence of inflectional morphology; for example, the use of adverbs to compensate for the absent plural marker.

Derivation.   By *derivation* we refer to those alterations of form that denote the part of speech of a word; for example, the -ion suffix that denotes noun. Phonological paraphasia apparently does occur in such affixes as well as in associated stress rules. The example in Table 11.1 where the patient produced *mathemadadic* for *mathematician* (from my own records) is somewhat suspect (note the preservation of *-ic*), and the patient's general imitative behavior was erratic (he repeated *condominium* as *kindaminimum*). There are, however, a number of good examples, as well as a detailed treatment of the nature of the phonological error in Schnitzer, 1972.

Morpheme Structure.   Morpheme structure rules describe the constraints on the sequences of phonemic segments allowed by specific language (the older term was phonotactics). (See Chomsky & Halle, 1968, for some discussion).

TABLE 11.1

Paraphasias

Type	Example
I. Phonological	
A. Major lexical items	falderbill, wednebby
B. Function words	*uth boy walked mut uth store
C. Inflection	*the boynu walkmer the store
D. Derivation	mathemadadic
E. Morpheme structure	*thuthe, ngip, zhirlp
F. Segmental	*/y/,/oe/,/bw/
G. Suprasegmental	?it's the boy who went? not the girl!
H. Adjustment	courageous (/k r j s/)
II. Semantic	
A. Major lexical items	I can't hear without my glasses
B. Function words	glare off the road/glare of the road
C. Inflection	more/most
D. Derivation	I couldn't talking anymore
E. Structures	he gave the doll and the kitty/ . . . doll to the kitty
III. Structural	
A. Phrase structure	*the little/boy is/playing
B. Transformations	*he do walks funny? (but, mood to talk/for talking)
C. Discontiguity	*he has been go, he ising go
D. Categorial	
1. Major lexical	*a nighturnal animal prowls at noct
2. Function words	*from boy went the with store
IV. Ordering	
A. Within phrase	*boy the little went to store the
B. Across phrase	*to the girl flowers the boy gave

*denotes unreported paraphasias

These rules are apparently never impaired by brain damage. Whitaker, 1970, refers to the " . . . rigid adherence to the laws of phonological organization of the particular language regardless of the severity of the dysfunction" (p. 51).

Suprasegmental. The phonology of suprasegmentals deals with the information-bearing aspects of stress, intonation, and disjuncture. These aspects of grammar are to be distinguished from those acoustic aspects of utterances that serve to convey information about the identity or emotional state of the speaker (See Heilman, Scholes, & Watson, 1975 for discussion of the latter). The existence of paraphasia of suprasegmental phonology is, I believe, unclear at this point. While Whitaker (1970) refers to "misplacing of stress" he views this as "reflecting in many cases an erroneous analysis of the grammatical form class" (p. 51). The unstressed status of function words in certain positions is viewed as a contributing factor in agrammatic imitations (Goodglass, 1976). However, reading a sentence in the manner described in Table 11.1 seems not only unobserved but even difficult to imagine. It should be noted that the tendency of the normal listener to supply the correct suprasegmental features as a function of his internalized knowledge of the language (Lieberman, 1967) may contribute to the rarity of such behavior.

(The only specific treatment of a selected suprasegmental feature from the point of view of language disorders, is, to my knowledge, a consideration of word boundary in Scholes, 1972).

Segmental.   While inventories of segmental phonemes and phonemic oppositions may be simplified or rearranged, no new (i.e., non-native) oppositions or segments are introduced. Rounding is not introduced to front vowels as a phonemic distinction, or labialization to stops, etc.

Adjustment Rules.   Low-level adjustment rules that alter the segments and stress of forms depending on derivation, inflection, and negation is treated extensively in the context of generative phonology in Schnitzer, 1972. Mispronunciations are, from this point of view, the result of mis-assignment of phonological features on a deeper level. By and large, the generative rules themselves appear to be unimpaired but operate in the normal fashion on incorrect input thereby yielding incorrect phonetic shapes.

Semantic Paraphasias

A semantic paraphasia occurs when some form or construction that is grammatically correct is used in such a way as to alter the intended meaning or create an anomolous proposition.

Major Lexical Items.   The commonly reported semantic paraphasia is typically limited to nouns, verbs, adjectives, and adverbs. A local patient said *beautiful* for *pretty* (adjective), *ducks* for *dogs* (noun), *write* for *read* (verb), and *finally* for *easily* (adverb) in a single interview. A thorough review of the neurolinguistic analyses of this type of paraphasia can be found in Caramazza and Berndt, 1978.

Function Words.   Semantic paraphasia of function words is fairly common. In general, these errors appear to be confined (like errors of major lexical items) to mistakes within categories—that is, one preposition for another, one determiner for another (*my* for *the*), one auxiliary for another. Like the semantic feature hierachy observed with nouns, the more frequent semantic paraphasias of function words appear to involve lower categorizations—for example, the replacement of *the* with *a* is more common than replacing *the* with *my*. (i.e., articles *vs* NP markers).

Inflections.   Semantic paraphasia of inflection is also common. Errors are within an inflection, never across inflections (e.g., a tense inflection is never substituted for a number marker, etc.) Thus, tenses are substituted, plural and singular are mixed up, and degree is confused.

Derivation.   Using a nominalizing derivation (gerund or participle) where a verb is indicated, as in the example, is observed with some frequency. This example is from Green, 1973. Whitaker, 1970, suggests that one common form of derivational paraphasia—using the gerund/participial form as a verb, as in the example—may be due to the latter "being easier to process" (p. 52).

Structure.   A semantic paraphasia of a structure occurs when one phrase structure is substituted for another with a resulting change in the reading of that sentence. The example given is a common behavior of children asked to imitate dative constructions. Before the dative is part of their grammar, they will convert such structures to conjoined accusatives—an earlier acquired structure.

I haven't actually observed this particular example in adult aphasics, but the conversion of passives to actives is commonly seen in imitation tasks, as is the conversion of complex embedded structures into simpler ones—for example, *He grinned and asked me . . .* became *He grinned. He asked me. . .*

Structural Paraphasias

In structural paraphasias we are looking for cases where one structure is substituted for another. This may be on any one of several levels of grammatical structure, as classified in the following.

Phrase Structure.   By a phrase structure paraphasia we intend cases in which the basic phrase structure components of sentences are given the wrong structural analyses. For example, suppose an aphasic patient indicated the structure of the sentence below to be as shown:

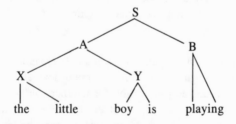

The only evidence for or against phrase structure paraphasia is found in the work of Edgar Zurif and his associates (Zurif, Caramazza, & Myerson, 1972; Zurif & Caramazza, 1976). In this research, subjects are asked to subjectively judge the

word-relatedness of pairs of words in sentences. In this way constituent structures for given sentences can be inferred as well as relative strengths of the
constituent relationships. In general, the parsings gained by this method with
normals resembles the tree diagrams of the test sentences as they would be
indicated by grammarians. Agrammatic aphasics generally preserve the structure
of the major lexical items of the sentence but class all function words as appen-
dices to the main structure. In some, but not all cases of judgments of "mixed
anterior aphasics," subject-verb-object phrase structure was given as $(S+V)+0$
(as opposed to the grammarians' $(S)+(V+0)$.

An interesting case of the retention of the intended phrase structure in the
absence of relevant function word information is provided in Zurif, et al., 1972,
in sentence #7, where *she loves the flying kites* is parsed as meaning she loves
kites that fly—note that without the article, the sentence is ambiguous and could
equally well be parsed as meaning she loves to fly kites.

On the basis of the work to date, one can only conclude that phrase structure is
subject to paraphasia in at most an inconsistent fashion and is, apparently,
limited to S + V + 0 parsings. Further, the work on hyper sentences (e.g., *I
know that* S, *I say that* S, etc.) by Buckingham, Avakian-Whitaker, and
Whitaker, (1975) indicates that all paraphasias are limited to the embedded S—in
itself a rather strong bit of evidence for the stability of phrase structure.

Transformation.   Paraphasias of transformational generations of surface
structure are seen in aphasia. One of our patients changed *I wasn't in the mood
for talking* to *I wasn't in the mood to talk,* in which a different transformation is
chosen, but the "deep structure" remains unchanged. Apparently, such
paraphasias are limited to cases in which underlying meaning is unchanged and
no illegal orders of elements are created. The second point is particularly relevant
here. While it is well known that children will incorporate one but not all rules of
a particular transformational derivation, uttering things like *My daddy do go?*
(where the DO particle is inserted, but not moved to the front as required by
interrogative), no such behavior is reported in aphasia.

Discontiguous Constituents.   Certain elements, such as verb auxiliaries, are
introduced by the phrase structure component of a grammar as unitary elements
whose constituents must be subsequently adjusted by transformational rules. The
progressive auxiliary, BE-ing, for example, is generated as a unit and is then
moved around so as to get *is going, is certainly going,* etc. It would appear, then,
feasible that some specific disorder might impair this sequence adjusting, but no
such strings as *he ising go* occur.

Grammatical Category.   Clear paraphasic cases of a word from one part of
speech being used as a different, erroneous category are not observed. Lexical
forms that are uniquely nouns are not used as verbs (e.g., *He pedestrianed*

across the street), variant forms of words with specific category assignments are not crossed (e.g., *Since it is a nighturnal creature, it only prowls at noct*). Saffran, Schwartz, and Marin (1980) report some cases of this kind, as "He shoppingcentered . . ."

Several studies (deVilliers, 1978; Gleason, 1978) show considerable semantic paraphasia within inflectional categories in both children and aphasics, but no errors across categories.

In my own observations, I have encountered paraphasias supplying possessive pronouns for articles, but both of these are in the class of noun phrase markers, and I have never encountered such things as articles in place of prepositions, auxiliaries in place of pronouns, etc.

In this regard, Vetter, 1975, discusses this issue from the point of view of the speech behavior of schizophrenic patients. He reports that he has never seen the kind of miscategoricization that is practiced by such writers as e.e. cummings, James Joyce, and Gertrude Stein. Vetter's examples from these authors—e.g., cummings' *but if a lark should april me*—provide excellent cases of what categorial paraphasia would look like if it should occur.

Major categorial paraphasias do occur in child language, as when my son asked me to *higher his handlebars,* and there are some possible exceptions to this lacuna in Green, 1973. It would appear, however, that Green's cases, including *I went to this place in the near house* (*near* as an adjective) and *something /elsid/ towards it out* (*toward* as verb) can be explained by other disorders (*near* as a paraphasia of *nearest*; /elsid/ as the verb).

Ordering Paraphasia

Misordering of either elements within phrases or of phrases themselves is not observed in aphasia. The kinds of utterances illustrated in Table 11.1 do not occur. Goodglass, 1976, offers one possible counter example (the only instance from a large corpus on a single case) of the object noun preceeding the verb—*wood, uh handling* (p. 254). The hesitancy would appear to indicate, however, a temporary block on the verb rather than a re-structuring of the normal verb-object sequencing for English.

It may be noted that children's orderings of constituents are often not that of the adult model (e.g., *allgone sugar*), but these variations appear to be phased out once the proper sequencing is acquired.

SUMMARY OF PARAPHASIC LACUNAE

In the typology of potential paraphasias just reviewed, several notable patterns of omission occur. By and large, phonological paraphasia does not occur. That is, while numerous types of nonsense forms appear in the speech of aphasics, these forms do not violate the morpheme structure rules of the language nor do they alter the segmental inventories in any significant manner. Thus, the nonsense forms that occur would appear to result from errors in the recovery of underlying phonologic representation of forms or in the misapplication of the correct set of generative phonological rules.

Nonsense forms ("phonemic paraphasia") of syntactic functors—free or bound forms—do not occur. This would verify the linguistic view (e.g., Jacobs & Rosenbaum, 1968) that such forms have no underlying phonological representation but are, rather, sets of semantic and functional features only.

These observations suggest that phonology, once acquired, is entirely automatized. This component would appear to be characterized along the lines of a computer program that blindly performs whatever operations are triggered by the configurations it receives. In the case of linguistic entities that have no underlying phonological specifications (inflectional formatives, function words), it has no input on which to operate and thus does not generate inappropriate phonetic shapes of these terms.

Major grammatical categories appear to be impervious to aphasic disorder. While derivational errors may result in inappropriate usages (e.g., *I couldn't talking*), base forms that are uniquely certain parts of speech are not used in other grammatical functions. This appears to apply to both the major lexical categories of noun, verb, adjective, and adverb and to syntactic functor categories such as preposition, auxiliary, determiner, etc.

Of primary interest here, however, is the noticable absence of sequencing errors. The orders of phonemes within words, the orders of bases and affixes within words, the order of words within phrases, the order of phrases within sentences, and the order of sentences within corpora are not disordered in aphasia. This claim, of course, is exactly the opposite of the view of many neurolinguists. Goodglass, 1976, for example, says that paragrammatism is marked by "confusions in the choice and ordering of words and of grammatical forms" (p. 240). The illustrative example of this pattern offered by Goodglass is: "I feel very well. My hearing, writing, been doing good, things that I couldn't hear from. In other words, I didn't know how. This year, the last three years, or perhaps a little more, I didn't know how to do me any able to" (p. 239).

Counter to Goodglass' interpretation, one is struck by the fact that sequencing and categorization are remarkably preserved in this passage. If we exclude the word salad sequence "me any able to" on the grounds that it fails to meet the condition of paraphasia (in that the normal form to which it might correspond is not at all obvious), there is just one candidate for a case of misordering or miscategorization—viz., *I couldn't hear from*. If this is a semantic paraphasia within the category of prepositional adverbs (i.e., the intended form is *before*), then there are no misorderings in the text. If semantic paraphasia is the wrong interpretation, there is still no ordering paraphasia since the items given in the utterance (*things, that, from, hear,* couldn't, I) don't re-order in any acceptable sequence.

If, then, the view proposed here to the effect that sequencing of linguistic entities is not disrupted by aphasia is accepted, it turns out that the term aphasia has exactly the right meaning in current usage—namely, that it is a disorder of the grammar of the language. This comes about since, if we combine Lashley's proposal with the observations and interpretations above of paraphasias, then there is an autonomous sequencing mechanism that is an important part of a model of language use, but not properly a part of the grammar of a language.

SYNTAX AND ORDER IN BEHAVIOR

What kinds of behavior would distinguish syntactic disorders from sequencing disorders? We consider here two areas; one in phonology and one in syntax.

In English, adjectives may, in general, preceed or follow the nouns they modify [if they follow, a form of the copula must intervene—*the red rose, the rose (that) is red*]. Not all adjectives may modify all nouns; some of these restrictions are pragmatic (i.e., the things denoted by the nouns don't have the properties described by the adjectives, as in *a hungry rock*) and some are syntactic or formal (e.g., while there is nothing semantically inappropriate between the modifying pair *near/close* and the noun pair *miss/call, call* takes *close* and *miss* takes *near*).

Thus, someone with a grammatical disorder with intact sequencing might produce *a near call* or *a close miss* but never *a call close* or *miss near a*. Someone with a sequencing disorder with intact grammar might produce (or accept as OK) *miss near a* and *a call close* but not *a close miss* or *a near call*. An autonomous sequencing disorder would require production and/or acceptance of misordered or unordered grammatically well-formed structures while an autonomous grammatical disorder would require production and/or acceptance of grammatically ill-formed structures of sequential well-formedness.

The most obvious case I can think of for a phonological restriction on English free forms that is independent of sequencing is that every such form must contain at least one vowel. Thus, articulable utterances such as "sh," "fs," "v," "fv," etc., cannot be English free morphemes. The question then may be formulated, has any English speaking jargon aphasic produced such forms in the context of free morphemes; e.g., *I had a fsh but the zh died?* Without scanning all such records, my impression is that the answer to this question is no. That is to say, jargon aphasics violate neither the sequential constraints nor the constraints of phonological integrity of their native language(s).

It is of some interest to note, in this regard, that while nearly everyone ever associated with aphasiology has remarked on the retention of sequencing constraints in jargon aphasia, no one—to the best of my knowledge—has investigated whether phonological integrity of the type illustrated here is ever violated.

Making a Tephelone Call

Phonological metathesis—exchanging the positions of two speech sounds within a given context—is relatively common in normal as well as disordered utterance production. Such errors as the articulation of *tephelone* for *telephone* are surely cases of sequencing disorders: All of the elements are there, and we can be reasonably sure what the correct form is (it is a true paraphasia).

Unfortunately, beyond the anecdotal reporting of such metatheses, little is known about them in terms of the location and/or severity of brain damage that may cause consistent patterns of such errors, their developmental patterns in childhood, or the grammatical function of the metathesized elements. There are, of course, treatments that deal with the featural comparison of the metathesized phonemes. To construct a "tongue twister" maximizing the chances for phonemic metathesis, use phones that differ by one feature—e.g., /f/ /ð/, /s/ /ʃ/. Try: "sick shiney soul shufflers." The fact that such patterns can be formulated would suggest that this is a true sequencing disorder—that is, the part of speech or grammatical function of the words in which the sounds occur appears not to matter so long as the sounds have particular phonetic characteristics.

For Lashley's claim to be supported by phonemic metathesis, we would need to find cases of such behavior that could be related to specific neurological disorders and clearly distinguishable from the more traditional phonemic paraphasia. We would need a case of an individual who consistently produces forms like *tephelone* for *telephone* and never forms like *mannerpate* for *telephone*.

SOME HEURISTICS REGARDING SEQUENCING IN PSYCHOLINGUISTICS

While considerable attention has been devoted to the acquisition, use, and debilitation of grammar, comparatively few studies have dealt with sequencing of linguistic elements in the same way. If one wished to find evidence for the acquisition, use, and debilitation of an autonomous sequencing mechanism for language, where and how would one look?

Most obvious is the search for instances of those paraphasias that are here claimed to be non-existent, and, if any are found, to attempt to associate each with discrete components of higher neurological structures.

Secondly, this view would require demonstration of the isolability of the grammar and the sequencing rules in language acquisition and use. One might ask, for example, at what age the linguistic fact of dative is learned and whether this knowledge is acquired before or after the sequencing rules for the expression of dative are mastered. For this particular example, one might explore the assignment of structure to grammatically ambiguous strings such as, *The man fed her cat food,* versus cases in which a reading is given by grammatical cues, e.g., *The man fed her the cat food.* Scholes, Tanis, and Turner, 1976, have investigated just this case and have shown separable acquisitions of the sequential interpretive strategy and the grammatical analysis.

As a further indication of the acquisition of grammatical rule versus sequencing strategy, it should be kept in mind that strategies are based on probability, and the accuracy of a prediction based on probability is a function of the data base or experience on which it is built: Grammatical rules have no such feature; i.e., the passive is the passive no matter how often or seldom one has encountered such structures. Developmentally, then, the tendency to interpret certain structures as having certain meanings where this is based on experience should be a slope whose curve gradually changes over time. The acquisition of a grammatical rule, however, is a onestep function (once learned, it is learned).

In aphasiology, the preservation of sequencing in the absence of grammatical capacity seems well documented. Not only does the speech behavior discussed above testify to this, but perceptual ability as well may be adduced as evidence. At the recent International Neuropsychological Society symposium on jargonaphasia (New York, 1979) A. R. Lecours reported that a patient of his asked for clarification when Lecours spoke to him in native-language jargon language while E. Weinstein reported that his patients requested that he stop speaking nonsense when he spoke to them in a foreign language. I submit that when Lecours used the patient's native-language sequencing contraints in his jargon and Weinstein violated the patient's sequencing constraints in using a non-native language, the former's acceptance of the jargon as properly formed and the latter's rejection indicate an awareness of native language sequencing constraints in the absence of any intelligibility.

While it would appear from these observations that intact sequencing mechanism with impaired grammar is the common case in aphasia, one wonders under what conditions the reverse would be observed. For a patient to have impaired sequencing but intact grammar would require a type of paraphasia in which each of the unordered elements maintains grammatical integrity. One way to demonstrate this disorder in comprehension would be to find a patient who could correctly associate scrambled sentences with pictured events; for example, pointing to a picture of a truck running over a toy (in an array of pictures) given the stimulus, *truck running toy the over is the.*

SEQUENCING AND SYNTAX A LA SAPIR

An informative historical note on sequencing and syntax is provided in Edward Sapir's *Language,* 1921. We find there a number of references showing that Sapir felt that syntactic relations in grammar were historically traceable to the "dynamic features of speech—sentence and stress—" (p. 114). He notes, for example, that the earlier meaning of *of* as "away, moving from" has given way to a syntactic function of "genitive marker" in such expressions as *the law of the land*. That is, while the lexical import of the term is independent of order (*of* would mean "moving from" no matter where it might occur in an utterance), its syntactic function is tied to its position between two noun phrases. Sapir's reasoning was that the sequential position of the term in these expressions under- lay its current functional interpretation.

Sapir's thesis is fascinating when we look at language acquisition in hearing and deaf children. Hearing children treat affixes and stems as wholes long before they are able to deal with them as separable components (Palermo & Molfese, 1972). In this regard, ontogeny does recapitulate phylogeny; i.e., a suffix such as -er is treated in terms of its lexical value by the young child and later, presumably by virtue of its consistent sequential position, as an agentive suffix. By such processes we clearly recognize the suffixal value of -er in *lawyer* but no longer think of its lexical interpretation as "one who." One might even speculate that the ability to deal with linguistic elements in terms of arrangements and syntactic function, without being very concerned with their semantic interpretations, is a characteristic of structural as well as generative transformational linguistics.

Particularly intriguing is the application of Sapir's ideas to the acquisition of English by deaf children. The reasoning is as follows: (1) Sequence and stress are features of the spoken form of a language (visual forms don't have stress and are not constrained to be sequenced in time); (2) sequence and stress are precursors to syntactic structures and relations; (3) the deaf child must acquire language with- out access to the sequence and stress characteristics of speech. (4) Therefore: Deaf children will not acquire syntax in the way hearing children do or to the extent hearing children do.

The conclusion of 4 is entirely compatible with data on language acquisition by deaf children (Russell, Quigley, & Power, 1976; Scholes, Cohen, & Brum- field, 1978; Scholes, Tanis, & Anderson, 1976).

SUMMARY AND CONCLUSION

Nearly thirty years ago Karl Lashley speculated on the nature of a mechanism that governs the sequential ordering of linguistic (and other) events in human behavior. These speculations seem particularly intriguing in the context of a discussion of the mental and neurological approaches to language. Contemporary linguistic theory has, in this writer's view, tended to obscure Lashley's insights in that the goal of linguistic work is specified as "providing structural descrip- tions" while the exemplars of this work (see McCawley) in fact provide struc- tural orderings. We have argued that it is possible and even desirable to separate the elements and structural relationships of the grammar of a language from the rules (or conventions) by which these elements and relationships are sequenced in utterances. Thinkers such as Thomas Bever and George Lakoff have provided instances of language use that clearly distinguish grammar and sequencing and have given us some of the necessary terminology as well as providing frameworks of research into these issues. Edward Sapir speculated on a causal relationship between sequencing in speech and syntactic function that is seen to provide some interesting heuristics on normal and deaf language acquisition.

Aphasiology is seen to be largely composed of the reporting and typologizing of disorders of grammar. Paraphasic behavior that could be univocally described as sequencing disorder is either non-existent or unreported. These lacunae suggest that the neurological impairments that yield aphasia and paraphasias do not impair the sequencing mechanisms for linguistic elements, and the question thus becomes, "What kind of impairment does yield mis-ordered utterances?" The question is raised, but not answered here.

Finally, some suggestions are made for the attainment of evidence for the acquisition and debilitation of sequencing (as opposed to grammar). While there are studies in the literature that can be interpreted as showing autonomous sequencing and grammatical abilities, much work remains to be done. It is our hope that the claims and challenges of this chapter will stimulate others to prove or disprove the "autonomous sequencing mechanism" hypothesis and thus advance our understanding of these issues.

Since writing this, an article on the same topic has come to my attention: James Eicher, Linguistics and the problem of serial order, *Papers in Linguistics 10:1-2*, 1977, 151-183.

REFERENCES

Aaronson, D., & Rieber, R. W., eds. 1975. *Developmental psycholinguistics and communication disorders. Annals of the New York Academy of Sciences*, pp. 263.

Becher, E. 1911. *Gehirn und Seele*. Heidelberg.

Bever, T. G. 1970. The cognitive basis for linguistic structures. In *Cognition and the development of language*, ed. J. R. Haynes. New York: Wiley.

Buckingham, H. W., Jr. 1977. The conduction theory and neologistic jargon. *Language and Speech* 20:174-84.

Buckingham, H. W., Jr., Avakian-Whitaker, H., & Whitaker, H. 1975. Linguistic structures in stereotyped aphasic speech. *Linguistics* 154/155:5-13.

Burt, M. K. 1971. *From deep to surface structure*. New York: Harper and Row.

Caramazza, A., & Berndt, R. S. 1978. Semantic and syntactic processes in aphasia: a review of the literature. *Psychological Bulletin* 85.4:898-918.

Caramazza, A., & Zurif, E. B., eds. 1978. *Language acquisition and language breakdown*. Baltimore: Johns Hopkins.

Chomsky, N. A. 1965. *Aspects of the theory of syntax*. Cambridge, Mass: MIT Press.

Chomsky, N. A., & Halle, M. 1968. *The sound pattern of English*. New York: Harper and Row.

Gleason, J. B. 1978. The acquisition and dissolution of the English inflection system. In *Language acquisition and language breakdown*, ed. A. Caramazza & E. B. Zurif. Baltimore: Johns Hopkins.

Gleason, J. B., Goodglass, H., Green, E., Ackerman, N., & Hyde, M. R. 1975. The retrieval of syntax in Broca's aphasia. *Brain and Language* 2:451–71.

Goodglass, H. 1976. Agrammatism. In *Studies in neurolinguistics,* ed. H. Whitaker & H. A. Whitaker, vol. 1. New York: Academic Press.

Goodglass, H., & Blumstien, S., eds. 1973. *Psycholinguistics and aphasia.* Baltimore: Johns Hopkins.

Green, E. 1973. Phonological and grammatical aspects of jargon in an aphasic patient: a case study. In *Psycholinguistics and aphasia,* ed. H. Goodglass & S. Blumstien. Baltimore: Johns Hopkins.

Heilman, K. M., Scholes, R. J., & Watson, R. T. 1975. Auditory affective agnosia (disturbed comprehension of affective speech). *Journal of Neurology, Neurosurgery and Psychiatry* 38:69–72.

Heilman, K. M., Scholes, R. J., & Watson, R. T. 1976. Defects of immediate memory in Broca's and conduction aphasia. *Brain and Language 3:* 201–208.

Jacobs, R. A., & Rosenbaum, P. S. 1968. *English transformational grammar.* Waltham, Mass.: Blaisdell.

Lashley, K. S. 1951. The problem of serial order in behavior. In *Cerebral mechanisms in behavior,* ed. L. A. Jeffries. New York: Wiley.

Lecours, A. R., & Rouillon, F. 1976. Neurolinguistic analysis of jargon-aphasia and jargonagraphia. In *Studies in neurolinguistics,* ed. H. Whitaker & H. A. Whitaker, vol. 1. New York: Academic Press.

Lieberman, P. 1967. *Intonation, perception and language.* Cambridge: MIT Press.

Palermo, D. S., & Molfese, D. L. 1972. Language acquisition from age five onward. *Psychological Bulletin* 78:409–28.

Russell, W. K., Quigley, S. P., & Power, D. J. 1976. *Linguistics and deaf children.* Alexander Graham Bell Association for the Deaf, Washington, D.C.

Sapir, E. 1921. *Language.* Harvest Books.

Schnitzer, M. L. 1972. *Generative phonology—evidence from aphasia.* University Park: Pennsylvania State University Press.

Schnitzer, M. L., & Martin, F. E. 1974. Sequential constraint impairment in aphasia: a case study. *Brain and Language* 1: 283–92.

Scholes, R. J. 1972. *Performance aspects of readjustment rules.* Proceedings of the 8th Annual Meeting of the Chicago Linguistic Society.

Scholes, R. J. 1978. Syntactic and lexical components of sentence comprehension. In *Language acquisition and language breakdown,* ed. A. Caramazza & E. B. Zurif. Baltimore: Johns Hopkins.

Scholes, R. J., Cohen, M., & Brumfield, S. 1978. Some possible causes of syntactic deficits in the congenitally deaf English user. *American Annals of the Deaf* 23.5:528–35.

Scholes, R. J., Tanis, D. C., & Turner, A. 1976. Syntactic and strategic aspects of the comprehension of indirect and direct object constituents by children. *Language and Speech* 19.3:212–23.

Vetter, H. J. 1975. Psychopathology and atypical language development. In *Developmental psycholinguistics and communication disorders,* ed. D. Aaronson & R. W. Rieber. *Annals of the New York Academy of Sciences.*

Villiers, J. G. de 1968. Fourteen grammatical morphemes in acquisition and aphasia. In *Language acquisition and language breakdown,* ed. A. Caramazza & E. B. Zurif. Baltimore: Johns Hopkins.

Whitaker, H. A. 1970. *A model for neurolinguists.* Colchester: University of Essex.

Zurif, E. B., & Caramazza, A. 1976. Psycholinguistic structures in aphasia: studies in syntax and semantics. In *Studies in neurolinguistics,* ed. H. Whitaker & H. A. Whitaker, vol. 1. New York: Academic Press.

Zurif, E. B., Caramazza, A., & Myerson, R. 1972. Grammatical judgments of agrammatic aphasics. *Neuropsychologia* 10:405–17.

12

Psycholinguistic Experiment and Linguistic Intuition[1]

Virginia Valian
Columbia University

The methodological questions discussed in this chapter are directed toward psycholinguistics but hold more generally for all dependent areas within psychology. By a dependent or derivative science I mean one that relies on and is constrained by concepts from another science in stating its theories and hypotheses. Biology, in this sense, is dependent on physics. The central claim here is that formal psycholinguistic experiments (including formal observational studies) test performance models directly, competence models only very indirectly. Intuitive judgments, which may be thought of as informal experiments, test competence models more directly, even though intuitive judgments are fallible.

First it is necessary to characterize and distinguish competence and performance. Two characterizations are possible, what may be called the *general distinction,* which is a priori, and what may be called the *particular distinction,* which is a posteriori (Valian, 1979). The general distinction is the one that will be important for present purposes.

The general distinction is between knowledge and use. It is a priori because it does not depend on data. It is applicable whenever one assumes that there is knowledge *of* or *that* something. The distinction is logical because there is a conceptual difference between, on the one hand, knowing of or that something and, on the other hand, making use of that knowledge. The distinction is at least implicitly presupposed by all branches of cognitive psychology. For example, all programs have knowledge stores.

The particular distinction, in contrast, is an empirical matter. It represents a particular claim about what the content of knowledge is, such that it is distin-

[1]My thanks to J. J. Katz for endless discussion of the issues touched on in this chapter.

guished from features of the use system in which it is embedded. Chomsky early proposed one claim about the particular distinction, namely that there exists a syntactic level called deep structure. That claim could be incorrect: It is subject to data; it is empirical.

To summarize, the general distinction is imprevious to data and asserts the non-identity of knowledge and use; the particular distinction depends on corroborating evidence about how to draw it, about, for example, what the content of knowledge is. Disagreements about how to draw the particular distinction have no bearing on the existence of the general distinction. Here we will neither make nor defend any claims about how to draw the particular distinction; we simply note the definitional necessary of the general distinction. (See Valian, 1979, for further discussion.)

Having noted that there is a difference between knowing something and making use of knowledge, we now turn to the question of what the subject matter of psycholinguistics is. Given the preceding discussion, the subject matter could be the nature of the knowledge, the use of the knowledge, or both. Since we are talking about language, we can rephrase the choice as follows: Psycholinguistics is about the knowledge necessary for any and all linguistic behavior to take place; it is about how that knowledge is represented, accessed, and used; it is about both. (It will not always be easy to tell which behaviors are "linguistic," and which "non-linguistic," but there are enough clear cases to allow the discussion to proceed: Making a pun is clearly linguistic behavior while tieing shoelaces is clearly not.)

There are two different routes we can follow to answer the above question, corresponding to two different conceptions of grammar. (There are other routes as well, but only two will be followed here.) One conception is that first put forward by Chomsky, which claims that linguistics is theoretical psychology, having as its subject matter the ideal speaker-hearer's knowledge of the language plus the structure of the language itself. A constraint is placed on theories in linguistics that they be psychologically realizable (though whether practicing linguists typically make decisions on such a basis is unclear). On that conception, psycholinguistics is the study of performance. That is, the goal of psycholinguistics is to develop an explanatory model of performance.

Another conception is that put forward by Katz (1981), which claims that linguistics is solely linguistics, having as its subject matter only the structure of the language. Theories in linguistics are neither about psychological representations nor constrained by psychological facts. On this Platonic conception it is not ruled out that speakers have knowledge of their language and its structure, but the existence of such knowledge is a matter of independent and contingent fact, and the nature of that knowledge is within the domain of psychology.

Thus, the two conceptions make different assignments of the subject matter of psycholinguistics: On a Chomskyan view it is limited to performance, on a Platonic view it includes competence and performance. Further, in practice, the psycholinguist often ends up making claims about competence. Two questions may still be raised. Why does such a practice exist? Does the practice make sense? The following discussion attempts to answer both questions.

Let us first assume that we are interested in finding out whether someone has knowledge of some hypothesized linguistic rule or entity K_g. Even though the question of whether a person *has* K_g is logically distinct from the question of whether or how that person *uses* K_g in some task T_i, the only access to K_g is through one or another T_i. For example, if we want to know whether people have knowledge of basic grammatical relations like "subject of the sentence," we can only find out by having them do various tasks: We could ask them to identify the subject of various sentences, or to sort sentences with or without a subject into two different piles, or to make judgments about sentences that require discrimination of subjecthood, and so on.

If, for all T, there is no evidence of K_g, our confidence in the existence of K_g will decrease as a function of how many T's are tried. If only T_1 and T_2 are tried, and no evidence for K_g is found, we ought to keep an open mind about K_g's existence. To return to the example of subjecthood, if none of the above-described "experiments" demonstrated people's knowledge of subjecthood, we should be just as inclined to worry about experimental error as about the nonexistence of knowledge of subjecthood.

An open mind would not be necessary if it could be proven that T_1 or T_2 had some special status with respect to K_g, for example, if it could be demonstrated that performance on T_1 or T_2 could not fail to disclose K_g if K_g existed. We assume for the moment, however, that all T's are equal. If $T_1, T_2, \ldots, T_{1000}$ are tried, and no evidence for K_g is found, we will be fairly certain K_g does not exist. Thus, experimental evidence for the absence of K_g requires many negative cases from a large and representative sample of T's.

If, in contrast, for T_1 or T_2 there *is* evidence of K_g, then we have reason to believe in the existence of K_g, even if other T's fail to disclose the existence of K_g. Only if T_1 or T_2 had some especially suspect status with respect to K_g would we distrust the evidence. Thus, all other things being equal, less evidence is needed to confirm the existence of K_g than to confirm the non-existence of K_g. A similar point is made by Kiparsky (1975, p. 203), thus:

> When we find a certain pattern of blips with the radio-telescope aimed at some point in the sky, we may have evidence for a pulsar, but when we fail to find such a pattern, there might be either no pulsar or the signals we are looking for are so weak that they are buried in all kinds of other stellar and terrestrial noise.

Our temporary assumption that all T's were equal can now be examined. That assumption must be false, since in all sciences some T's are better sources of data than others. There are at least two determinants of how much confidence we place in a given T_i. The first is how successful a theory one can build by making use of data from a particular T_i; the second is how explicable it is that a particular T_i should yield superior data. To justify using T_i it is sufficient to show that by doing so one can construct a fine-grained comprehensive consistent theory. A good theory testifies to the adequacy of its associated data-collection procedures, simply by virtue of its existence. What solidifies confidence is an explanation for why T_i works so well. Such an explanation is not required for confidence, since a technique may work without anyone's knowing why, but it solidifies confidence.

The conclusion of this section of the argument is that, to find out if K_i exists, one should use the T that yields "good" data. You know if you have good data by whether you have a good theory. Thus, at one level, a theory justifies the data, just as, at another level, the data justify the theory.

The linguists' technique of choice is having intuitions. That "task" has made possible the construction of a comprehensive finely-grained theory of, on a Chomskyan view, people's (more accurately, of ideal speaker-hearers') knowledge about language (more specifically, knowledge about the structural properties of language). The theory is not about intuitions, any more than physics is about meter readings. It is about linguistic knowledge; having intuitions is a tool, an informal experimental procedure, allowing one to find out what one knows about a language. Grammar-constructing systematizes that knowledge and also projects claims about the object of the knowledge, namely the language in question.

If intuitions are "good" data for the construction of powerful theories about linguistic knowledge and language itself, why don't psycholinguists take for granted the linguists' claims about the nature of knowledge, and concentrate on determining access and use? Why, instead, do psycholinguists commonly make competing claims about the nature of linguistic knowledge? It is not because psycholinguists have a Platonic conception of grammar; none have espoused Platonism. But, even if psycholinguists did subscribe to a Platonist view, they would still be in error to rely on psychological experiment rather than linguistic intuition as a basis for information about a speaker-hearer's knowlege, or competence. To demonstrate that, however, it will first be necessary to go through psycholinguists' actual reasons for making claims about competence. There are three reasons.

The first is that linguists disagree about what the nature of linguistic knowledge is. The second is that many psycholinguists distrust the linguists' method as one that yields artifactual results. The third is that psycholinguists have erroneously concluded from failure to find evidence of aspects of K (e.g., transformations) in a few T's, that success via the T of having intuitions is only apparent, not true, success. There are several discussions of this third mistake. (See, for example, Fromkin, 1975; Kiparsky, 1975; Wirth, 1975; Valian, 1979. See also Foss & Fay, 1975, and Gough & Diehl, 1977, for a discussion of the limitations of experiments and the lack of strong evidence against the use of transformations.) Here the discussion will center on the first two reasons psycholinguists make competing claims about competence.

The first is that linguists disagree among themselves at any particular time about the contents of linguistic knowledge, and they change their minds over time (see McCawley, this volume). As a result, the psycholinguist is usually in a quandary about which theory to incorporate into a performance model. That quandary, however, is integral to any dependent science. There are always disagreements in basic science, often about very fundamental issues, such as how many basic particles compose matter. But no dependent science can afford to wait until the ultimate truth is arrived at in its allied basic science(s). Choices must be made with no guarantee of having made the right choice, and, in any event, advances can be made in the dependent science with an incomplete or even incorrect basic science. Newtonian physics, for example, is useful over a very large range.

It is tempting, however, to think that where linguistics has failed, psycholinguistics may succeed, especially if the experimental procedure of linguistics is intrinsically flawed. We now arrive at the second reason psycholinguists concern themselves with questions of knowledge as well as use. In most dependent sciences there is more agreement that the methods their allied basic sciences use are appropriate; seldom do dependent scientists criticize the main techniques used by basic scientists as being inherently flawed.

What are the properties of having intuitions that make it seem so suspect a technique? They should be quite serious in order to justify relinquishing a technique that allows for the construction of fine-grained theory and substituting techniques that, thus far, have explored only fairly gross aspects of linguistic knowledge and had difficulty establishing them.[2]

The major criticisms that have been made against using intuitions as data are: They are fallible; they are unstable; they are often in apparent conflict with each other and with data gathered in other ways; they are biased by one's theoretical orientation and by context. There are many discussions of the nature of intuitions and their role in the linguist's enterprise. See, for example, Bever (1970); Greenbaum (1976); Spencer (1973); Householder (1965, 1966); Derwing (1973); Ringen (1977); Labov (1972); Carroll, Bever, and Pollack (1979). By and large, intuitions are seen as necessary data, though the linguist's dependence on intuitions is often seen as unfortunate, because of the problematic character of intuitions.

The list of problems seems formidable until one realizes that the same criticisms hold, and to the same extent, for formal experimental results. All experimental procedures are fallible. They all yield data which are subject to more than one interpretation. There is always some datum in conflict with other data. The

---

[2]I will not take up the possible difficulty of fitting theories to intuitive data since there is no a priori reason to suppose that that task is more difficult for intuitions than for other data.

same procedure may yield one result in the hands of a scientist with one theoretical orientation and another in the hands of a scientist with a different orientation. Some experimenters get results when others do not. To begin with, then, there seems to be parity between having intuitions and doing formal experiments in terms of the likelihood of each to error.

Perhaps what makes having intuitions seem more likely to error is that it is subjective. There are no pieces of apparatus either in producing the stimuli or measuring the responses. The factor of human error, because there are no other error sources and because nothing is available to hide the human factor, looms large. But many subjective judgments are both reliable and valid. To buttress this claim I will compare making judgments about language with making judgments about wine, or tea, or cheese. There is an important disanalogy in the comparison that I mention first. In making judgments about food and drink one is making judgments about physical objects; neither linguistic knowledge nor language is a physical object. For present purposes the disanalogy is unimportant. It may seem that there is another disanalogy, in that tasters lack a theoretical bias, but that is not true. A Bordeaux lover, for example, will accept defects in a Bordeaux, like excessive tannin, that a Burgundy lover will not.

Tea companies have tea-tasters; champagne and sherry houses have taste specialists; wine shippers rely on their tongue. Tea- and wine-tasters taste in order to make quality judgments between different examples of the same tea or grape type, and in order to make analytical judgments that a blended tea or wine needs more or less of one or another component. Only people can produce a blend that will taste the same from year to year. In other words, companies hire tasters and smellers because their skills are needed, not because of ritual. Tasters are not infallible, but their errors are within acceptable limits, in part because they know what steps to take to keep their errors at a minimum. Interestingly, many of the procedures tasters deliberately use to reduce errors of judgment are similar to procedures linguists use.

Here are some examples of the similarities between tasters and linguists. Tasters arrange the order in which they will taste samples. Wines or teas expected to be light-bodied will precede those expected to be heavy-bodied. Tasting in the other order would dull or coarsen the palate. The fact that order of presentation of samples affects judgment is not taken as an indication that the judgment-making process is so flawed as to be useless, but as a fact to be exploited so as to reduce errors of judgment. Linguists support their analyses by presenting examples in a particular order, a practice that is similarly reasonable.

Tasters also make better judgments if they do not taste completely ''blind.'' By visual inspection and smell they are able to narrow the range of possibilities as to the identity and quality of the wine. Further, knowing in advance that a wine is, say, a French wine, will enable a taster to make a more accurate judgment about the exact geographical origin of the wine than if she had been given no prior information. Prior information can also be misleading, but that will be discovered in the long run. As mentioned earlier, tasters' preferences for wine of a certain type may also lead to erroneous judgments, but it should be noticed that although a Bordeaux lover will be too forgiving of excess tannin, she will simultaneously be more likely than a Burgundy lover to detect a critical absence of tannin in a young wine.

Linguists armed with a theory similarly have a greater possibility of making finer judgments, and a greater possibility of making certain kinds of errors. Theories, depending on their content, make it more likely that some distinctions will be missed and more likely that others will be noticed. In the long run, the competing theoretical claims and their attendant intuitions will be adjudicated. One easy method both tasters and linguists employ in the short run is to check their judgments with others who hold the same, different, or neutral theory and then re-judge.

The erroneous expectation that is operative here is that it is preferable to approach samples with a completely open mind. The only completely open mind is an ignorant, inexperienced one. Only someone who knows nothing about wine can approach samples of it with no preconceptions. Common reports of beginning tasters include: They all taste the same; they taste different but it's all a jumble; I can't remember anything about the ones I tasted last week, and so on. The untrained palate pays a heavy price for its "open-mindedness," namely, lack of ability to make fine discriminations. Again, the fact that training and experience are necessary is not a sign that the technique is suspect. Similarly, intuition-having is a skill at which all are capable at some level, but which training and experience can cultivate.

Another characteristic of tasters is that some tasters are better than others at detecting certain flavor components. For example, some people are very sensitive to bitterness and can detect it at lower concentrations than other people can. That is, not only do some people have better palates than others—since talent is unequally distributed—but some people excel in making certain kinds of judgments. Again there is a parallel with linguistics: Some people have better ears in general than other people, and some people excel at syntactic judgments, while others excel at semantic judgments. Again, the fact that people with talent, training and experience will have intuitions that people lacking them will not have is not an argument against using intuitions as data.

This is not to claim that intuition-having is such a privileged activity that only professionals should engage in it. We all have intuitions, because we all possess one necessary property, knowledge of our language. But having good intuitions requires more than knowing a language, and the other requirements will be met to various degrees from person to person. Therefore it should be recognized that while everyone is capable of having intuitions, there is also a talent and skill involved that are presumably more highly cultivated in professional linguists than in the person on the street.

To summarize this section of the argument, having intuitions is on a methodological par with using other experimental procedures except for its more apparent subjective character. The subjectivity is not a disqualification, however, since subjective judgments can be both reliable and valid. Further, we know something about how to improve our ability to produce good intuitions, such as via training, checking with others, and so forth.

Now we can return to the issue of the domain of psycholinguists from a Platonic viewpoint. Were psycholinguists to adopt a Platonist view of linguistics they would be free to make claims about the nature of competence but, I will argue, should give greater weight to intuitions than to psychological experiment, continuing to reserve the latter principally for claims about performance.

Intuitions have two aspects. The Platonic linguist is only concerned with what intuitions are about, namely, language. But the psychologist is also interested in what can be inferred about the intuiter's knowledge from the intuitions. The intuitions are not hallucinations. By virtue of the fact that linguists can construct good grammars by using intuitions as a starting point, there is evidence that the intuitions do reflect, on the intuiter's part, linguistic knowledge.

Thus, the role that intuitions play in the construction of grammars testifies to the existence of linguistic knowledge, independent of whether that knowledge is considered to be in the domain of linguistics or psychology. On a Platonist view it is necessary for the psychologist to integrate the information about speakers' linguistic knowledge obtainable from linguistic intuition with that from psychological experiment. The psychologist cannot ignore the implications about knowledge offered by intuitions (unless intuitions are somehow suspect, which the preceding discussion claimed was not true).

If anything, then, the psycholinguist who adopts a Plantonist framework must give more weight to intuitions than one who adopts a Chomskyan framework. If intuitions yield information about linguistic knowledge (as well as information about the structure of the language), and if linguistic knowledge is the province of the psychologist, then the psycholinguist must make full use of that information. Further, since the picture of competence that we get from intuitions is richer and more detailed that the picture we get from psycholinguistic experiments alone, and since in general we are ill-advised to throw data away, we are better off taking the richer offering (again, supposing there is nothing suspect about intuitions).

Any lingering unease about the method of having intuitions is probably due to how little we understand about why the method works, what makes for a good intuiter, what is responsible for faulty intuitions, what makes some intuitions clear and certain while others feel questionable, and so on (see Bever, 1974; Carroll et al., 1979). We earlier stated that a good theory testifies to the adequacy of its data-collection procedures, but that an explanation of why the procedures worked so well would solidify confidence in the procedures. That explanation is missing. Answers to the just-posed questions are needed to explain *why* the task of having intuitions yields better data than other tasks, even though they are not needed to prove that the task of having intuitions is superior to other tasks.

I have suggested elsewhere (Valian, 1979) that one possible reason intuitions are a better source of information about competence is that intuitions have as their focus and object the structural properties of the language. In contrast, most psycholinguistic experiments are designed to keep subjects from explicit awareness of the linguistic structure of the materials. The effects are intended to operate unconsciously. Further, subjects' responses are frequently nonlinguistic (e.g., pressing a button), so that inferences must be drawn about the interaction between the nonlinguistic and linguistic aspects of the task. The suggestion does not prove that intuitions are by their nature more informative about competence, but makes somewhat more reasonable the fact that they are.

There is, then, no a priori claim being made here that intuitions are the only source of knowledge about knowledge, nor that intuitions are always correct. Their use is not being justified on the basis of the claim that they have an a priori privileged status. Rather, their use is being justified on the basis of the fact that they work. It is as a matter of fact that we make the claim that having intuitions produces more direct information about the contents of knowledge, or competence, than psycholinguistic experiments do, and the further claim that psycholinguists should be more hesitant in making statements about the competence component than the performance component, if their statements are only based on psycholinguistic experiment.

REFERENCES

Bever, T. G. 1970. The cognitive basis for linguistic structures. In *Cognition and the development of language,* ed. J. R. Hayes. New York: Wiley.

Bever, T. G. 1974. The ascent of the specious or, there's a lot we don't know about mirrors. In *Explaining linguistic phenomena,* ed. D. Cohen. Washington, D.C.: Hemisphere.

Carroll, J. M., Bever, T. G., & Pollack, C. 1979. *The nonuniqueness of linguistic intuitions.* Unpublished manuscript, Columbia University.

Derwing, B. L. 1973. *Transformational grammar as a theory of language acquisition.* Cambridge: Cambridge University Press.

Foss, D. J., & Fay, D. 1975. Linguistic theory and performance models. In *Testing linguistic hypotheses,* ed. D. Cohen & J. R. Wirth. Washington, D.C.: Hemisphere.

Fromkin, V. A. 1975. When does a test test a hypothesis, or, what counts as evidence? In *Testing linguistic hypotheses,* ed. D. Cohen & J. R. Wirth. Washington, D.C.: Hemisphere.

Gough, P. B., & Diehl, R. L. 1977. Experimental psycholinguistics. In *A survey of linguistic science,* ed. W. O. Dingwall. 2d ed. Stamford, Conn.: Greylock.

Greenbaum, S. 1976. Contextual influence on acceptability judgments. *International Journal of Psycholinguistic Research,* pp. 5–11.

Householder, F. W. 1965. On some recent claims in phonological theory. *Journal of Linguistics* 1:13–34.

Householder, F. W. 1966. Phonological theory: A brief comment. *Journal of Linguistics* 2:99–100.

Katz, J. J. 1981. *Language and other abstract objects.* Totowa, N.J.: Rowman & Littlefield.

Kiparsky, P. 1975. What are phonological theories about? In *Testing linguistic hypotheses,* ed. D. Cohen & J. R. Wirth. Washington, D.C.: Hemisphere.

Labov, W. 1972. *Sociolinguistic patterns.* Philadelphia: University of Pennsylvania Press.

Ringen, J. 1977. *Linguistic data: Intuitions and grammar testing.* Paper presented at the 12th International Congress of Linguists, Austria.

Spencer, N. J. 1973. Differences between linguists and nonlinguists in intuitions of grammaticality-acceptability. *Journal of Psycholinguistic Research* 2:83–98.

Valian, V. 1979. The wherefores and therefores of the competence-performance distinction. In *Sentence processing: Psycholinguistic studies presented to Merrill Garrett,* ed. W. Cooper & E. Walker. Hillsdale, N.J.: Lawrence Erlbaum Associates.

Wirth, J. R. 1975. Logical considerations in the testing of linguistic hypotheses. In *Testing linguistic hypotheses,* ed. D. Cohen & J. R. Wirth. Washington, D.C.: Hemisphere.

13 Metaphor and Mental Duality

Stevan Harnad
Behavioral & Brain Sciences
Princeton, New Jersey

I am going to attempt to argue that, given certain premises, there are reasons, not only empirical, but also logical, for expecting a certain division of labor in the processing of information by the human brain. This division of labor consists specifically of a functional bifurcation into what may be called, to a first approximation, "verbal" and "nonverbal" modes of information-processing. That this dichotomy is not quite satisfactory, however, will be one of the principal conclusions of this chapter, for I shall attempt to show that *metaphor,* which in its most common guise is a literary, and hence a fortiori a "verbal" phenomenon, may in fact be more a function of the "nonverbal" than the "verbal" mode. (For alternative attempts to account for cognitive lateralization, see e.g. Bever, 1975; Wickelgren, 1975; Pendse, 1978.)

The bulk of this chapter will be discursive and general. I will proceed from a consideration of learning and perception to language and metaphor chiefly by what I hope will be conceded to be a logical route. (In the process, I shall have to introduce a number of special terms and concepts from what will at first appear wildly disparate domains of discourse; a glossary is provided to orient the reader). I reserve facts about the real world and real brain for a brief *coda* at the end.

PREMISES

We must first agree upon the following premises:

(1) Action and thinking are in fact a function of the brain.

This, paradoxically enough, is my least crucial premise, and could perhaps be replaced by some abstract epistemological principle. At worst, its rejection may render some of my concluding references to actual data concerning brain function less compelling in terms of their real-world locus: "Right" and "left" would have to be replaced by some less ontologically-committed terms. However, the underlying cognitive bifurcation to which they allude would still have some claim to validity.

> (2) At least a significant portion of both action and thinking are governed by learning; i.e. they are somehow derived from experience by *induction* (Harnad, 1976).

This will be made more precise shortly. For now, it is sufficient to note that to deny this premise is to claim that there is no need to account for the "origins" of action and thinking through any general empiristic principles. They just "are" as they are, and ours is but to analyze the consequences of already "having" them, not to conjecture as to how they got that way (see footnote 1).

Perhaps I have depicted the denial of this premise in so peculiar a way as to assure that no one would actually endorse such a gambit. And yet this is the only coherent way I can formulate what I take to be the position of rationalists, extreme nativists, and any others who deny the existence of radical induction (see, for example, Chomsky, 1980).

> (3) The brain (or, in the case of the denial of (1), some abstract epistemological principle) does not have an infinite rote memory; i.e. we cannot remember "everything."
>
> (4) The experiential (phenomenal) world is of at least one order of complexity greater than that of memory (or its equivalent); i.e. there is always more "out there" than we can remember.

DISCRIMINATION AND MEMORY LIMITS

That premises (3) and (4) can be taken as empirical hypotheses rather than merely as premises is illustrated by the following: In a famous paper summarizing a good deal of research in psychophysics, George Miller (1956) showed that there are some rather narrow limits on our capacity to remember stimulus information (See Broadbent, 1975, for a recent updated version of these findings). Given a one-dimensional sensory continuum, say, the amplitude (loudness) spectrum of a sound of fixed timbre and pitch, human beings seem to be very restricted in the number of absolute levels of loudness they can remember. Up to seven distinct values along the amplitude spectrum can be reliably remembered, as demonstrated by the ability to assign an instance from each level a unique name whenever it is encountered. However, as the number of absolute judgments is pushed beyond this limit, as one attempts to segment the loudness spectrum more minutely, reliability falls off rapidly, and errors and confusion abound.

This phenomenon is by no means restricted to loudness. It is exhibited by other sensory continua as well, and is also demonstrable (with suitably generalized "limit" parameters) in higher-dimensional cases.

Miller interprets such psychophysical data as evidence for limits on our capacity to perform *absolute discrimination*. An absolute discrimination is any judgment requiring a unique memory. The best index of the possession of a unique memory in this sense is the capacity to assign a unique name: to *identify* the remembered input.

Miller contrasts these apparent orderly limitations of our absolute judgment with our relatively unpredictable capacities for *relative discrimination* or similarity judgment. To relatively discriminate is to distinguish two inputs (presented simultaneously or in rapid succession) as being identical or different, and to judge the degree and direction of the difference. Here no memory is required, but merely the capacity to make concurrent comparisons.

Miller remarks that not only do the limits on our capacity to perform relative discrimination not seem to obey the "magical number seven" rule, capriciously depending instead upon the particular input modality involved, but that invariably these limits dramatically exceed the absolute judgment limit. We are in all cases capable of far fewer absolute than relative judgments.

Now how are premises (3) and (4) borne out by this? There is support for (3) in an even stronger form than stated, for not only is it demonstrable that we *remember* less than we can perceive (which implies, a fortiori, that we remember less than there "is") but limits also on relative judgment show that we *perceive* less than there "is" (where "perceive" is taken to mean "being able to resolve by relative discrimination"). Therefore, not only is our memory (i.e., our capacity to remember experiences) finite, but even the instantaneous perceptual resolution of these experiences is limited. There is more information "out there" than we can perceive directly—which also strongly confirms (4).

Having established that at least (3) and (4) are not unreasonable, I shall now attempt to erect upon them some systematic generalizations. All I can vouch for besides, is clarity. (For a more elaborate development of this viewpoint, see Harnad, 1973.)

INDUCTION AND REDUCTION

Given that the real world is informationally richer than our finite processing capacities, it follows that if there is to be any learning from experience, this must involve some *reduction* of experience. That is—and here I mobilize (1) as well:

caveant idealists, mentalists, and disciples of Karl Lashley (1960)—the *engram,* or structural record of the experience, which is extracted and stored in the brain as a memory, will not be a faithful copy of the experience.

Otherwise stated, I deny that we have *analogue* memories (at least insofar as absolute judgments are concerned). In fact, I claim that even if we did have potentially infinite rote memories, our brains would still be obliged to perform *some* reduction, i.e., some discarding or suppression of information. This follows from the induction postulate (2), since the rote registering of each unique experience in its *full uniqueness* would make it impossible for one to be anything but a reflex automaton with a very rich spiritual life. To be able to learn by induction is to be able to extract regularities from the flux of experience: to select the invariant and recurrent, and discard the irrelevant and "unique."

To illustrate with the Miller paradigm: If, in learning to identify a sound of a specific loudness, one had attempted to incorporate into the engram *all* the unique information potentially available upon first hearing—including, of course, the polysensory context in which it had occurred, the concurrent state of one's gut and of one's soul, not to mention one's (presumably) unique sense of each temporal instant—then *nothing* could ever be subsequently identified, for nothing could ever exactly recur. Hence induction would be a logical impossibility. (No induction without reduction!)

I did promise a more precise definition of induction. The paradigm for induction (otherwise known as the absolute discrimination paradigm, for obvious reasons) is the following:

> An *inductor* is said to have performed *induction,* if, having been confronted with experiential inputs, some of which (*positive instances*) are *invariant* with respect to the presence of some property (or properties) and some of which (*negative instances*) are invariant with respect to the absence of this property (or properties), the inductor can, after a sufficiently large sample of inputs, reliably produce, exclusively in the presence of the positive instances, a *unique, arbitrary output.* This output must be *unique,* in the sense that it is associated with the positive instances and the positive instances alone; and it must be *arbitrary,* in the sense that (a) it was demonstrably not already associated with the positive instances prior to the induction ("non-apriority") and (b) it is not structurally isomorphic with the positive instances ("non-iconicity").

Precision has its drawbacks. Expressed in the vernacular, induction, or absolute discrimination learning, consists of learning to uniquely identify something from experience. The rule is that you must not have been able to identify it previously, and that your means of identification must not be *iconic* (i.e. not an analogue copy of what you are identifying).

That the first of these conditions (non-apriority) actually implies the second (non-iconicity) is easily shown. If the identification were allowed to be a structural copy of some sort, we would be in danger of falling into an analogue of the analogue-memory problem discussed earlier. Suppose one were allowed to "identify" a certain loudness by simultaneously vocalizing with commensurate loudness, or perhaps matching it by turning the potentiometer of an oscillator that emits a sound of continuously variable amplitude. This task one could presumably accomplish without the need of prior experience (ignoring now the improvement that may result from "mere exposure" to such a task), which would violate the constraint that one must have been *demonstrably* unable to perform the identification a priori. (Mark well, for future reference, the similarity of this iconic pseudo-induction to *relative* judgment.)

CONTEXT AND CONTINUITY

It should also be apparent why "absolute discrimination" is a more accurate term for induction than "identification." To illustrate: If I place an object on a table (let it be, for the sake of argument, a bowl of potato soup) and demand that you "identify" it, you may be justifiably perplexed as to what it is that I want you to say. In fact, you would be entitled to reply with anything from "a concrete visual object" to "potato-soup-Charlie at time t." On the other hand, if it were flanked on either side by a plant and a hat, you may be more comfortable in identifying it as "the food"; or, if surrounded instead by various soups, as "the Vichyssoise," etc.

These more determinate cases reveal that in any identification, a discrimination or distinction from among a definite set or *context of alternatives* is either implicitly or explicitly involved. Technically, the receipt of "information" means the reduction of *uncertainty,* and uncertainty is defined against a set of alternative outcomes, much as in the casting of dice. A foray into information theory would not be appropriate here, but let it be understood that what I mean by the *context* associated with every identification could be formulated quite rigorously (Garner, 1974; Olson, 1970).

The role of context is as critical in the actual *learning* of an absolute discrimination as it was in the above cases, which involved the mere exercise of an already-learned absolute discrimination. In the simplest sort of induction, consisting of only the dichotomy of positive and negative instances, it is the *negative instances* that provide the balance of the context against which the *invariant properties* underlying the absolute discrimination are extracted. Without such a clearly-defined complement to the positive instances, the number of invariants underlying identification would quickly escalate into that indeterminate, irreducible state-of-affairs, already twice avoided in this discussion, in which an instance would have to be encoded in its infinite (and inutile) uniqueness (cf. Luria, 1968; Borges, 1969; Harber, 1979).

What I am claiming is that we do not tell apart "potato soup" from "the rest of the world," but only from various definite subclasses of the rest of the world.

Notice that in this particular case I say that we "do not" rather than "cannot," for there do of course exist what philosophers have called "natural kinds" to simplify a good deal of our inductive life (Marler, 1976; Rosch & Lloyd, 1978). However, I have throughout this discussion always been keeping one eye on the most difficult sort of case, namely that in which the experiential inputs vary *continuously* along several sensory dimensions, rather than falling neatly into certain prefabricated physical or perceptual categories.

The example of sound amplitude was just such a difficult case. And of course there are innumerable others, of multidimensional and polysensory varieties, such as complex geometric forms, acoustic timbres and sound sequences, complex daily events and sequences of experiences—in fact, any experience that varies along an actual continuum (or a "virtual" continuum, in virtue of unresolvable informational complexity). And this is not yet to have mentioned purely *abstract* cases, such as the "space" from which I discriminated the foregoing list of examples.

In fact, *space* itself is the best example. Loci in space do *not* constitute "natural kinds," and when we name loci according to an imposed set of coordinates, these constitute a *reduction,* with a certain definite grain, adapted to some specific discriminative context.

Suppose I see a man standing somewhere in a large circular field, and someone asks me where he is ("Identify his locus"). I may say that he is "between center and five o'clock," or "in the fourth quadrant," or "in the circle," or "out there"—depending on what I conceive to be the alternatives. In fact, if there were a dozen people out there, that would simplify things for me considerably (provided they were not standing too close together). But I can no more state his "absolute" locus than any object's "absolute" identity (cf. Rosch & Lloyd, 1978).

ENGRAMS, INVARIANTS, AND CATEGORY
BOUNDARIES

These examples are meant to illustrate that absolute discriminations are not performed "in vacuo" (and so they are, in this sense, not really "absolute"). They are performed within a context of alternatives that *focus* that reduction of experience necessary for the practice of induction. In fact, I claim that experience is reduced to what is in each case very close to the *minimal* set of invariants required to perform a particular identification. These, and these only, are "committed to memory," in the sense of being encoded in an *engram* constituting a "record" of that experience.

Such a record provides a finite and tractable package that can be stored and reliably recalled by name. In fact, the role of the identifying *response,* the arbitrary, unique name, is to provide a reliable, exclusive means of access to the engram.

I call such encoding "categorical" because it has well-defined category *boundaries*. In particular, any input continua involved have been "quantized," in the sense that certain entire regions of continuous variation have been reduced to an effectively equivalent discrete unit. Instances have been reduced to their invariants.

Here are some examples: A "zebra" belongs to a prefabricated physical category, which, when it is learned, involves ignoring the within-category variation from a "zebra-Charlie" to a "zebra-Fred." "Red" is (probably) a prefabricated perceptual category, a segment of a physical continuum that is innately quantized by the visual system (Bornstein, 1975). Within its boundaries, the differences between a "scarlet" and a "vermillion" are ignored. The musical-acoustic categories "A" or "C#" (Siegel & Siegel, 1977) and the phonemic categories "/ba/" or "/ga/" (Eimas, 1975; Liberman, 1976; Pastore, 1976) may (perhaps) be quantized by the process of induction alone (this is not yet known for sure[1]); within the boundaries of these categories too, variation is ignored. Finally, if we focus upon "zebra-Charlie," "vermillion," "C#," and "/ga/," we may find that we have been reduced to the limits of categorial grain altogether, so that we could not make further absolute discriminations even if we cared to.

A COGNITIVE BIFURCATION:
BOUNDED AND UNBOUNDED ENGRAMS

At this point an interesting paradox ought to be suggesting itself. What have I been doing here, contemplating these various absolute discriminations that I can and do make? I have claimed that, due to limits on my memory (and constraints on induction) I am forced to encode experiences in a highly reduced form. As a consequence, I extract certain information from instances and store that information alone, under some name or other, discarding all else. If this is indeed the case, then at some particular time t when I am either perceiving or contemplating in my mind an instance out of one of my categories, I ought to be aware only of some sort of abstract skeleton. And yet I seem to be aware of a good deal more! In particular, when I see or imagine a man on a large field, he seems to be

---

[1]Every time a category turns out to be innate, it entails passing the epistemological burden to evolution. The inductivist holds himself accountable for the acquisition of our categories, the nativist only for their structure and deployment. Radical inductivism, which is the position adopted here, assumes that there *is* significant category acquisition during ontogeny. See Harnad, 1976 and Dennett, 1980.

occupying a very specific, unique position, even though, in the case of actually perceiving him, I may be unable to recall after a few moments what the unique position was, precisely; and in the case of imagining him, I may be unable to *describe* my image beyond a definite (verbal) grain of resolution. What sort of processing is involved in my immediate perception and in my iconic imagery?

In fact, forget about induction and absolute discrimination for the moment: How is it that I am able to perform *relative discrimination* or *similarity judgment* at all? If my engrams consist of reduced extractions and abstractions, how is this (albeit ephemeral from the anamnestic viewpoint) holistic experience, similarity judgment, possible at all? It would seem that if *ab ovo* I am reducing and quantizing and ignoring as I learn, the world should be getting steadily more and more fragmented—not to mention that I can hardly conceive how it ought to have looked to me prior to my ever having extracted any categories at all! And yet my experience seems to be, and always to have been, uniformly and continuously whole for as long as I can recall![2] Is that sense of "recall" a contradiction in terms?

This is the stage at which a cognitive bifurcation appears to be forced upon us. Perhaps we do not establish engrams (let us call them *bounded engrams*) only of the kind I have already described. Perhaps we have another representational system as well, one that also registers a trace or "engram" worthy of being called a "memory" (cf. Pylyshyn, 1973). However, I am not prepared to retract any of my premises, and consequently this second representational system, if it exists, must occupy a rather peculiar status. Its engrams, if they are not of the same highly reduced sort as the bounded ones, cannot be expected to subserve absolute discrimination. Moreover, they cannot have names. They cannot be addressed reliably; and being thus overdetermined in their uniqueness, there must be considerable overlap and confusability among them (from the absolute discrimination point-of-view).

In fact, if this second species of engram consists of analogues of my naive, continuous, instant-to-instant experience, then it seems impossible to think of them as "bounded" at all, as I am not aware of any "quantization" of my experience. Certainly the "natural kinds" and other wholesale categories I inherit *gratis* provide a kind of intrinsic segmentation, but they are probably already named and encoded in bounded engrams, and probably also best handled via that system. What about everything else? What about timbres and melodies, forms and spatial configurations I've never named? How do I remember a face? Is *all that detail* that distinguishes faces I know (and name) encoded in bounded engrams somewhere? Could I go ahead and quantize the spectrum of Chinese faces that way too? What about instance-to-instance variation of a face—all its subtle nuances of expression? I see those too, but from the standpoint of naming

---

[2]Indeed, this could be taken as a fifth postulate, mediating the strong confirmation of (3) and (4): viz, (5) Immediate experience seems phenomenally continuous and holistic.

and quantizing, they seem to present literally boundless alternatives for one lifetime!

So the engrams of this second representational system cannot be "bounded" in the same sense as those subserving absolute discrimination. They must to a great extent blend continuously and namelessly into one another, preserving their irreducible uniqueness, but doing so anonymously, without benefit of an absolute identity. They may be available in an immediate sense for short-term iconic memory, and they may be more-or-less available later on, in mental imagery. But they are bound to be less *tractable* than bounded engrams.

Note that naming is something you *do*. It is a motor act, and the motor system is a *voluntary* one. Likewise, verbal imagery seems to have retained a degree of this conative control. Hence the apparent possibility of "thinking" in words.

Iconic imagery, on the other hand, never enjoyed a voluntary status in overt behavior—or did it? Certainly not in overt *verbal* behavior. However, recall the forbidden class of iconic responses: responses such as drawing, singing, playing a musical instrument, mimicry, etc. Could these not provide a substrate for rendering some unbounded engrams more tractable? Being *continuous,* iconic responses cannot, of course, provide boundaries such as the category boundaries provided by names. But they *can* subserve a modicum of conation, so that we are, to a degree, able to "think" iconically. However, to the extent that these images have *not* been under such prior motor control, they are destined to be a good deal more "self-willed" (in the sense of *their* will, not ours) than mental verbalization.[3]

INTERACTIONS BETWEEN BOUNDED AND UNBOUNDED REPRESENTATIONAL SYSTEMS: LANGUAGE AND IMAGES

One avenue of possible control over unbouded engrams has not yet been explored. Are they not, after all, *associated* somehow (even if only indirectly and unreliably) with their bounded counterparts? Obviously this association is not unique or one-to-one, but many-(many-many)-to-few, in virtue of the uniqueness and multiplicity of the unbounded engrams relative to the reduced bounded ones. Moreover, it is not clear, given the unbounded nature of unbounded engrams, how effective any association of this sort can be conceived to be. However, it seems reasonable to suppose that, among the various *gradients of association* from engram to engram provided by variables such as structural similarity,

---

[3]The mental analogues of scanning eye-movements (which are, to an approximation, iconic responses) may facilitate visual imagery, but not reliably. Images persist in maintaining a perverse degree of independence, so we must often be resigned to being passive spectators of a relatively autonomous, dreamlike display.

temporal or spatial contiguity in experience, "natural kinds" and iconic responses, a special relationship with corresponding bounded engrams should not be excluded. Hence, if I think "zebra," it seems reasonable to suppose that I might be more likely to stir one of the unbounded engrams of "zebra-Fred" than of "potato-soup-Charlie."

So language, as one manifestation of this interaction between bounded representations and their homologous unbounded counterparts,[4] does seem to have some sway over images, even if not a strong or absolute one. And, *apropos* of language, it also seems appropriate to inquire whether there might not be unbounded engrams of a purely "linguistic" sort. I did make some enigmatic allusion earlier to "abstract" spaces from which I had "pulled" certain verbal illustrations. What might that mean?

I confess that I have some difficulty in being specific about this (principally because the "images" underlying my conceptions at this point wax elusively abstract), but perhaps it is not unreasonable to suppose that abstract properties and relations have *structural* characteristics that are, as such, amenable in principle to an iconic representation.

For example, suppose that we are learning an absolute discrimination: that of naming "quadrupeds" (within the context of creatures possessing various quantities of limbs). Why shouldn't the property of "four-limbedness" (or even just "fourness"), which is extracted during such a piece of induction, have, parallel to its "bounded" duties, an unbounded representation as well? I do not mean the "fourness" that is intrinsically embedded in each unbounded engram of a particular quadruped, but a bonus unbounded encoding on the basis of fourness's disembodied existence in the bounded representation: an (unbounded) engram of a (bounded) engram. If it has not been too far-fetched to suppose an interaction between bounded and unbounded representations in my earlier suggestion that the name of a bounded engram may (sometimes) evoke an unbounded image, then perhaps it does not go too much farther now to suppose that the abstract properties of bounded engrams have their unbounded images too. If that is the case, then these derivative unbounded engrams are in a sense "linguistic" (if

---

[4]That there is *interaction* (of this and other sorts, discussed later) between the bounded and unbounded representational systems is an extremely important feature of the model proposed here. (For one thing, it implies that a portion, at least, of my title is a misnomer: we are dealing, not with "mental" duality, but with *cognitive* duality, within one "mind.") The two representational systems, neither viable alone, work in concert in information-processing, each making its unique contribution. Some tasks may have a stronger "loading" on one than the other, but the presence of the other is still felt. For example, after absolute-discrimination learning, relative discrimination is demonstrably modified, such that intracategory similarities are enhanced and intercategory differences are accentuated. This is the "perceptual boundary" effect in categorical perception whereby /ba/'s sound more like /ba/'s and /ga/'s like /ga/'s, although the underlying acoustic variable, the formant transition, is continuous.

the naming process in absolute discrimination is conceded to be linguistic), or at any rate an abstract offshoot of a linguistic process.

A third sense in which language might impinge upon unbounded representations would be the converse of the above, namely, the formation of a bounded engram on the basis of input from unbounded engrams. This is a very important case, and in fact much less tenuous than the preceding one. I will return to this case later, and will now add only that there is nothing in the nature of induction which would rule out the possibility of learning on the basis of *internal* inputs: Since unbounded representations, too, are derived from experience, the establishment of a bounded category, later demonstrable externally, but essentially based upon internal hypothesis-testing with unbounded "memories" as raw material, would certainly be a *bona fide* case of induction.

Yet another sort of interaction between language and unbounded representations would of course be via the icons of words themselves: words in their pure sound value, or in song, or verse.

PROPOSITIONS AND COMMUNICATION

There may well have been some readers who were not prepared to grant that in this discussion of discrimination, naming and memory I have hitherto broached upon "linguistic" matters at all. For their benefit I shall immediately introduce: the *proposition*.[5] It seems clear that in a universe in which inductors are busily displaying their capacity to perform induction, they are likely to be confronted with many of the same or similar instances in different contexts. "Potato-soup-Charlie" may put in a number of appearances as "food" or as "Vichyssoise" or as "a concrete visual object." It does not seem reasonable to treat him as a total stranger on every occasion. In particular, if I already know "potato-soup-Charlie," I really only have to hear his *name* in learning to discriminate "Vichyssoise." I need only be *told* that "Vichyssoise" *is*, in point of fact, good old "potato-soup-Charlie," in order to be able to perform (at least in part) that new discrimination.

Now, one might be inclined to argue that such a state-of-affairs does not satisfy my criteria for induction: that under such conditions one could identify correctly from the first actually-encountered instance onward (following the proposition), implying that the learning was a priori.

In one sense this would certainly be true, for if you had not previously known "potato-soup-Charlie" you would not have known "Vichyssoise" from being

---

[5]I do not wish to enter into the philosophical dispute as to whether there "exist" special abstract entities underlying sentences. My propositions merely constitute the information conveyed by declarative sentences.

told that it was he. But were you incapable of understanding a proposition, then even possessing prior acquaintance of Charlie you could not benefit from the additional propositional information in learning to name "Vichyssoise." Furthermore, ignorance is certainly demonstrable prior to the actual receipt of the propositional information. So the capacity to comprehend and encode propositional information must be regarded as a means of learning: a very rapid and powerful means.

I will not attempt to enter into the problem of the nature of propositional understanding (see e.g. Katz, 1976, Steklis & Harnad, 1976a), but it seems clear that propositions provide information about category relations, in particular, those of membership and category-inclusion. *Negation* is presumably mastered from positive and negative instantiation, and the logical connectives, quantifiers, and rules of inference can be picked up by induction (to the extent that they are not already inherent in induction). With such an arsenal, an inductor can spare himself a lot of learning from experience (as long as there is someone else around to provide him with the pre-emptive propositional information).

It is also clear that the propositional *communication* of information—for communication it is, as contrasted with the perceptual *extraction* of information by discrimination learning from instances—must be intimately linked with *bounded* representations, upon which it must draw for its atomic terms, and upon which it acts via the information it provides. In particular, I will claim that category relations are *revised and updated* on the basis of propositional information, as demonstrable, for example, by an altered use of names subsequent to the receipt of such information.

BIVALENCE

The orderly state of affairs in the bounded system (names, categories, revision, updating) in contrast to the unreliability and intractability of the unbounded system, owes its existence in large part, I claim, to a certain critical property of the *boundaries* of bounded engrams. These boundaries have the property of being *bivalent,* that is, governed by (two-valued) logic. More precisely, within a particular discriminative context, category boundaries have the remarkable property of enforcing *exclusive membership.*[6]

I shall illustrate with the simplest kind of context: the dichotomy. An (intracontextual) instance must be either *in* the positive category, or *not in* it; not both, and not neither. In such a consistent (and hence, in principle, learnable)

---

[6]I do not, of course, deny the existence of probabilistic, "fuzzy" sets (Zadeh & Fu, 1975) in perception and cognition. However, in naming, absolute discrimination and categorical perception it is clear that bivalent boundaries prevail. For reasons too complicated to discuss here, I also regard the so-called "nonbivalent" logics (see, for example, Rescher, 1969) as irrelevant to the considerations at hand.

paradigm, the mutual-exclusiveness of positive and negative instances is rigidly reflected in the nature of the bounded engram, and in particular in the nature of its boundary, which is "impermeable" to membership. There is nothing mysterious here, just a faithful reflection of a real-world consistency, as evidenced by the rational use of names. Given that he is a contextual candidate for the category "food," "potato-soup-Charlie" either is or is not a member; not both, not neither.

The same can definitely *not* be said of the various unbounded engrams of "vermillion," for example. Bereft of names and not absolutely discriminable, it is not possible to place boundaries between them, and hence it makes no sense to attempt to make bivalent distinctions.

At the propositional level (which is clearly the territory of the bounded system) bivalence is also eloquently operative. If you tell me that "Socrates" is a "man," then I duly assign him membership in that category. This, in turn, determines that he is "mortal," for my category "man" is contained in my category "mortal." It follows that my category structure is such that if you told me "Socrates" was "immortal" I would either not believe you, or begin to ponder as to where my categories might require revision. (Needless to recall, underlying any such reshuffling of categories are the very bounded engrams—names, invariants, bivalent boundaries—of which I have been speaking.)

PROPOSITIONS AND APPOSITIONS

But what about the unbounded system? Suppose I had learned that "Socrates" was indeed a "man," and then you insisted that he was "*im*mortal." I have already said that it is likely that—in accordance, perhaps, with a Quinean principle of "minimal mutilation" of the categorical structure (Quine, 1969), my bounded system would reject this. Does my unbounded system do likewise? First it would be well to check if it has understood the question!

I have already suggested that names may somehow weakly resonate in their unbounded counterparts. Suppose in this case they in fact do so. I have accessed some of the unbounded "Socrates'" and the unbounded "immortals." What then? In the propositional case, the critical link is the copula "is" (or "is not"). That link embodies the propositional claim (or denial) to the tune of which the bounded engrams perform so admirably. In the present case, they have given their answer: "That does not compute."

What do the unbounded engrams say? First, it must be ascertained just what it is that they have heard. Have they heard the "is"? Or, more precisely, have they *understood* the "is," which is to say, have they understood what it is that is being *proposed* here? I claim that they have not.

Abandoning the anthropomorphic rhetoric: Whatever it is that the bounded system "has" in being able to process propositional information, the unbounded system hasn't got it. I would venture the guess that the critical property has a lot to do with bivalence and category boundaries. Whereas in the bounded case the propositional information is decoded as something proposed or claimed concerning category relations, in the unbounded case the information is merely construed as the *apposition* of (the unbounded engrams of) the subject and the predicate.

By apposition[7] I simply mean the *juxtaposing* or *pairing* of the engrams, in much the way they are paired in a relative discrimination or similarity judgment. In fact, a *similarity judgment* is precisely what the essence of such an apposition is.

EXEGESIS

The apposition of unbounded engrams yields a *holistic comparison* in which the irrelevant, continuous properties vanquished from bounded engrams by reduction are free to reveal *structural congruities* to which the bounded system was "blind." This is not to say that the bounded system can never by privy to such revelations. On the contrary, the interaction between the two systems of which I spoke earlier allows the bounded system to extract invariants with unbounded engrams as *input*. All that the "blindness" of the bounded system is meant to imply is that it cannot "discover" these structural congruities by its own devices: It can only *exegesize* them once they are presented.

This concept of the *exegesis* of appositions by the bounded system is a rather critical one, and so I will attempt to explicate it in some detail. Consider the apposition of "Socrates" and "immortal": "Socrates is immortal." This proposition is *literally* false. But I have said that, as far as the unbounded system is concerned, this is not a proposition, but an apposition. Now if a proposition is literally false, it makes sense to *deny* it. But does it make sense to deny an apposition?

Consider first that an apposition can be regarded as trivially "true" if it is formulated as: "I have apposed the unbounded engrams "Socrates" and 'im-

---

[7]The term "appositional" is due to one of the most imaginative and articulate of the exponents of hemisphere differences, the neurosurgeon Joseph E. Bogen, who has generously left its meaning open for later users:

> The difficulty in characterizing the ability of the right hemisphere arises largely from our ignorance— we have barely scratched the surface of a vast unknown. We would do well therefore to choose arbitrarily a word, homologous in structure with the word "propositional" but sufficiently ambiguous to permit provisional use. For example, we can say that the right hemisphere has a highly developed 'appositional' capacity. This term implies a capacity for apposing or comparing of perceptions, schemas, engrams, etc., but has in addition the virtue that it implies very little else. If it is correct that the right hemisphere excels in capacities as yet unknown to us, the full meaning of 'appositional'' will emerge as these capacities are further studied and understood. (Bogen, 1969, pp. 149–156)

mortal'," or "It is possible to appose. . . . " However, this would be to construe it as a propositional claim, which it is not.

Second, one might be inclined to infer that what is really meant by the apposition is that "Socrates" is *like* an "immortal": that they are in some sense *similar*. I reply that this too is true, but not quite to the point. Certainly, since there is structural congruity, there is similarity. But one may still be inclined to deny that there is "relevant" similarity.

Given the unbounded nature of unbounded engrams, anything is potentially "similar" to anything else, in the sense of being potentially apposable and sharing some structural attributes. This is yet another manifestation of the "analogue memory" phenomenon discussed at the outset; for experiences, in their unbounded uniqueness, grade continuously into one another, with no basis for any categorical distinctions. Things may be *more* similar or *less* similar, but not "non-similar."

So one can deny "relevant" similarity of an apposition, but not similarity *simpliciter*. And even this is to construe the apposition propositionally, which is to beg the question. However, the matter of "relevant" similarity does cast some light on the phenomenon of *exegesis* I mentioned earlier. One is inclined to ask: "Relevant with respect to what?", and the only reply I can conceive of is: "The categories."

What I mean by the "exegesis" of an apposition is the testing of whether the structural congruities it reveals are in any sense "relevant" to the bounded representation, and if so, to update the latter accordingly. In that sense, appositions may be very important in the generation of models and hypotheses in science (Hesse, 1966).

To exegesize an apposition is to find or impose a categorial context that makes a corresponding (nontrivial) proposition *literally* true. The holistic comparison is replaced by a categorical approximation, with a *categorial invariant* substituted for the *structural congruity:* a reduction of the type always attendant upon category extraction. The similarity is quantized: "Socrates is like an immortal in that his ideas are still actively discussed today, etc." (See Verbrugge & McCarrell, 1977).

AFFECT

I have discussed the role of apposition in intellectual creativity elsewhere (Harnad, 1973). At this time I would like to consider another sort of "relevance." For this purpose I must make a brief foray into the domain of *affect*.

It is certainly the case that emotions have "natural kinds" (anger, fear, desire, etc.), for which we no doubt have bounded categories. But in a much more important sense, emotions are *continuous*, and it is their subtle nuances and blends that are so salient to us. These ineffable and indeed often *unique* variations are not amenable to categorical encoding. Moreover, in the reductive process involved in the establishment of bounded engrams, surely "emotion" would be the first thing to be dropped as irrelevant! Attention has often been drawn to the relative "freedom from affect" that so strikingly characterizes language as distinct from other symbolic and communicational systems (Steklis & Harnad, 1976).

So emotion is much more likely to be handled via the unbounded system, both in the sense that emotional experience is more amenable to iconic representation, and in the sense that the affective context of cognitive experience is more likely to be incorporated into the unbounded engram.

METAPHOR

Now, for those who have been straining for some time to hear an explicit formulation of the role of the unbounded system in *metaphor,* let me count the ways:

a. I have argued that a name may have some better-than-chance probability of evoking corresponding unbounded images.
b. Names themselves have iconic properties as pure sound.
c. There may be unbounded engrams of bounded engrams; i.e., abstract and indeed verbal properties have iconic structure.
d. Unbounded engrams have the potential to reveal, through apposition, structural properties and congruities to which the bounded system is blind (Socrates *is* immortal).
e. Bounded engrams can be extracted from unbounded engrams, by the exegesis of an apposition, a form of internal hypothesis-testing.
f. Unbounded engrams have a *"de re"* emotional quality, of which the bounded ones have been purged.

I claim that a *metaphor* constitutes an apposition in the sense I have defined it earlier. It is not a proposition. (Does it make sense to "deny" that "Night is a blanket"?)[8] The apposition is based upon structural congruities between the

---

[8]Originally, I relied heavily on the "mismatch" or incongruity view of metaphor, according to which the literal construal of a metaphor should be false or anomalous. Although I still feel that this holds for most metaphors, counterexamples such as "No man is an island"—arising from a seminar on metaphor at Princeton University in 1980–81, attended by Andrew Ortony, George Miller and others (see Ortony, 1979b)—have persuaded me that the literal construal may also merely be trivial or irrelevant. In any event, there must be some cue, inherent or contextual, that the literal construal is not the appropriate one to consider.

The Princeton metaphor seminar also had the unintentional effect (certainly not endorsed by the

unbounded engrams evoked by the words. These unbounded engrams may be chiefly sensory (as in a above) or they may be more abstract (as in c). The apposition may be at several levels at once, e.g. in that the names used may themselves have iconic properties (b). The apposition may have "relevant" cognitive consequences (d) that may even result in new bounded categories (e), but their "relevance" may also be a purely emotional one (f). Moreover, the structural congruities that emerge from appositions may have an intrinsic emotional value of their own, a criterion of "relevance" more likely to be appreciated by the unbounded system than the bounded one.

THE REAL WORLD AND THE REAL BRAIN

It remains only to add that, in the real world, the two sides of our real brain appear to function in certain specialized ways that bifurcate along lines suggestive of those I have been discussing here (Harnad, 1973).

---

other participants) of radicalizing my view of metaphor to the extent of making me provisionally conjecture that *any* literal utterance can be construed as a metaphor—that any proposition can be treated as an apposition—although not necessarily a *good* one. By way of taking up my challenge to propose the most doggedly literal of utterances for me to try to turn into a trope, the seminar (or, rather, A. Ortony) proposed $\sqrt{27} = 3$.

Although grumbling that I could have discounted the example as part of a formal proprietary vocabulary—*in* English but not *of* it—I accepted the challenge, even eschewing pun-like tricks—appositionally quite cricket—such as in the (literal) construal: "The cube (-shaped) root of (tree number) twenty-seven is three (years old)." Here are my two candidates, the first admittedly involving a few extra appositions, but the second (drawing on numerology), entirely self-contained:

Meta-Form

I love thee
As sev'n and twenty's cube root's three.
If I loved thee more,
Twelve squared would overtake one-forty-four.

That same ubiquitous Platonic force
That sets prime numbers' unrelenting course
When its more consequential work is done
Again of two of us will form a one.

Roots

One short of perfection
Mortal and mean
Yet inside twenty-seven
Nobler roots to be seen

Another issue that loomed large in the Princeton seminar was that of the difference between literal and "metaphoric" similarity, especially the asymmetry of the latter (Ortony, 1979a). In brief, the

If certain parts of the left cerebral hemisphere are injured, various aphasias, or language disorders result. Among these may be: the loss of the capacity to name objects (Benson, 1979), inability to generate or understand sentences (Hécaen, 1967), and deficits in analytic reasoning and the formation of abstract concepts (Goldstein, 1948; Jackson, 1958). The role of the left hemisphere in language-related behavior is also confirmed in people without brain injury by monitoring the electrical activity over various regions of the scalp during the performance of verbal tasks (Galin & Ornstein, 1972).

The functions of the right hemisphere are not that well defined. Its injury disrupts "nonverbal IQ," which, if examined minutely, consists of sensory-perceptual performance, the perception of spatial relations, the perception and production of musical sounds, and the recognition of faces (Hécaen, 1962; Wertheim, 1969; see review by Bradshaw & Nettleton, 1981). There is also evidence that the right hemisphere may be more involved in emotional experience (Steklis, 1978; Denenberg, 1981), and dreaming (Goldstein & Harnad, 1977). The isolated right hemisphere, after an operation that splits the brain, has been shown to be initially unable to speak, and capable only of rudimentary understanding of isolated nouns (Sperry & Gazzaniga, 1967) (although there is evidence for considerable recovery years later, Zaidel, 1978). Many of these results have also been confirmed in the normal, uninjured brain (Harnad, Doty, Goldstein, Jaynes, & Krauthamer, 1977).

The neurologist Head (1963) has noted that "When an aphasic [left-hemisphere injured] cannot employ more abstract terms, he often uses descriptive phrases, similes and metaphorical expressions in an appropriate manner."

---

difference between the two kinds of similarity in the appositional/propositional model is that literal similarity is based on shared invariant properties and category co-membership, which is in turn governed by the categorical distinctions we have made: Co-categorized things appear more alike, and things separated by category boundaries seem more different. Appositional or "predistinctive" similarity, on the other hand, is governed by any of the structural features of the objects (or engrams) being apposed, irrespective of category boundaries: congruities of form, shared associations, or any other commonality that is perceived upon apposing them. Such similarities are *pre*distinctive, in the sense that they have the *potential* to subserve categorical distinctions (given an appropriate context of alternatives—see main text concerning "exegesis"), but they are not yet based on having made those distinctions.

Finally, in my view the "asymmetry" of metaphoric similarity derives from the asymmetry of the (explicit or implied) underlying subset/set relations expressed by propositions. "A is B"—which is, not coincidentally, the canonical form for a metaphor, and only secondarily yields "A is a kind of B" and "A is like B"—is equivalent to "A is a member of B" or "A is a subset of B," which is an asymmetric relation. It may be that some stage of the appositional process is symmetric, but the process of exegesis is constrained by the categorical, hierarchical structure of our bounded representational systems, so eventually the membership/containment relation must prevail. (And even in literal comparisons of objects at the same hierarchical level there is the useful—and asymmetric—convention of expressing the unfamiliar in terms of the familiar: "a tangello is like an orange" rather than "an orange is like a tangello" was the example much debated in the Princeton seminar.)

And, in an uncannily apt extended metaphor of his own, an appositional allegory,[9] Bruner (1962, p. 2-5) has written:

> The right is order and lawfulness, le droit. . . . Reaching for knowledge with the
> right hand is science. Yet to say only that much of science is to overlook one of its
> excitements, for the great hypotheses of science are gifts carried in the left
> hand . . . it has been proposed that art students can seduce their proper hand to more
> expressiveness by drawing first with the left. . . . And should we say that reaching
> for knowledge with the left hand is art? Again it is not enough, for as surely as the
> recital of a daydream differs from the well-wrought tale, there is a barrier between
> undisciplined fantasy and art. To climb the barrier requires a right hand adept at
> technique and artifice. . . . One thing has become increasingly clear in pursuing the
> nature of knowing. It is that the conventional apparatus of the psychologist—both
> his instruments of investigation and the conceptual tools he uses in the interpreta-
> tion of his data—leaves one approach unexplored. It is an approach whose medium
> of exchange seems to be the metaphor paid out by the left hand. It is a way that grows
> happy hunches and 'lucky' guesses, that is stirred into connective activity by the
> poet and the necromancer looking sidewise rather than directly. Their hunches and
> intuitions generate a grammar of their own—searching out connections, suggesting
> similarities, weaving ideas loosely in a trial web. . . . If he is lucky or if he has
> subtle psychological intuition he will from time to time come up with hunches,
> combinatorial products of his metaphoric activity. If he is not fearful of these
> products of his own subjectivity, he will go so far as to tame the metaphors that
> have produced the hunches, tame them in the sense of shifting them from the left
> hand to the right hand by rendering them into notions that can be tested.

GLOSSARY

Assumptions:

1. Action and thinking are a function of the brain.
2. A significant portion of action and thinking are governed by learning; i.e.,
   they are derived from experience by *induction*.
3. The brain does not have an infinite rote memory.
4. The experiential world is of at least one order of complexity greater than

---

[9]Was the present chapter itself anything more than an "appositional allegory," with no literal
connection to the real brain and real cognitive processing? In my introductory chapter for this volume
I conceded that the present chapter was not yet "neoconstructive." And I have certainly given
evidence of having little sympathy for hemisphere "mythology" (Steklis & Harnad, 1976b), even
going to the length of repudiating an instance of my own earlier intemperate zeal (Harnad, 1972). I
fondly regard this chapter as an exegesis of that earlier work, but whether the categories and
invariants it has extracted (bounded and unbounded engrams, proposition and apposition, context,
exegesis) are apt or relevant enough to warrant revising and updating his category structure, the
reader must be the one to judge.

memory; i.e. there is always more "out there" than it is possible to remember.

[*5. Immediate experience seems to be continuous and holistic.]

Definitions:

ABSOLUTE DISCRIMINATION: the identification of a class of inputs by the reliable assignment of a unique arbitrary motor response, i.e. a name.

ANALOGUE MEMORY: an engram that is *isomorphic* with the experience of which it is a record: a one-to-one correspondence that transforms but does not *reduce* input information.

APPOSITION: the collation or juxtaposition of two unbounded engrams (as contrasted with the predication of properties of subjects in the case of the proposition); propositions are bivalent, appositions are not.

BIVALENCE: two-valued logic, consisting of the truth values "true" and "false," which stand in a mutually exclusive and exhaustive relation to one another (either-or, not both, and not neither).

BOUNDED ENGRAMS: engrams underlying the categories formed during absolute discrimination or induction; the information encoded in bounded engrams consists of that minimal set of invariants which must be retained so as to perform reliable absolute discrimination.

CATEGORY: an absolutely discriminated class of inputs for which a bounded engram has been formed.

CATEGORY-BOUNDARY: the limits of the extension of a category; these may be concrete, as in the case of a quantized sensory continuum (the boundary between *red* and *orange* or /ba/ and /da/) or abstract, as in the case of conceptual categories.

CONTEXT: a set of alternatives that is associated with every absolute discrimination; the simplest context is a dichotomy, consisting of the class of positive and negative instances.

ENGRAM: the structural trace of an experience as retained in the brain; the physical substrate of memory.

To EXEGESIZE an apposition is to find or impose a categorial context that makes a corresponding (nontrivial) proposition literally true. The holistic comparison is replaced by a categorical approximation, with a categorial invariant substituted for the structural congruity.

ICONIC RESPONSES: responses that are isomorphic to—analogues of—stimulus input (as contrasted with *arbitrary* responses, having no systematic relation to the structure of the input).

INDUCTION: learning to perform absolute discrimination from experience with instances.

An INDUCTOR is said to have performed *induction* if, having been confronted with experiential inputs, some of which (*positive instances*) are invariant with respect to the presence of some property (or properties) and some of which (*negative instances*) are invariant with respect to the absence of this property (or properties), this inductor can, after a sufficiently large sample of inputs, reliably produce, exclusively in the presence of the positive instances, a *unique, arbitrary output*. This output must be *unique* in the sense that it is associated with the positive instances, and the positive instances alone; and it must be *arbitrary* in the sense that (a) it was demonstrably not already associated with the positive instances prior to the induction ("non-apriority") and (b) it is not structurally isomorphic with the positive instances ("non-iconicity").

INVARIANT PROPERTY: any property that is shared by a class of inputs, as distinguished from another class that lacks it.

PROPOSITION: a claim that something is the case; always formulable as a statement about category relations; e.g. "Socrates is a man" claims that the member of the singular category "Socrates" is contained in the category "man."

REDUCTION: the discarding or suppression of irrelevant information in the formation of the engram underlying absolute discrimination; what is discarded or suppressed is always determined by the context of alternatives; only invariants are retained.

RELATIVE DISCRIMINATION: (or *similarity judgment*): the comparision of two inputs (presented simultaneously or successively) yielding a response that indicates whether the inputs are identical or different, and if different, the magnitude and direction of the difference (relative to other pairs of inputs).

STRUCTURAL CONGRUITY: the unbounded counterpart of invariant property; the structural properties shared by two unbounded engrams; a kind of similarity.

UNBOUNDED ENGRAMS: engrams that are analogues of experience; because they are not reduced, they cannot be assigned names, and cannot subserve absolute discrimination.

REFERENCES

Aaronson, D. & Rieber, R. eds. 1975. *Developmental psycholinguistics and language disorder*. New York: Annals of the New York Academy of Sciences 263.

Beach, F. A., Hebb, D. O., Morgan, C. T., & Nissen, H. W. eds. 1968. *The neuropsychology of Lashley*. New York: McGraw-Hill.

Benson, D. F. 1979. Neurological correlates of anomia. In *Studies in neurolinguistics,* Volume IV, eds., Whitaker & Whitaker. New York: Academic Press.

Bever, T. G. 1975. Cerebral asymmetries in humans are due to the differentiation of two incompatible processes: holistic and analytic. In *Developmental psycholinguistics and language disorder,* eds., Aaronson & Rieber.

Bogen, J. E. 1969. The other side of the brain III: An appositional mind. *Bulletin of the Los Angeles Neurological Society 34:* 135-162.

Borges, J. L. 1969. Funes the memorious. In *Labyrinths,* eds., Yates and Irby.

Bornstein, M. H. 1975. The influence of visual perception on color. *American Anthropologist 77:* 774-798.

Bradshaw, J. L., & Nettleton, N. C. 1981. The nature of hemispheric specialization in man. *The Behaviorial and Brain Sciences 4:* 51-91.

Broadbent, D. E. 1975. The magic number seven after fifteen years. In *Studies in long term memory,* eds., Kennedy & Wilkes.

Brunner, J. S. 1962. *On Knowing: Essays for the left hand.* Cambridge, Mass.: Harvard

Buser, P. A. & Rougeul-Buser, A. eds. 1978. *Cerebral correlates of conscious experience.* Amsterdam: North Holland.

Chomsky, N. 1980. Rules and representations. *The Behavioral and Brain Sciences 3:* 1-61.

Darley, F. L. & Millikan, C. H. eds., 1967. *Brain mechanisms underlying language and speech.* New York: Grune & Stratton.

Denenberg, V. H. 1981. Hemispheric laterality in animals and the effects of early experience. *The Behaviorial and Brain Sciences 4:* 1-49.

Dennett, 1980. Passing the buck to biology. *The Behaviorial and Brain Sciences 3:* 19.

Desmedt, J. E. ed. 1977. *Language and hemispheric specialization in man: Cerebral ERPs.* Basel: Karger.

Eimas, P. D. 1975. Distinctive features codes in the short-term memory of children. *Journal of Experimental Child Psychology. 19:* 241-251.

Galin, D., & Ornstein, R. E. 1972. Lateral specialization of cognitive mode: An EEG study. *Psychophysiology 9:* 412-418.

Garner, W. R. 1974. *The processing of information and structure.* Hillsdale, N.J.: Lawrence Erlbaum Associates.

Goldstein, K. 1948. *Language and language disturbances.* New York: Grune & Stratton.

Goldstein, L., & Harnad, S. 1977. Quantitated EEG correlates of normal and abnormal interhemispheric relations. In *Language and hemispheric specialization in man,* ed., Desmedt.

Haber, R. N. 1979. Twenty years of haunting eidetic imagery: where's the ghost? *The Behavioral and Brain Sciences 3:* 583-629.

Harnad, S. 1972. Creativity, lateral saccades and the nondominant hemisphere. *Perceptual and Motor Skills 34:* 653-654.

Harnad, S. 1973. *Interhemispheric Division of Labour.* Presented at Bucke Society *Conference on Transformations of Consciousness* Montreal 1973 (unpublished manuscript available from author).

Harnad, S. 1976. Evolution, induction and accountability. In *Origins and evolution of language and speech,* eds., Harnad *et al.*

Harnad, S., Doty, R. W., Goldstein, L., Jaynes, J. & Krauthamer, G. eds., 1977. *Lateralization in the nervous system.* New York: Academic Press.

Harnad, S. R., Steklis, H. D., & Lancaster, J. B. eds., 1976. *Origins and evolution of language and speech.* New York: Annals of the New York Academy of Sciences 280.

Head, H. 1963. *Aphasia and kindred disorders of speech* Volume I. New York: Hafner.

Hécaen, H. 1962. Clinical symptomatology in right and left hemispheric lesions. In *Interhemispheric relations and cerebral dominance,* ed., Mountcastle.

Hécaen, H. 1967. Brain mechanisms suggested by studies of parietal lobes. In *Brain mechanisms underlying language and speech,* eds., Darley & Millikan.

Hesse, M. B. 1966. *Models and analogies in science.* Notre Dame, Indiana: University of Notre Dame Press.

Jackson, J. H. 1958. *Selected writings of John Hughlings Jackson,* ed., J. Taylor. New York: Basic.

Hirsh, S. K., Eldredge, D., Hirsh, I. J., & Silverman, S. R. eds. 1976. *Hearing and Davis.* St. Louis. Mo.: Washington University Press.

Katz, J. J. 1976. A hypothesis about the uniqueness of natural language. In *Origins and evolution of language and speech,* eds., Harnad *et al.*

Kennedy, A. & Wilkes, A. eds., 1975. *Studies in long term memory.* London: Wiley.

Lashley, K. S. 1968. In search of the engram. In *The neuropsychology of Lashley,* eds., Beach *et al.*

Liberman, A. 1976. Discussion paper. In *Origins and evolution of language and speech,* eds., Harnad *et al.*

Luria, A. R. 1968. *The mind of a mnemonist.* New York: Basic.

Marler, P. 1976. An ethological theory of the origin of vocal learning. In *Origins and evolution of language and speech,* eds., Harnad *et al.*

Miller, G. A. 1956. The magical number seven, plus or minus two: Some limits on our capacity for processing information. *Psychology Review 63:*81–97.

Mountcastle, V. B. ed., 1962. *Interhemispheric relations and cerebral dominance.* Baltimore: Johns Hopkins Press.

Olson, D. R. 1970. Language and thought: Aspects of a cognitive theory of semantics. *Psychological Review 77:* 257–273.

Ortony, A. 1979a. Beyond literal similarity. *Psychological Review 86:* 161–180.

Ortony, A. 1979b. *Metaphor and thought.* New York: Cambridge University Press.

Pastore, R. E. 1976. Categorical perception: A critical re-evaluation. In *Hearing and Davis,* eds., Hirsh *et al.*

Pendse, S. G. 1978. Category perception, language and brain hemispheres: An information processing approach. *Behavioral Science 23:* 421–428.

Pylyshyn, Z. 1973. What the mind's eye tells the mind's brain: A critique of mental imagery. *Psychological Bulletin 80:*1–24.

Quine, W. V. 1969. *Ontological relativity and other essays.* New York: Columbia.

Rescher, N. 1969. *Many-valued logic.* New York: McGraw-Hill.

Rosch, E. & Lloyd, B. L. eds., 1978. *Cognition and categorization.* Hillsdale, N.J.: Lawrence Erlbaum Associates.

Siegel, J., & Siegel, W. 1977. Absolute identification of notes and intervals by musicians. *Perception & Psychophysics 21:* 143–152.

Sperry, R. W., & Gazzaniga, M. S. 1967. Language following surgical disconnention of the hemispheres. In *Brain mechanisms underlying language and speech,* eds., Darley & Millikan.

Steklis, H. D. 1978. Of gonads and ganglia. *The Behavioral and Brain Sciences* 1:317–318.

Steklis, H. D., & Harnad, S. R. 1976a. From hand to mouth: Some critical stages in the evolution of language. In *Origins and evolution of language and speech,* eds., Harnad *et al.*

Steklis, H. D., & Harnad, S. R. 1976b. Comment on Paredes & Hepburn's "The split-brain and the culture-cognition paradox." *Current Anthropology 17:* 320–322.

Verbrugge, R. R., & McCarrell, N. S. 1977. Metaphoric comprehension. *Cognitive Psychology 9:* 494–533.

Vinken, P. J., & Bruyn, G. W. eds. 1969. *Handbook of clinical neurology,* Vol. IV, *Disorders of speech, perception and symbolic behaviour.* Elsevier: North Holland.

Wertheim, N. 1969. The amusias. In *Handbook of clinical neurology,* eds., Vinken and Bruyn.

Whitaker, H. A., & Whitaker, H. eds., 1979. *Studies in neurolinguistics,* Volume IV, New York: Academic Press.

Wickelgren, W. A. 1975. Relations, operators, predicates, and the syntax of (verbal) propositional and (spatial) operational memory. *Bulletin of Psychonomic Society* 6:161–164.

Yates, D. & Irby, J. E. eds. 1969. *Labyrinths.* New York: New Directions.

Zadeh, L. A., & Fu, K. S., 1975. *Fuzzy sets and their applications to cognitive and decision processes.* New York: Academic Press.

Zaidel, E. 1978. Lexical organization in the right hemisphere. In *Cerebral correlates of conscious experience,* eds., Buser & Rougeul-Buser.

14 Computations and Representations

Karl H. Pribram
Stanford University

INTRODUCTION

Gilbert Ryle (1949) has pointed out that the term "mind" is derived from "minding." When an organism minds (or does so in the negative), we are apt to endow it with all sorts of psychological attributes: Attention, perception, conception, consciousness, intention, will, satisfaction, thought, and talk are only a few of the labeled concepts that we use to identify these attributes. When brain tissue is severely damaged these psychological attributes become distorted or even destroyed. Furthermore, the distortion (or destruction) is not uniform: Damage to different parts of the brain differentially interferes with the various psychological attributes. This differential, selective interference is especially marked in man with regard to his ability to talk—to communicate audio-vocally. In most right-handed human adults speech is interfered with most critically when lesions occur in the left hemisphere, in a centrally located zone that surrounds the Sylvian fissure.

Mind and brain are thus shown to be related and we examine here the relationship with special reference to one psychological attribute—the ability to make, use, and comprehend language(s). A question that arises immediately, therefore, is whether language functions are localized in brain tissue. As audio-vocal communication becomes severely disturbed by and essentially only by lesions in a restricted portion of the brain, the question arises as to whether speech communication is synonymous with language. This question cannot be answered by fiat: Social consensus must, in the long run, decide how we are to define what we mean.

But, in the meanwhile, we can use the term language with considerable precision provided we employ some modifiers. Thus, spoken language is called the natural language; music can be considered a language-like system (see e.g. Bernstein, 1976; Jackendoff & Lerdahl, 1979; Pribram, 1981); and gestural communications are often referred to as "sign" languages (Klima & Bellugi, 1979).

When the issue is phrased in this fashion, it becomes clear that different regions of the brain partake in different sorts of language-like systems. For instance, gestural communications are not as dependent on the perisylvian cortex as are spoken natural languages. However, it might still be the case that some specific brain locus or some special brain process dependent on overall connectivity or chemistry might account for a single language ability and only its expression was dependent on diverse brain loci.

Against this possibility are observations on mentally retarded children who despite their overall incapacities can speak fluently and understand when spoken to: also, cases of idiot-savants whose incredible computational or musical abilities fail to be matched by any other form of intelligence. Though not conclusive, such observations argue strongly that the several language-like systems have diverse substrates that share, however, some overall capability that reaches its greatest development in man.

RE-PRESENTATION

What then, is this overall capability that makes man human? What brain function becomes so markedly enhanced that human languages distinguish man from all other animals? The evidence to be reviewed makes it likely that it is the brain's ability to construct hierarchies of representations that is critical.

Hierarchies imply levels. A level can be defined as a presentation (description) that is simpler than if it were made in terms of the constituents of that level. Thus each level can be characterized by a description, a presentation, and by components that are described in some different fashion—i.e., the component level of presentation is distinct from the level of the whole. Further, there would be no need for a presentation at the wholistic level were it not in some non-trivial sense, simpler. By simpler I mean simply simpler to use (see e.g. Pribram, 1971, Chapters 4 & 13 for examples). Bytes (which transform a binary code into an octal) are simpler to use than the equivalent description in bits. A presentation of a program in Fortran is infinitely simpler to use than a presentation of the successive switch settings that characterize the hardware equivalent of the program. Of interest here is whether psychological processes can be considered to be re-presentations of functions of the brain.

In the sense of hierarchical levels of presentation, the analogy between computer software (programs) and hardware can serve as a model. The psychological, mental level is described in a presentation that is analogous to the program level. The wetware of the brain is of course analogous to the hardware of the computer (e.g., Miller, Galanter, & Pribram, 1960). There is an equivalence between program and successive switch settings. Can we therefore say that in some real sense the switch settings are re-presented in the program? And vice-versa? If so, in that same sense psychological processes re-present brain function and vice-versa.

ISOMORPHISM

Are the equivalences between levels of presentation isomorphic to one another? Again, the answer to this question depends on reaching some consensus on the definition of isomorphic. Shepard (Shepard & Chipman, 1970) has recently suggested that processes that map into each other readily such as perspective transformations can be regarded as displaying secondary isomorphism. Where are we to draw the line between representations that display the *same* form (are ismorphic) and those that do not?

Isomorphy is not a trivial problem when one tries to understand the nature of brain representations. Köhler (1964) attempted to show that the geometry of cortical electrical activity conforms to the geometry of the physical events producing the stimulation of the organism. This line of reasoning suggested that brain representations "pictured" the significant environment of the organism or at least caricatured it.

By contrast, the computer program-hardware analogy suggests that significant transformations can occur between levels of presentation: indeed that the utility of re-presentations is derived from these transformations. Both isomorphic and transformational processing may, of course, characterize brain representations. But at least the computer analogy has liberated brain scientists from searching exclusively for "pictures" and set them to search for computations that transform sensory input and motor output and state that search in "information (bits and bytes type) processing" terms.

COMPLEMENTATION AND COORDINATE STRUCTURES

An added dividend has accrued from this new freedom. Even where isomorphism between presentations might initially be sought, the naive realism of brain "pictures" gives way to a more sophisticated view of the relationship between the sentient organism and its significant environment. Gibson (1966), Turvey (1973), and Shaw (1977), among others, have proposed that the organism becomes attuned to its environment and that the relationship between the two is one of complementation. They argue that representation suggests an *iso*morphic replica: Note that earlier I have argued the opposite—that a re-presentation involves a *trans*formation. They therefore suggest that complementation, which implies a duality, a mirror image of sorts, is more appropriate. But the distinction between complementation and representation does not clearly define the issue. A complement need not be a "picture," even a mirrored picture, any more than other presentations: Many musical instruments complement the fingers of the hand, yet a piano keyboard, violin string and clarinet stops have completely different configurations. The issue is whether the presentations are isomorphs or transforms of each other.

What types of transformational mechanism within the nervous system could be responsible for bringing it into a complementary relationship with the environment? Below the cortex these mechanisms are composed of iterative feedback loops (see Miller, Galanter, & Pribram, 1960; Pribram, 1977; Granit, 1955; Gel'fand, Gurfinkel, Tsetlin, & Shik, 1971) "coordinate structures" or TOTES (test-operate-test-exit mechanisms) that adjust the organism to changes in receptor load. At the cortex these changes in load are directly encoded (see e.g. Evarts, 1967). Anatomically there is considerable receptor-cortex isomorphism. How then can "load," which is environmentally engendered, become represented in the cortex?

Consider the anatomical connectivity of an array upon which environmental events operate. If the cortex is to encode these environmental operations there must be some transformation exerted upon the limit of the array—some transfer function that preserves an equivalence between environmental input and its cortical representation.

NEURAL HOLOGRAMS

There is good evidence that this transfer function is effected by lateral networks of mostly axonless (local circuit) neurons (Rakic, 1976) neurons whose dendrites extend perpendicularly to the receptor-cortical connectivity (see Bekesy, 1967; Ratliff, 1965; Pribram, 1977a). These networks of neurons operate in large part without generating propagated nerve impulses. Their mode of functioning is by way of graded local potentials—hyperpolarizations and depolarizations. Their operation can be considered to impose a spatial filter on the receptor-cortical pathway. The characteristics of this filter transform the input into its linear equivalent in the frequency domain. In short, the filters perform something like a Fourier transform on the input from the receptors.

Just as there is a radical difference between octal bytes and binary bits, so there is a radical difference between an input and its Fourier transform. In the transform domain frequencies are encoded and information becomes distributed—mathematically the transform is called a spread function. Further, the frequency domain allows extremely rapid correlations to be made. (This was the basis for the invention of X-ray tomography by which three dimensional brain scans can be produced.)

Computers are artifacts that enact the power of hierarchically organized list structure programs. Holograms are artifacts that enact the power of transforms in the frequency domain. Holograms encode the interference patterns created by wave forms of different frequencies—much as an FM radio signal encodes information by virtue of the modulations of the frequency of an electromagnetic wave. In a hologram, however, the wave forms are two dimensional rather than unidimensional as in radio waves. Thus, considerably more information can be transmitted and stored provided the carrier frequency is high enough.

Over the past decade the evidence that the brain functions as a frequency analyzer has accumulated rapidly. Over a century ago Helmholtz (1867) supported Ohm's (1843) suggestion that the auditory system operates in this fashion. Bekesy's classical studies extended these concepts to the somatosensory modality (1957). In the olfactory mode, Freeman (1975) has presented evidence that a similar mechanism is operative. And most recently the work of Campbell and Robson (1968), of Schiller, Finlay and Volman (1976), of Movshon, Thompson, and Tolhurst (1978), of Pollen and Taylor (1974), of Maffei and Fiorentini (1973), of Ikeda and Wright (1974), of de Valois, Albrecht, and Thorell (1978), of Glezer, Ivanoff, and Tscherbach (1973), and our own work (Pribram, Lassonde, & Ptito, 1981) have established beyond any reasonable doubt that the visual system also operates in this fashion.

Two mysteries that had plagued the brain-mind problem have been resolved by these data that demonstrate a stage of processing in which the frequency domain is important. First, the resistance to brain damage of discrete memory traces is explained by the distributed nature of the holographic-like store. Second, image construction with its wealth of texture and its projection away from the receptor surface are now readily understood. Thus far there has been no other mechanism by which texture can be simulated (see Szentagothai & Arbib, 1975; Campbell, 1974). Projection is accomplished as in stereophonic high fidelity audio systems when there is disparity between the phases from two sources (see Bekesy, 1957).

For the mind-brain problem these are indeed striking contributions. The projected images are in fact the Ghosts in the Machine that Gilbert Ryle (1949) was attempting to excise in his behavioristic approach to the problem. Once images are admitted, the entire range of ghostly mental phenomena comes tumbling along bag and baggage. If brain mechanisms can generate images, why not feelings? And thoughts? And languages?

NEURAL-MENTAL RE-PRESENTATIONS

Note that this analysis concerned various levels of neural functioning: e.g., receptors, coordinate structures, cortical holograms. Only when we examine the functioning whole do we achieve the mental—and of course the whole includes the environmental events that excite the receptors and make possible effector action. To keep faith with the spirit of the analysis we must conclude that brain is re-presented in mind and mind in brain. This does not mean, however, that the presentations of mind and of brain are identical or need be isomorphic—in fact, we have seen that they are disparate: Transformations characterize the relationship. Re-presentation is a realization in a specific domain of a presentation realized in another domain. The fact that the two presentations can be related to each other by a specifiable transformation indicates that some underlying unity is involved. In the case of complementation this unity has been suggested to be due to a symmetry structure (see Shaw & Pittenger, 1977). One type of symmetry is achieved in the complete reversibility which is the hallmark of holonomic frequency transforms (to decode a Fourier hologram the original transform—now called the inverse—needs only to be repeated). At present we have no other name than re-presentation for the unity that becomes realized in the variety of computational dualities and holonomic transformations.

INFORMATION PROCESSING

Complementation, coordination, and imaging account for a type of brain-mind relationship that in older neurological literature was called sensory-motor functioning. In this type of relationship "mind" closely binds the organism to its environment and through behavior, the environment to the organism. (This "binding" function operates through constraints similar to those that limit the distribution of hydrogen and oxygen once they are bound as H_2O, to which we give a new representational name—water.) Psychophysics, perception of Gestalts and illusions, and motor skills are the psychological processes that are studied when this aspect of mind is considered.

But there are other mental phenomena that do not fit these constraints. Cognitive problem-solving processes and social-emotional skills, for example, involve dimensions of mind that are distinctly different from those discussed in the previous sections.

It is easiest to begin with problem-solving processing because a quantitative measure of what constitutes a problem can be given in terms of "information." A bit of information reduces uncertainty in half—uncertainty being a measure of the number of specified alternatives that characterize the choices an organism faces in a situation. The measure on uncertainty and information is therefore identical and simply reflects the choices made with respect to possible choices.

Note that alternatives, choices, break up, partition an organism-environment relationship into segments (sets and subsets). In order to do this, segments must be differentiated. This is the problem of similarity and of categorizing—a problem recognized as fundamental to cognitive psychology, (see e.g. Tversky, 1977).

The brain locus involved in information processing is distinctly separate from that in which complementation takes place. Complementation as we have seen is a function of the sensory-motor projection systems of the brain. Information processing, differentiation among alternatives is disrupted by resections of what is usually called "association" cortex of the posterior convexity of the brain (for review, see Pribram, 1974). In man, lesions of these areas produce agnosias, deficits in recognizing, in cognitive processing. Experimental analysis has shown that resection of this cortex reduces the ratio of possible alternatives sampled by the organism (Pribram, 1960).

As noted earlier, one of the most pressing problems in psychology is to decipher the transformations that re-present images as information (and vice-versa). The linear complementary functions of the sensory-motor systems must be transformed into nonlinear choices. How do the "association" systems of the brain effect these nonlinear transformations? We do not as yet know, but to date we have shown that the operation of this cortex in making discrimination possible is intimately dependent on its efferent, downstream connections to the basal ganglia of the brain and from there to the sensory-motor systems (Spinelli & Pribram, 1967; Lassonde, Ptito, & Pribram, 1981).

Several possibilities for research are opened by these results. Radar operators have faced the problems of digitizing holographic presentations. They have relied on the mathematics of Hadamard and Walsh transforms to differentiate the infinitely multivalued Fourier domain into a finite multivalued one (Hadamard, 1972) and then into a bivalued (binary) system (Walsh, 1972). The efferent operators from the association cortex that have been found to modify the lateral connectivities in the projection system may convert an essentially continuous "field" into a binary matrix (see Wilson & Cowan, 1973). Or, these efferent operators may be band-limiting in such a manner that logons, units of information suggested by Gabor (1946), are produced (see MacKay, 1969; Brillouin, 1962, for review).

EPISODIC PROCESSING

There is an entirely different mode of central processing that is reciprocal to the information and cognitive mechanism just described. Resection or electrical excitation of the frontolimbic forebrain almost always produces effects on projection cortex opposite to those produced by these methods applied to the convexal association cortex (see Spinelli & Pribram, 1967; Lassonde, Ptito, & Pribram, 1981). According to the analysis pursued here, frontolimbic processing should therefore result in integration rather than differentiation.

According to the results of neurobehavioral experiments, the frontolimbic forebrain subserves context dependent, episode specific constructions (see Pribram, Ahumada, Hartog, & Roos, 1964; Pribram & Luria, 1973; Pribram, 1977c). This type of construction involves taking the continuum of experience and "chunking" it into coherent episodes (see Miller, 1956; Simon, 1974). The chunks are, of course, arbitrary but effective in enhancing the utility of the re-presentation. Encoding binary bits into octal bytes is such an operation. Experimental evidence (see Pribram & Tubbs, 1967; Pribram, Plotkin, Anderson, & Leong, 1977) has been obtained to show that frontal cortex is in fact critical to such parsing or chunking operations.

One can conceptualize the difference between behavioral differentiation and chunking in terms of the distinction between mathematic differentiation and integration. Differentiating a wave form emphasizes consistent changes (invariances). Each invariant can become an alternative—a bit (binary digit) of information. Integration, by contrast, encompasses the entire area contained by the wave forms. All that needs to be specified are the limits over which the integration should proceed, and these limits—the windows—are established arbitrarily or on the basis of some extraneous (contextual) criterion. Episodic integration is thus context sensitive. Arbitrary (token) rules for integration must be established—e.g. as by social convention. But brain states (such as the neurochemical states that are regulated by limbic system functioning and responsible for basic emotional and motivational feelings) also furnish the momentary contextual limits for integration. In economic theory these contextual parameters are called "probable availability" (social and arbitrary) and "desireability" (based on attraction between available input and need). The frontolimbic forebrain deals with the organism's economy (Pribram, 1965)—sometimes wisely—while the posterior cortical convexity is involved in formulating knowledge (informs cognitions).

COGNITIVE CONTROLS

A model of brain function emerges from these considerations. This model envisages complementation between brain and the environment. Complementation takes place via sensory transduction on the one hand and behavioral adjustment on the other. Hierarchically organized coordinate structures in the peripheral and central nervous system become organized to re-present the transductions and adjustments. This is in part accomplished by transformations of the presentations into the frequency domain in which correlations are readily performed.

The encoded frequency representations are in turn operated upon by controls from the "association" systems of the brain. Two classes of such systems, operating reciprocally have been identified, one originating in the posterior cortical convexity and the other in the frontolimbic forebrain. Control from the convexity tends to differentiate the representation making possible, "choices" among its "bits" and therefore information and cognitive porcessing. By contrast, control from the frontolimbic forebrain tends to integrate portions, episodes, of the complement, chunking it according to felt needs and/or environmental contingencies.

HUMAN LANGUAGES

The transformations produced by these information (cognitive) and episodic (economic, sapient) controls can, in man, serve as the basis for re-presentation at still another level of presentation. Neurally this level is probably made possible by the increase of the proportions of cortex not directly committed to complementation (see Young, 1962; Pribram, 1962; also, Pribram, 1971). Encoding this level in an enduring culture is equally important (see Pribram, 1964, 1975b, 1976, and Popper & Eccles, 1977). The re-presentation now partakes both of the structure of information process and that of the arbitrary chunking of the episodic process. At a deeper level, its semantic store re-presents the distributed frequency domain and even the coordinate structures that compose complementation.

The nature of transformations that re-present cognitions (knowledge) and context sensitive episodic constructions (wisdom) in language and language-like process is not at all clear. Chomsky has chosen to emphasize syntax (1980) and there is good evidence that this approach to natural language and to musical phrasing (Bernstein, 1976; Lerdahl & Jackendoff, 1977; Pribram, 1981) can be fruitful. However, this emphasis on syntax fails to point out that equally important syntactic advances characterize all cultural achievements (Pribram, 1971). This, then poses the problem of what distinguishes them—what is the difference between natural languages, musical compositions, sport, dance, architecture, and painting? I have in a preliminary fashion attempted to frame this question by examining the relative roles of semantics (cognition) and pragmatics (sapience) with regard to natural languages (Pribram, 1976; 1978; 1980) and music (1981).

Much more needs to be done—languages, cognitions, and wisdom apparently do not spring from the isolated operation of any single neural mechanism—still, there is the haunting evidence of the linguistically competent retardates and of the savants to continually remind us of the uniqueness of the combinations that characterize each of these mental processes.

EPILOGUE

Since this was written a great deal of interest has been devoted to the problems of cognitive computations and psychological representations. For instance, a recent issue of *The Brain and Behavioral Sciences* (Spring, 1980) was devoted to these problems, as is Volume III of the Pennsylvania State Series on Ecological Psychology (1981). The views expressed in my presentation here can be readily compared with others, therefore. On the whole, there appears to be considerable agreement overall, but with sharp differences in detail (such as whether brain facts are critical—see, e.g., the excellent discussion by Churchland of Pylyshyn's otherwise superb contribution in *The Behavioral and Brain Sciences*), and definition (as to whether by representation is meant an isomorph or a transform or both).

REFERENCES

Bekesy, G. von 1957. Neural volleys and the similarity between some sensations produced by tones and by skin vibrations. *Journal of the Acoustical Society or America* 29:1059-69.

Bekesy, G. von 1967. *Sensory inhibition*. Princeton: Princeton University Press.

Bernstein, L. 1976. *The unanswered question*. Cambridge: Harvard University Press.

Brillouin, L. 1962. *Science and information theory*. New York: Academic.

Campbell, F. W. 1974. The transmission of spatial information through the visual system. In *The neuroscience third study program*, ed. F. O. Schmitt & F. G. Worden. Cambridge: MIT Press.

Campbell, F. W., & Robson, J. G. 1968. Application of Fourier analysis to the visibility of gratings. *Journal of Physiology* 197:551-66.

Chomsky, N. 1980. *Rules and representations*. New York: Columbia University Press.

Churchland, P. S. 1980. Neuroscience and psychology: Should the labor be divided? *The Behavioral and Brain Sciences*, 3(1):133.

Evarts, E. V. 1967. Representation of movements and muscles by pyramidal tract neurons of the precentral motor cortex. In *Neurophysiological basis of normal and abnormal motor activities*, ed. M. D. Yahr & D. P. Purpura, New York: Raven.

Freeman, W. 1975. *Mass action in the nervous system*. New York: Academic.

Gabor, D. 1946. Theory of communication. *Journal of the Institute of Electrical Engineers* 93(3):429.

Gel'fand, I. M., Gurfinkel, V. S., Tsetlin, H. L., & Shik, M. L. 1971. Some problems in the analysis of movements. In *Models of the structural-functional organization of certain biological systems*, ed. I. M. Gel'fand, V. S. Fomin, & M. T. Tsetlin, pp. 329-45. Cambridge: MIT Press.

Gibson, J. J. 1966. *The senses considered as perceptual systems*. Boston: Houghton Mifflin.

Glezer, V. D., Ivanoff, V. A., & Tscherbach, T. A. 1973. Investigation of complex and hypercomplex receptive fields of visual cortex of the cat as spatial frequency filters. *Vision Research* 13:1875-1904.

Granit, R. 1955. *Receptors and sensory perception*. New Haven: Yale University Press.

Hadamard, J. 1972. In *Transmission of information by orthogonal functions*, ed. H. F. Harmuth, pp. 30-33. New York: Springer-Verlag.

Helmholtz, H. von. 1867. *Handbuch der physiologishen Optik*. Leipzig: Voss.

Ikeda, H., & Wright, M. J. 1974. Evidence for "sustained" and "transient" neurons in the cat's visual cortex. *Vision Research* 14:133-36.

Jackendoff, R., & Lerdahl, F. 1979. Generative music theory and its relation to psychology (unpublished manuscript).

Klima, E. S., & Bellugi, U. 1979. *The signs of language*. Cambridge: Harvard University Press.

Köhler, I. 1964. *The formation and transformation of the perceptual world*. New York: International Press.

Lassonde, M. C., Ptito, M., & Pribram, K. H. 1981, Intracerebral influences on the microstructure of visual cortex. *Experimental Brain Research,* in press, 1981.

Lerdahl, F., & Jackendoff, R. 1977. Toward a formal theory of tonal music. *Journal of Music Theory* Spring:111–172.

MacKay, D. M. 1969. *Information mechanism and meaning.* Cambridge: MIT Press.

McGuinness, D., & Pribram, K. H. 1981. The origins of sensory bias in the development of gender differences in perception and cognition. In *Toward theories of cognitive functioning and development,* ed. M. Korkner, G. Turkewitz, & J. Tizard.

Maffei, L., & Fiorentini, A. 1973. The visual cortex as a spatial frequency analyzer. *Vision Research* 13:1255–67.

Miller, G. A. 1956. The magical number seven, plus or minus two, or, some limits on our capacity for processing information. *Psychological Review* 63:81–97.

Miller, G. A., Galanter, F., & Pribram, K. H. 1960. *Plans and the structure of behavior.* New York: Holt.

Movshon, J. A., Thompson, I. D., & Tolhurst, D. J. 1978. Spatial summation in the receptive field of simple cells in the cat's striate cortex. *Journal of Physiology* 283:53–77.

Ohm, G. S. 1843. Über die Definition des Tones, nebst daran geknüpfter Theorie der Sirene und ähnlicher tonbildener Vorrichtungen. *Annalen der Physik und Chemie* 59:513–65.

Pollen, D. A., & Taylor, J. H. 1974. The striate cortex and the spatial analysis of visual space. In *The neurosciences third study program,* ed. F. O. Schmitt & F. G. Worden, Cambridge, MIT Press.

Popper, K. R., & Eccles, J. C. 1977. *The self and its brain.* New York: Springer.

Pribram, K. H. 1960. The intrinsic systems of the forebrain. In *Handbook of physiology,* ed. J. Field, H. W. Magoun, & V. E. Hall, *Neurophysiology,* vol. 2. American Physiological Society, Washington, D.C.

Pribram, K. H. 1964. Neurological notes on the art of education. In *Theories of learning and instruction,* ed. E. Hilgard, pp. 78–110. Chicago: University of Chicago Press.

Pribram, K. H. 1971. *Languages of the brain: experimental paradoxes and principles in neuropsychology.* Englewood Cliffs, N.J.: Prentice-Hall. 2d ed. Monterey: Brooks/Cole.

Pribram, K. H. 1974. How is it that sensing so much we can do so little? In *The neurosciences third study program.* ed. F. O. Schmitt & F. G. Worden. Cambridge: MIT Press.

Pribram, K. H., ed. 1975. *Central processing of sensory input.* Cambridge: MIT Press.

Pribram, K. H. 1976. Language in a sociobiological frame. In *Origins and evolution of language and speech, Annals of the New York Academy of Sciences* 280:798–809.

Pribram, K. H. 1977a. Modes of central processing in human learning and remembering. In *Brain and learning,* ed. T. J. Teyler. Stamford, Conn.: Greylock.

Pribram, K. H. 1977b. New dimensions in the functions of the basal ganglia. In *Psychopathology and brain dysfunction,* ed. C. Shagass, S. Gershon, & A. J. Friedhoff, pp. 77–95. New York: Raven.

Pribram, K. H. 1978. The linguistic act. In *Psychiatry and the humanities: Vol. 3: Psychoanalysis and language,* ed. J. H. Smith. New Haven: Yale University Press.

Pribram, K. H. 1980. The place of pragmatics in the syntactic and semantic organization of language. In *Temporal variables in speech, studies in honour of Frieda Goldman-Eisler,* The Hague/Paris: Mouton.

Pribram, K. H. 1981. Brain mechanisms in music: Prolegomena for a theory of the meaning of meaning. In *Music, mind and brain.* ed M. Clynes. New York: Plenum.

Pribram, K. H., Ahumada, A., Hartog, J., & Roos, L. 1964. A progress report on the neurological process disturbed by frontal lesions in primates. In *The frontal granular cortex and behavior,* ed. I. M. Warren & K. Akert, pp. 28–55. New York: McGraw-Hill.

Pribram, K. H., Lassonde, M. C., & Ptito, M. 1981. Classification of receptive field properties. *Experimental Brain Research,* in press, 1981.

Pribram, K. H., & Luria, A. R., eds. 1973. *Psychophysiology of the frontal lobes*. New York: Academic Press.

Pribram, K. H., Plotkin, H. C., Anderson, R. M., & Leong, D. 1977. Information sources in the delayed alternation task for normal and "frontal" monkeys. *Neuropsychologia* 15:329-40.

Pribram, K. H., & Tubbs, W. E. 1967. Short-term memory, parsing, and the primate frontal cortex. *Science* 156:1765-67.

Rakic, P. 1976. *Local circuit neurons*. Cambridge: MIT Press.

Ratliff, F. 1965. *Mach Bands: quantitative studies in neural networks in the retina*. San Francisco: Holden-Day.

Ryle, G. 1949. *The concept of mind*. New York: Barnes and Noble.

Schiller, P. H., Finlay, B. L., & Volman, S. F. 1976. Quantitative studies of single-cell properties in monkey striate cortex. *Journal of Neurophysiology* 39:1288-1374.

Shaw, R. E., & Pittenger, J. 1977. Perceiving the face of change in changing faces: implications for a theory of object perception. In *Perceiving, acting, and knowing*, ed. R. Shaw & J. Bransford, pp. 103-32. Hillsdale, N.J.: Lawrence Erlbaum Associates.

Shepard, R., & Chipman, S. 1970. Second-order isomorphism of internal representations: shapes of states. *Cognitive Psychology* 1:1-17.

Simon, H. A. 1974. How big is a chunk? *Science* 183:482-88.

Spinelli, D. H., & Pribram, K. H. 1966. Changes in visual recovery functions produced by temporal lobe stimulations in monkeys. *Electroencephalography and Clinical Neurophysiology* 20:44-49.

Spinelli, D. H., & Pribram, K. H. 1967. Changes in visual recovery function and unit capacity produced by frontal and temporal cortex stimulation. *Electroencephalography and Clinical Neurophysiology* 22:143-49.

Szentagothai, J., & Arbib, M. A. 1975. *Conceptual models of neural organization*. Cambridge: MIT Press.

Turvey, M. T. 1973. Peripheral and central processes in vision: inferences from an information processing analysis of masking with pattern stimuli. *Psychology Review* 80:1-52.

Tversky, A. 1977. Features of similarity. *Psychology Review* 84:327-52.

Valois, R. L. de, Albrecht, D. G., & Thorell, L. G. 1978. Spatial tuning of LGN and cortical cells in monkey visual system. In *Spatial contrast*, ed. H. Spekreijse. Amsterdam: Royal Netherlands Academy of Sciences, Monograph Series, forthcoming.

Walsh, D. M. 1972. In *Transmission of information by orthogonal functions*, ed. H. F. Harmuth, pp. 22-30. New York: Springer-Verlag.

Wilson, H. R., & Cowan, J. D. 1973. A mathematical theory of the functional dynamics of cortical and thalamic nervous tissue. *Kybernetic* 13:55-80.

Young, J. Z. 1962. Why do we have two brains? In *Interhemispheric relations and cerebral dominance*, ed. V. B. Mountcastle, pp. 7-24. Baltimore: Johns Hopkins.

15 The Cognitive Sciences: A Semiotic Paradigm

Charls Pearson
Georgia Institute of Technology

INTRODUCTION

Given the importance and ubiquity of cognition as well as the power of the scientific method and the inquisitiveness of scientists themselves, it is no wonder that several sciences have focused on cognition itself as their prime target of study. These sciences such as psychology, linguistics, logic, semiotics or information science, etc. may be considered sciences of second intention in that their ultimate concern is that object—cognition—that the other sciences merely use in the observation of their objects of ultimate concern, be they parameciums and plants, or protons and planets.

Among these sciences, which may for ease of reference be called the cognitive sciences, an important problem, and one that appears to provide a unifying concept for this emerging discipline, is the problem of representation. For instance, Piaget has suggested that the ability to represent objects and events is a necessary prerequisite for the development of any system of cognition for the acquisition of knowledge and experience (1951). Representation is a semiotic concept in that a trinary relation, called a 'sign,' is involved essentially in the notion of representation. This indicates that semiotics may not only provide a unifying viewpoint but empirical semiotics may even offer our first hope of a unifying methodology for the cognitive sciences. We may call this the semiotic paradigm for cognitive science.

Other candidates have attempted to supply this paradigm. Among these perhaps the leading contender is language and linguistics. But language and linguistics have been criticized as offering too narrow a viewpoint for unifying the cognitive sciences, and yet there is strong argument supporting the feeling

225

that cognition is essentially a language process. This paradox arises because of the ambiguity of the terms 'language,' 'language process,' and 'linguistics.' When 'language' and 'linguistics' are interpreted in the narrow sense of ordinary natural language as interpreted by many linguists today, it is obvious that there are many cognitive processes that do not employ natural language words. However, it is thought that these same processes do involve some kind of language mechanisms. This feeling is so strong that many investigators define cognitive thought in any of its forms to be "language." When language and linguistics are interpreted in this broader sense they do encompass, even if only by definition, all of cognitive science.

To avoid ambiguity it is best to use distinctive terms for the different senses of 'language' and 'language process' involved here. John Locke coined the terms 'semiotic,' and 'semiosis' for the broader sense of these words. Charles Peirce adopted these words in the development of his system of semiotic (1931–58), and Charles Morris made them popular amongst philosophers and logicians (1938). Modern usage employs 'semiotics,' 'semiosis,' and uses 'semiotician' for one who studies semiotics philosophically or speculatively, and 'semioticist' for one who studies it empirically.

Therefore the suggestion that semiotics may be a unifying viewpoint for cognitive science is not essentially different from the suggestion that the study of language yields this unifying framework, but is an explication of it that eliminates certain objectional paradoxes.

SEMIOTIC BACKGROUND

Cognitive processing of any kind, whether it involves perception, memory, recognition, or *merely* external communication, can be viewed as the processing of signs. In this view, cognitive performance depends both upon the goal, or purpose, of the processing and the structure of the signs used in the processing. In semiotics, we attempt to understand the basic nature of cognitive processing by investigating the structure of signs and sign systems, and the relation between sign structure and the cognitive process: perception, classification, communication, memory, recognition, etc. The goals of cognitive processing are not, properly speaking, a part of semiotics. The study of cognitive goals may belong to either psychology or ethics, or even to semiotic engineering, but not to basic semiotics itself.

Experiments in semiotics bear a remarkable likeness to experiments in other cognitive disciplines. For instance, many semiotics experiments are similar to certain psychological experiments; i.e., on the surface there appears to be no difference at all. However, this superficial similarity covers a very essential difference. In psychology, we use the known structure of signs of probe the structure of behavior. In semiotics we use the known structure of behavior to probe the structure of signs. For instance, in psychology we might choose a fixed set of word pairs and use these to explore the communication ability of both arbitrary normal speakers and arbitrary schizophrenics; however, in semiotics we select a fixed panel of normal speakers and, subjecting them to the same experimental paradigm, use this to measure a certain kind of "synonymity" between arbitrary word pairs. It is this inversion of emphasis from the usual psychological viewpoint that gives semiotics its broad powers of unification and integration.

UNIVERSAL SIGN STRUCTURE THEORY

My purpose in developing a theory of sign structure is to have a tool for explicating the nature of cognition and representation and their relationship to semiotic processes, and for classifying cognitive processes according to their semiotic dimensionality and interrelationships. Throughout my investigations I have had occasion to use several different taxonomies, or classification schemes, for signs. Of these only the classification by Charles Peirce (1931–58) has proved to be satisfactory in every empirical setting for which a classification was wanted. I therefore ascribe the Peircean scheme, an empirical reality, and would like my theory of sign structure to explain the applicability and usefulness of the Peircean scheme in terms of the structure of the sign.

Peirce defines the sign as a three-place relation:

> A sign, or *representamen,* is something which stands to somebody for something in some respect or capacity (1931–58, vol. 2. 228).

> In consequence of every representamen being thus connected with three things, . . . the science of semiotics has three branches (1931–58, 2.229).

Peirce called these three branches "pure grammar," "logic proper," and "pure rhetoric." Subsequently, Charles Morris called these the three 'dimensions' of semiotics and gave them their current names: syntactics, semantics, and pragmatics (1938).

Peirce's taxonomy has three classification schemes, leading to nine categories of signs. Definitions 1–3 pertain to a syntactic classification; definitions 4–6 to a semantic classification; and definitions 7–9 to a pragmatic classification of signs.

Definition 1: A sign which exists as an abstract quality both in itself and in its relation to other signs is called a '*TONE.* '[1]

Definition 2: A sign which exists as a general kind, both in itself and distinguishable from other signs is called a '*TYPE.* '

Definition 3: A sign which exists as an actual, single, physically existing individual is called a '*TOKEN.* '

---

[1]It must be remembered that Peirce employed a great number of different and differing nomenclatures. The one adopted here was used in Pearson, 1977.

Definition 4: A sign which is related to its object by an actual, single, existential, cause and effect relation is called an *'INDEX'*.

Definition 5: A sign which is related to its object by a concrete similarity between the shape of the sign and its object is called an *'ICON'*.

Definition 6: A sign which is related to its object by an arbitrary convention, agreement, or general law, is called a *'SYMBOL'*.

Definition 7: A sign whose interpretant represents it as a sign of possible reference to its interpreter is called a *'RHEME'*.

Definition 8: A sign whose interpretant represents it as a sign of fact or actual reference to its interpreter is called a *'PHEME'*.

Definition 9: A sign whose interpretant represents it as a sign of reason to its interpreter is called a *'DOLEME'*.[2]

Because of the rather opaque nature of several of these definitions it may be well to give some examples. An example of a tone in linguistics would be a nonterminal node of a phrase structure diagram, a context category, or a set of allowable (including obligatory) transformations on a sign (word, sentence, or discourse). An example of a tone in logic would be a functional combinator; i.e., a categorical analysis of a sign. An example of a type in linguistics would be a terminal node of a phrase structure diagram or a lexical item (word, sentence, or discourse) at the morphological level, before the phonetic transformations have been embodied. An example of a type in logic would be a well formed expression (term, formula, argument). An example of a type in statistical linguistics would be a general sign of which a particular occurrence token is a specific instance. Classical linguistics and classical logic do not concern themselves with the study of tokens. An example of a token in statistical linguistics would be the single, particular occurrence of some sign that actually occurs at a specific point in the computer scan of a machine readable text. An example of a token in psycholinguistics is one actual stimulus that is exposed in a T-scope.

An example of an index in cognitive psychology is Bruner's 'enactive response' (Bruner, Olver, & Greenfield, 1966). An example from ordinary life would be a pillar of smoke in a dry forest taken by a ranger as a sign for fire, or a knock on a closed door taken by someone on the inside as a sign that someone or something was present on the outside. An example of an icon from cognitive psychology is Bruner's 'ikon.' An example from ordinary life is a paint chip that denotes paint in a can, of the same color as the chip, or a rhythmically repeated note in a melody that holds the music together by the similarities that it establishes. An example of a symbol from cognitive psychology is Bruner's 'symbol.' Natural language signs are all symbolic, including those called 'indexical' and those called 'onomatopoetic.'

---

[2]Peirce's actual term was 'deloam' from the Greek δελωμ.

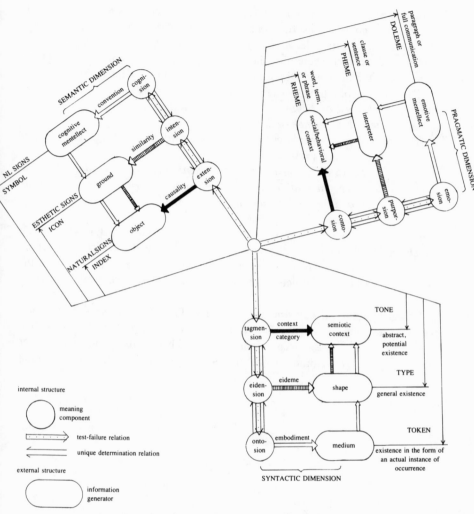

FIG. 15.1   The Universal Sign Structure Model.
© Copyright 1977 by Charls Pearson

An example of a rheme in logic would be a term; an example of a rheme from natural language would be a word or a phrase. An example of a pheme from logic is a statement; from natural language a clause or sentence. An example of a doleme from logic is an argument; from natural language, a paragraph or a complete communication.

The proposed theory of sign structure is embodied in the Universal Sign

Structure Model shown in Fig. 15.1. In order to show how this model explains the Peircean taxonomy, I must first state the following three principles of the theory.

The Trinarity Principle: *A sign must consist of a trinary relation.*

To be consistent, therefore, the model has three parts called the Syntactic Dimension, the Semantic Dimension, and the Pragmatic Dimension.

The Principle of Internal/External Balance: *The internal and the external structure of a sign must be balanced, consisting of exactly one internal component for each external component and vice versa.*

The internal components are called components of meaning. The external components are called information generators.

The Principle of Additional Structure: *Whenever a sign has more than the minimum structure, the additional structure is built up from the center out (as per Fig. 15.1), and for each dimension independently.*

Example. From Fig. 15.1 we isolate the minimum structure (Fig. 15.2) which we shall later find is the structure of the indexical rhematic tone. If we want to add to it one layer of semantic structure, we derive (according to the Principle of Additional Structure) the structure of the iconic rhematic tone (Fig. 15.3).

Using the universal sign structure diagram of Fig. 15.1 and these three principles we can now explain the Peircean Taxonomy of signs by means of nine representation theorems. ('Representation' is used here in its mathematical rather than its cognitive or semiotic sense.) Certain rules of interpretation or translation

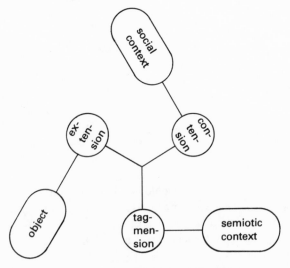

FIG. 15.2. The minimum semiotic structure.

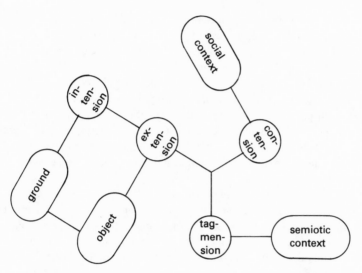

FIG. 15.3.   A sign with the minimum additional semantic structure.

between the theoretical vocabulary and the observational (or less theoretical) vocabulary are required for the proofs of these theorems. The rules of interpretation are obvious, and they form an integral part of the theory. The nine representation theorems are as follows.

Theorem 1: A sign is a tone iff (if and only if) it has exactly one level of syntactic structure. It therefore has one component of syntactic meaning (tagmension) and one external syntactic component (the semiotic context).

Theorem 2: A sign is a type iff it has exactly two levels of syntactic structure. It therefore has two components of syntactic meaning (tagmension and eidension) and two external syntactic components (the semiotic context and the shape of the sign).

Theorem 3. A sign is a token iff it has all three levels of syntactic structure. It therefore has three components of syntactic meaning (tagmension, eidension, and ontosion) and three external syntactic components (the semiotic context, the shape of the sign, and the medium in which it is embodied).

Theorem 4: A sign is an index iff it has exactly one level of semantic structure. It therefore has one component of semantic meaning (extension) and one external semantic component (the object of the sign).

Theorem 5: A sign is an icon iff it has exactly two levels of semantic structure. It therefore has two components of semantic meaning (extension and intension), and two external semantic components (the object of the sign and its ground).

Theorem 6: A sign is a symbol iff it has all three levels of semantic structure. It therefore has three components of semantic meaning (extension, intension, and cognesion), and three external semantic components (the object, the ground, and the cognitive mentellect of the sign).

Theorem 7: A sign is a rheme iff it has exactly one level of pragmatic structure. It therefore has one component of pragmatic meaning (contension) and one external pragmatic component (the social/behavioral context of the sign).

Theorem 8: A sign is a pheme iff it has exactly two levels of pragmatic structure. It therefore has two components of pragmatic meaning (contension and purposion) and two external pragmatic components (the social/behavioral context of the sign, and its interpreter).

Theorem 9: A sign is a doleme iff it has all three levels of pragmatic structure. It therefore has three internal pragmatic components (contension, purporsion, and emosion), and three external pragmatic components (the social/behavioral context, the interpreter, and the emotive mentellect of the sign).

The proofs of the nine theorems are relatively simple. Their nature is illustrated by proving Theorem 1.

Proof of Theorem 1: By the Trinarity Principle and the Principle of Additional Structure any sign must have at least one level of syntactic structure and this must be the innermost, or tagmatic, level. According to the Universal Sign Structure Model (Fig. 15.1), the outermost syntactic level consists of the embodiment of a sign in a physical medium. But if a sign had an embodiment in a physical medium it would exist as an actual, single, physically existing individual and could not exist merely as an abstract quality. It would be a token, not a tone; therefore a tone cannot have an ontotic level of syntactic structure. Also from Fig. 15.1, the second (or middle) syntactic level consists of the distinguishability of a sign by a shape. But, if a sign had a distinctive, distinguishable, shape, it would exist as a concrete general, serving as an archtype for all tokens of the same type and could not exist, etc. It would be a type, not a tone. Therefore, a tone cannot have an eidontic level of syntactic structure.

Thus a tone has exactly one level of syntactic structure, which is the tagmatic structure. By the Principle of Internal/External Balance, this structure will consist of both an internal component and an external component. From Fig. 15.1 we see that the internal component is tagmension, the meaning component abstracted from the semiotic context, and the external component is the semiotic context itself. *Q.E.D.*

Interested readers will find all proofs stated in Pearson and Slamecka (1977a; 1977b).

Theorems 1–9 explain the three trichotomies proposed by Peirce—the syntactic classification (Theorems 1–3), the semantic classification (Theorems 4–6), and the pragmatic classification of signs (Theorems 7–9). The proposed sign structure model is universal in the sense that it displays the structure of all categories of signs. The theory presented in this section is the outgrowth of my dissertation research into the structure of the symbolic rheme (see Pearson, 1977). In this work the meaning of the sign is identified with its internal structure. A later work identified the generation of information with the external structure of signs.

The proposed theory is a relatively elementary beginning pertaining to relational phenomena. In the future, cognitive science should develop more refined theories of sign structure, particularly ones capable of predicting quantitative phenomena. To do so, cognitive science research must focus heavily on the fundamental questions of sign structure and sign processing, both from the experimental and the theoretical side. In my opinion, significant progress along these directions may establish cognitive science as a new paradigm for an alternative group of sciences.

SEMIOTIC ANALYSES OF REPRESENTATION

It is generally recognized that the problem of representation is fundamental to many of the cognitive sciences, including cognitive psychology, semiotics, information science, linguistics, and computer science. For instance, selecting an admissible way of structuring information about a task inside a computer is directly related to the effectiveness and efficiency of execution of the task (see Amarel, 1971). Likewise, it is assumed that thinkers do not deal with their problem environment directly; instead, they formulate abstract models and representations of the external environment.

Representational structures can sometimes prevent a thinker from solving a particular problem. He must then be able to shift to other representations in order to solve the problem. One extreme example is the well-known nine-dot problem. The problem-solver is asked to connect nine dots presented in a square formation with four continuous straight lines. Representing the problems as a directed graph with vertices limited to a subset of the nine dots precludes any solution to the problem. On the other hand, representing the problem as a graph with arcs that may be connected to vertices outside the boundary of the nine dots, gives rise to four potential solutions. The nine-dot problem is an extreme case, but one that points out how fundamental the representation problem is for the cognitive sciences.

While the emphasis in both artificial intelligence and information processing psychology in the past has been on designing and understanding processes, procedures, and algorithms for artificial and natural systems, research on the representation-of-knowledge question has lately been on the increase (see Amarel, 1971; Minsky, 1975; Quillian, 1968; Schank, 1973; Simmons, 1973).

Linguistic research has concentrated on syntactic and semantic representation (see Chomsky, 1957), much work in perceptual psychology is based on the representation of information (see Garner, 1974), and developmental psychologists have based much of their recent work on cognitive representation (see Bruner, Olver, & Greenfield, 1966). Despite the importance of representation to each of the cognitive sciences, it has not led to any unification or integration of them. In fact, heretofore, there has been very little cross-fertilization among the cognitive sciences. Part of the problem is the status of the representation concept itself. Many concepts of representation abound in the literature. Often each of the cognitive sciences has used its own unique concept of representation with some of the sciences even using more than one representation concept ambiguously and equivocally within the same discipline. These concepts need to be clarified, explicated, systematized, and integrated.

We begin our analysis by listing some of the many concepts of representation that have appeared in one or more of the cognitive sciences. These are shown in Fig. 15.4 where they are classified into syntactic concepts, semantic concepts, or pragmatic concepts according as they deal with the sign vehicle, the object of the sign, or the interpretation of the sign (see Morris, 1938, sec. 3). One sense of representation that includes all those of Fig. 15.4 considers representation to be a coding process where coding is regarded as a morphism of an external sign component into some other structure. According to the Universal Sign Structure Theory, cognitive coding processes can be divided similarly to Fig. 15.4 into syntactic coding processes, semantic coding processes, and pragmatic coding processes (altho these latter play a lesser role in cognition).

Syntactic coding processes relate to the *sign vehicle* rather than to either the object of the sign or the interpreter of the sign. They include coding of the medium, the shape, and the semiotic—e.g., linguistic—context of the sign (see Fig. 15.1).

Many processes of syntactic representation are studied statistically by the Shannon Calculus, or what is variously called "Information Theory," "Communication Theory," or the "Uncertainty Calculus." Other syntactic coding processes are sometimes studied analytically by the methods of operational calculus and spectral analysis. However, only a bare beginning has been made and a better understanding of syntactic sign structure and the vehicle of representation is necessary for improved understanding of syntactic coding processes. These concepts of representation are important for perceptual psychology, information science, communication science, linguistics, statistical linguistics, computer science, ontology, mathematics, and the logical calculuses, etc.

Other syntactic concepts of representation include representation as a modeling of the phenomena of the physical environment or of the interpreter or intepretation process as in "a representation of Phonemic memory" (Clark & Clark, 1977). As a last syntactic example, 'representation' can be used as a synonym for

PRAGMATIC

1. Representation as the interpretation of a sign's standing for an object in the mind of the interpreter.

2. Representation as an idea formed by the mind or state of mind underlying the interpreter's attitude.

3. Notions emphasizing the various aspects of interpretation, behavior, disposition, preference, goal-oriented action, etc. by and of subjects, animate or inanimate, related to and conditioned by representations within these subjects (i.e., "internal representations").

SEMANTIC

1. Representation as the other object which a sign stands for.

2. Representation as serving in the capacity of a specimen, example, or instance.

3. Notions emphasizing the relation between objects (material or abstract) and their representations.

1. Representation as the sign which stands for a particular idea, view, impression, etc. reflecting the state of the object or the interpreter.

2. Representation as a modeling of the phenomena of the interpreter or his external world.

3. Notions emphasizing the rules of formation of representations, formal structures of systems of representations, as well as rules of formation and admissible transformations of representations in some such system.

SYNTACTIC

FIG. 15.4. The Multiple Concepts of Representation.

'description' as in "The Structure of an utterance is a representation of its parts and their properties and interrelationships" (Hays, 1964, p. 517).

Semantic coding processes relate to the *other objects* which a sign stands for. They can be carried out by indexical (or enactive) coding, iconic (or ikonic) coding, (see Bruner, Olver, & Greenfield, 1966), and symbolic coding (see Fig. 15.1). These various coding strategies can access various cognitive memories: as the immediate memory, short-term memory, and long-term memory. The interactions and interrelations of all these are but poorly understood at present. A better understanding of semantic coding processes will require better understanding of the semantic structure of signs.

These semantic concepts of representation are important for cognitive psychology, information science, semantics, epistomology, philosophy of science, and logic.

Other semantic concepts of representation include the use of 'representation' as a synonym for 'theory,' as "a representation of the perceptual process" (Garner, 1974) or "semantic representations" (Chomsky, 1957); and representation as serving in the capacity of a specimen, example, or instance.

Pragmatic coding processes relate to the *interpretation* of a sign as standing for an object. They include coding of the social context, coding of the interpreter, and coding of the cognitive mentellect of the sign (see Fig. 15.1). These are the poorest understood of all the coding processes and it is fortunate that they play a lesser role in cognition and in all the cognitive sciences. Other pragmatic concepts of representation include representation as an idea formed by the mind or state of mind underlying the interpreter's attitude.

The above analysis and systematization leads quite naturally to a general semiotic concept of 'representation' that includes each of the above concepts as special cases. This general concept of 'representation' is the expression or designation by something that serves as a sign or symbol for something else. If a sign is defined as a vehicle that stands for something else (i.e., other than the sign itself) to, or for someone, then representation is the act or process of standing for something else.

It can be seen that signs are modeled mathematically by trinary relations. One branch of semiotics (represented by Charles Peirce) treats representation as any essential trinary relation (one that cannot be factored into any number of binary relations) especially in his logic of relations. Thus for Peirce representation becomes the key to all the trinary sciences (which Peirce calls the semiotic sciences). These include all of the sciences that contribute to an understanding of cognition. However, cognition does not include all of semiotics. While cognition is essentially semiotic—that is, it includes relationships and processes that are essentially trinary—it places primary emphasis on the syntactic and semantic dimensions. The pragmatic dimension, which is so important in the affective sciences such as ethics and esthetics, plays a more subdued role in the cognitive sciences. This suggests that cognitive science may be identified with syntactic and semantic semiotics.

According to the Universal Sign Structure Theory the syntactic dimension includes the medium, shape, and semiotic context of the sign, while the semantic dimension includes the real object, ground and cognitive mentellect of the sign. Both the syntactic and semantic dimension of the sign contain meaning components as well as the external components mentioned above (as does also the pragmatic dimension). An understanding of these meaning components is necessary to any understanding of how any knowledge of external reality is represented in the mind.

REPRESENTATION AND COGNITIVE SCIENCE

The problem of representation thus cuts across all of the cognitive sciences and provides a methodological unification as well as a unification of concern.

It is the general semiotic concept of representation outlined above that can serve as this bridge to integrate and unify the individual cognitive sciences and to synthesize a new science of cognition. By an empirical exploration of the structure of representation using an experimental methodology that benefits from the successful techniques of all the cognitive sciences by means of the semiotic inversion discussed in the second section of this chapter, the successes in each area can be integrated into each of the other areas so as to feedback and multiply these successes and thereby achieve an exponential explosion of growth.

An analysis of the coding problems involved for each sign component appearing in the Universal Sign Structure Theory reveals each to be a problem that is of great concern to one or more of the cognitive sciences and to cognitive science in general. For example, an examination of eidontic coding, or coding the shape of the sign, discovers problems of interest to both information theory and grammar. For instance, semiotic theories of symbol structure relate the mathematical concepts of information theory to the type and token concepts of statistical linguistics. Those same theories use other aspects of symbol structure to relate the mathematical concepts of complexity theory to the "strangeness" of word shapes and the difficulty of decoding them. Eidontic coding is a problem of syntactic representation (Pearson & Slamecka, 1977a).

As an example of a coding problem in an entirely different dimension, we may glance at deictic coding, or coding the object of the sign. Here we find problems of interest to troth cognitive psychology, developmental psychology, and semantics. For instance, the object of a sign may be coded in three distinct ways, indexically, iconically, and symbolically. Bruner's studies suggest that deictic coding in the child develops in the order indexical, iconic, and symbolic, thus matching the semantic structure of the sign given by the Universal Sign

Structure Theory (see Bruner, Olver, & Greenfield, 1966, sec. 3). Experiments in semantic structure of symbols and many unstated assumptions in cognitive psychology appear to relate the method of deictic coding to the type of cognitive memory that may be accessed. Deictic coding is a problem of semantic representation (see Pearson & Slamecka, 1977a, b).

By using the semiotic concept of representation to integrate and unify the individual cognitive sciences the way is opened up for developing a common language for discussing problems within any of the disciplines presently recognized as impacting cognitive science. By using a common language it is then possible to compare, contrast, and evaluate concepts, problems, methodology, and solutions across the boundaries of the traditional individual cognitive sciences. This common language would thus lead to a common, or at least a more unified and more powerful, methodology for the cognitive sciences. Problems raised within one of the traditional disciplines could be translated into the language of another discipline where a solution is already available, or more easily obtained, and then the solution translated back into the language of the original problem.

This viewpoint of semiotics and representation as unifying concepts for cognitive science leads to the conclusion that there are many more disciplines impacting the cognitive sciences than commonly recognized. These include all of the semiotic sciences. Some major examples are: psychology, linguistics, logic, philosophy, ontology, epistomology, sociology, economics, esthetics, theology, historiology, anthropology, communication science, information science, computer science, artificial intelligence, ethology, neuroscience, and hypnosis. Indeed, upon examination, it turns out that each of these traditional disciplines do have something to say about how we—or other cognizing bodies, such as animals and machines—represent knowledge.

This analysis also leads to the conclusion that the problems associated with coding each of the components of the sign will turn out to be important ones for cognitive science. We may therefore anticipate the importance of some previously unrecognized problems in cognitive science. For instance, the semiotic (or linguistic context) of the sign is studied in such disciplines as linguistics, esthetics, and mathematics. However, none of these have traditionally been concerned with the representation of external reality. We may therefore expect cognitive science to find itself interested one day in determining how our knowledge of the external world is represented in and by the tagmatic structures of a Pollock or a Motherwell painting. As another example we may briefly look at a pragmatic component of the sign, such as the social and/or behavioral context of the sign. Sociology and psychology have traditionally interested themselves in this component, but not in its use to represent knowledge. I therefore predict that one day cognitive science will be asking how we represent our knowledge of the external world thru our social conventions.

SUMMARY

This chapter presents a preliminary analysis of representation from the semiotic viewpoint that demonstrates the possibility of using a common language to discuss problems within many of the disciplines presently recognized as impacting the cognitive sciences. One conclusion of this analysis is that there are many more disciplines impacting the cognitive sciences than commonly recognized. These include all of the semiotic sciences. Some major examples are: psychology, linguistics, logic, ontology, epistomology, philosophy, sociology, economics, esthetics, theology, historiology, anthropology, communication science, information science, computer science, artificial intelligence, ethology, neuroscience, and hypnosis.

This analysis of representation treats it as a coding process and uses an eighteen component theory of sign structure, called the Universal Sign Structure Theory, to analyze the coding problems involved for each sign component. Each such problem analyzed turns out to be a problem that is of great concern to one or more of the cognitive sciences and to cognitive science in general. Two examples involve eidontic coding, or coding the shape of the sign, a problem of interest to both information theory and grammar, and deictic coding, or coding the object of the sign, a problem of interest to troth cognitive psychology, developmental psychology, and semantics. Several problems of cognitive science not previously recognized were suggested.

The semiotic dimensions of syntactics, semantics, and pragmatics, suggested by Morris, provide a convenient method of classifying and systematizing these problems. An initial attempt to carry this out suggests that cognitive science may be identified with syntactic and semantic semiotics.

ACKNOWLEDGMENTS

This work was partially funded by the National Science Foundation, Division of Information Science and Technology, by grant IST-7827002. This support is gratefully acknowledged. I wish to thank Al Badre, Vladimir Slamecka, and Pranas Zunde who helped by criticizing all or parts of the paper and for their many constructive suggestions.

REFERENCES

Amarel, S. 1971. Representations and modeling of problems of program formation. In *Machine intelligence,* ed. B. Meltzer & D. Michia. Edinburgh: Edinburgh University Press.
Bruner, J. S., Olver, R. R., & Greenfield, P. M. 1966. *Studies in cognitive growth.* New York: Wiley.
Chomsky, N. A. 1957. *Syntactic structures.* The Hague: Mouton.

Clark, H. H., & Clark, E. V. 1977. *Psychology and language*. Atlanta: Harcourt Brace Jovanovich.

Garner, W. R. 1974. *The processing of information and structure*. Hillsdale, New Jersey: Lawrence Erlbaum Associates.

Hays, D. 1964. Dependency theory. *Language* 40:511–25.

Minsky, M. L. 1975. A framework for representing knowledge. In *The psychology of computer vision*, ed. P. H. Winston. New York: McGraw-Hill.

Morris, C. W. 1938. Foundations of the theory of signs. *International Encyclopedia of Unified Science* 1.

Pearson, C. 1977. Towards an empirical foundation of meaning. Ph.D. dissertation, Georgia Institute of Technology.

Pearson, C., & Slamecka, V. 1977a. *Semiotic foundations of information science*. Final Project Report, National Science Foundation Grant GN-40952. School of Information and Computer Science, Georgia Institute of Technology.

Pearson, C., & Slamecka, V. 1977b. A theory of sign structure. *Semiotic Scene* 1:1–22.

Peirce, C. S. 1931–58. *The collected papers of Charles Sanders Peirce;* vols. 1–6, ed. C. Hartshorne & P. Weiss; vols. 7–8, ed. A. Burks. Cambridge: Harvard University Press.

Piaget, J. 1951. *Play, dreams and imitation in childhood*. New York: Norton.

Quillian, M. R. 1968. Semantic memory. In *Semantic information processing*, ed. M. L. Minsky. Cambridge: MIT Press.

Schank, R. C. 1973. Identification of conceptualization underlying natural language. In *Computer models of thought and language*, ed. R. C. Schank & K. M. Colby. San Francisco: Freeman.

Simmons, R. F. 1973. Semantic networks: their computation and use for understanding English sentences. In *Computer models of thought and language*, ed. R. C. Schank & K. M. Colby. San Francisco: Freeman.

16 Animal Communication as Evidence of Thinking

Donald R. Griffin
The Rockefeller University

The close linkage between human language and thought has been so widely recognized as to seem overwhelmingly self-evident. Yet it is obvious that we do not express every one of our thoughts at the very moment it is experienced; and this rules out any exact one-to-one equivalence between thinking and speaking. Unexpressed thoughts might entail some sort of internal, inaudible process akin to talking to oneself. But no neurophysiological correlates of such talking to oneself have yet been identified. Averaged evoked potentials recorded from human and animal brains do sometimes correlate with the presence or absence of discrimination between patterns of sensory stimulation that differ in importance to the person or animal concerned. But these electrical correlates have so far been detected only for gross differences in levels of activity in relatively large portions of the brain. It would require an enormous extension and refinement of any experiments yet reported to offer any hope of detecting electrical correlates of a specific mental image, for example, of imagining oneself swimming through through an underwater cavern among tropical coral reefs when actually straphanging in a crowded subway.

The dependence of thinking upon language must thus be formulated as an assertion that the capacity for more than trivially elementary thinking requires the capability of using language. Despite a variety of thorough and ingenious investigations such as those reviewed by Liberman and Pisoni (1977) and Green (1977) we have only speculative and sketchy ideas about the neurophysiological processes that underlie the production and interpretation of verbal communication.

Perhaps these ancient and thoroughly debated questions might be illuminated and clarified by a new look from a fresh perspective. The perspective I have in

241

mind is a zoological, ethological one based on recent discoveries about the rich variety of behavior displayed by various groups of animals. Especially important is the communication between individuals which serves to coordinate social behavior. It may not be going too far to suggest that the title of this entire volume might be "Language*s*, Mind*s*, and Brain*s*." There is no doubt that animals possess a wide variety of brains, including a few that are larger than our own, and insofar as minds are linked to the functioning of brains they too may exist in a sufficient variety of forms to provide fruitful opportunities for comparative investigation. Whether language occurs in more than one species is a question to which I will return later. Insofar as nonhuman animals may think at all, a biologically comparative analysis might be fruitful, as has been the case with other human attributes. Perhaps a better understanding of thinking as it may occur in simpler form in other species would throw helpful light on the operations of our own minds.

Such a suggestion tends to arouse visceral reactions related to our gut feel'ngs of human uniqueness and superiority. But as scientists and scholars we should be able to escape the limitations of our autonomic nervous systems and examine such questions with a willingness to learn about important human attributes such as language and thinking from any helpful source of information and understanding. It is widely believed that we are the only species capable of linguistic communication, at least the only one to be found on this planet. And since linguistic capability is believed essential for significant thinking, acceptance of one assumption of human uniqueness seems to entail the other as a necessary consequence.

This sort of faith in a qualitative human intellectual uniqueness has been somewhat shaken in recent years by several discoveries about the communication behavior of animals. The most obvious challenge comes from the work of the Gardners and their successors who have convincingly shown that chimpanzees and gorillas can be taught to use vocabularies of a few hundred gestures that serve to all intents and purposes as words. Only a few years earlier outstanding linguists and philosophers had dogmatically asserted that such an accomplishment by any nonhuman animal was unthinkable. Of course more stringent criteria of linguistic competence can easily be erected, and the defenders of absolute human uniqueness have had little difficulty in setting up new lines of defense based on criteria of syntax or linguistic structure. For example Limber (1977) seems to accept the use of sign language by chimpanzees as roughly equivalent to the speech of two year old children. But Limber argues that "The ability of apes or even 2-year-olds to communicate and use simple names is not sufficient reason to attribute the use of human language to them."

Another approach is, in essence, to accept the Great Apes into the "nearly human" fold and attempt to dig in on a second line of defense between them and the monkeys. These discoveries and their implications have been so widely discussed and analyzed from so many pertinent viewpoints that I can add nothing significant. Instead I should like to broaden the inquiry and consider the degree to which a wide variety of other nonhuman animals also communicate with others of their species in ways that may provide evidence of thinking.

To the degree that human language is considered to be closely linked, if not absolutely identical, with human thinking, I suggest the communication behavior of animals can be viewed with equal justification as evidence of some sort of thinking. To put the matter in slightly different words: When animals communicate, to what degree does this indicate that they understand the information they are communicating? Merely asking such a question tends to open a floodgate of outraged denials. People talk and think about an enormous variety of topics, many remote in time or space from the immediate situation. Human thinking shows great spontaneity and creativity. Animal communication, on the other hand, is said to be stimulus-bound and related only to immediate circumstances. It is very easy, as I have done elsewhere (Griffin, 1976, 1977), to collect eloquent quotations in which unqualified assertions of this sort are vigorously proclaimed. It is so generally and firmly believed that nonhuman animals lack any capacity for conceptual thought that we tend very strongly to interpret whatever evidence becomes available in such a way as to avoid challenging this assumption.

To take a familiar, and I believe a highly significant, example, Karl von Frisch and Martin Lindauer convinced most biologists 25 years ago that a particular species of social insect, the honeybee, is capable of conveying information about distance, direction, and desirability of not only foodstuffs but also other quite different things such as water or cavities into which a swarm of bees can move (reviewed by Frisch, 1967; and Lindauer, 1971). But we resist vigorously any notion that these insects might understand even the simple messages they have been shown to convey from one to the other; because insects are supposed to be genetically programmed automata, reacting to immediate stimuli in a rigid mechanical fashion whereas people are capable of an almost infinite variety of nuances in their linguistic communication and the thoughts thereby communicated.

It is important to bear in mind the severe limitation on our sources of information about animal communication and any thoughts that may underlie it. Ethologists are in a position comparable to scientists from a remote galaxy observing human behavior through powerful telescopes while cruising in a spaceship, and dangling microphones into our midst. Tremendously complex sounds would frequently be recorded, and highly varied motions observed and analyzed. Some sort of interaction between conspecifics would be obvious, if only because certain of the motions and most of the sounds are emitted only in their presence. But how much would such extraterrestrial ethologists be able to deduce from their spaceship if limited solely to the kinds of observations ethologists are now carrying out with animals?

Of course animal communication is not the only source of at least suggestive evidence that animals engage in some sort of thinking. Psychologists have developed a wide variety of ingenious experimental techniques for teaching many kinds of animals to make discriminations between stimuli varying in almost every conceivable dimension. Such relatively complex learned behavior, and many behavior patterns observed under natural conditions, can be interpreted as evidence that the animal understands the relationships to which it is responding. But responsiveness and awareness are not the same thing, as we all know from considering our own behavior and awareness. We do many things of which we are unaware, and consequently even such complex behavior as driving an automobile does not demonstrate awareness of all the discriminations and reactions that are involved. Thus while complex and appropriate behavioral reactions are suggestive that some may involve awareness, additional evidence is required before we can assign a high probability to the inference that the animal is not only capable of performing a certain behavior pattern but is also aware of what it is doing. With other members of our own species we ordinarily accept linguistic communication as evidence of this kind, and I am simply suggesting that this general procedure might profitably be extended to other species.

Another perspective on the situation is to imagine oneself trying to learn a wholly new foreign language solely by watching television programs. In theory, a sufficiently persistent and exhaustive correlation of the sounds and gestures with the subsequent behavior might allow decoding the language being used, but this is scarcely a practicable procedure. If one did not know that these were real people, it would be far easier instead to close one's mind and cling to the assumption that they were automata incapable of any sort of thinking.

When then do animals actually communicate? Linguists and philosophers tend to consider, for the most part, only a narrow range of animal communication compared to the rich variety discovered by ethologists in recent years. Usually domestic animals are used as examples, and the communication signals discussed are limited to those used to obtain food, to be let out the door of a house, and the like. On the basis of this sort of common observation of pets and other domestic animals, those concerned with language and thinking have tended to conclude that animal communication always relates to very pressing and immediate situations and stimuli. But our hypothetical extraterrestrial ethologists studying human behavior would very likely conclude that most human vocalizations also resulted from immediate stimuli. In the absence of the sort of detailed information available to us as thinkers and talkers, it is not easy to determine what else may be influencing a living organism, and it is therefore natural to assume a simple stimulus-response relationship.

Are there cases in which convincing evidence is available that animals do communicate about objects, events, or relationships that are more than trivially remote from the immediate pattern of stimuli impinging on their sense organs? The communicative dances of honeybees are important for just this reason; and they have been so thoroughly studied they provide some of the clearest examples.

The *Schwänzeltänze,* often called in English waggle dances, occur only when a colony of honeybees is severely in need of something. This is usually food, but under special circumstances it may be water, which is used in hot weather to cool the hive by regurgitating small droplets and fanning the wings to accelerate evaporation of the water. Or in a very rare circumstance, ordinarily experienced only once during the lifetime of any individual worker bee, the dances are used to communicate the distance, direction, and desirability of a cavity where a swarm consisting of thousands of individual bees may move and continue its existence. There is always a delay of a few minutes, and sometimes of many hours, between the visiting of a food source or other important object outside the hive and the communication with other bees. Thus the communication conveys information about things that are remote in both time and space from the sensory stimuli reaching the communicating animals at the time the communication takes place.

When the dances are used by scouts from a swarm of honeybees, and perhaps also under some conditions when the dances concern food, individual bees can alternate between acting as senders and receivers of information. In the case of swarming, individual bees ordinarily dance about different cavities for some hours or days but gradually reach a sort of consensus in which almost all dances refer to the most suitable cavity. In the course of reaching such a consensus the same bee may visit one cavity that, if it is of only mediocre quality, will elicit dances of moderate intensity. After many such dances, however, this bee may be stimulated by the more vigorous dances of one of her sisters and then visit the cavity thus announced. On returning she may dance with appropriate directional and distance indications, and appropriate enthusiasm about the second cavity. Thus communication behavior on the part of one insect competes with that by another, and the end result of such competition of what it seems appropriate to call imperatives leads to the consensus that in turn is followed by a synchronous flight by the entire swarm to the new cavity (Lindauer, 1955, 1971). This sort of communication certainly satisfies the basic requirements of the argumentative function of human language that Karl Popper and others have held to be beyond the capability of any animal communication system (Popper & Eccles, 1977, p. 59).

The fact that one or two milligrams of insect central nervous system is capable of producing and interpreting a versatile communication system means that the specific properties of human brains are not uniquely required for communicative dialogues and their use to organize cooperative behavior. If other people were observed to behave in the way Lindauer has described, we would not hesitate to infer at least simple levels of thinking and planning. Why not apply comparable criteria to honeybees?

Many ethologists have minimized the significance of the bee dances on the ground that they are unique among *known* examples of animal communication in the degree to which they exhibit symbolism and displacement. For example, Krebs (1977) calls them "an evolutionary freak." But one example suffices to establish that argumentative dialogues can be conducted by means of central nervous systems that are much smaller than ours and very different in gross anatomy.

It has not been customary to interpret these communicative dances of honeybees as evidence that these insects think about or understand the relationships they communicate, but I suggest as open mind concerning this and other instances of animal communication. If we allow ourselves to entertain the thought that perhaps animals understand what they are doing, we must be careful to avoid simply inverting the customary dogmatic insertions to the contrary with equally dogmatic assertions of reversed sign. Given the difficulties of gathering relevant evidence, we are obliged to proceed in a tentative fashion asking appropriate questions and weighing the balance of evidence at every stage in seeking to judge the likelihood that particular kinds of animal behavior, and especially of communication, may or may not be accompanied by awareness, understanding, or anything appropriately called thinking.

Just what do animals communicate about, aside from apes taught elements of human sign language and honeybees dancing about distance, direction, and desirability of things important to their colony? Two recent and very thorough reviews facilitate an attempt to answer this question (Sebeok, 1977; Smith, 1977). Virtually all groups of animals communicate to some degree with other members of their species, and instances have been found in which every sensory channel is used for social communication even including electric signals used by certain species of fish. But the nature of the signal or the receiving system are of minor interest compared to the actual message conveyed. In the great majority of known cases the messages appear to be relatively simple and to be roughly described by such terms as threat, courtship, appeasement, reassurance, announcement of discomfort or distress, or warning of danger. These messages, thus described, seem coarse and crude compared to the words of human language. They resemble many types of nonverbal human communication. Some caution is indicated, however, because of the limitations of available methods of decoding animal signals. Before von Frisch's insights, the frenzied gyrations of dancing bees appeared chaotic and meaningless. If one observed people talking to one another but had no idea that detailed information was being exchanged, it would be easy to conclude that only such general messages as threat, reassurance, distress, or affection were being transmitted.

One common opinion about animal communication is that it is rigid and uniform, that a given type of signal is either emitted or not in all-or-nothing fashion. Nothing could be farther from the truth, however, and enormous variability is evident once animal communication signals are studied in detail. The most obvious axis of variability can be loosely described as intensity. Signals are emitted with various degrees of vigor, sounds may be loud or faint, visual displays may be brief or of long duration, and specialized display postures may be exaggerated to varying degrees from noncommunicative postures. Duty cycle or the fraction of the time during which a communication signal is emitted is another variable that often correlates with the apparent urgency of the communication. But in addition to these variations in intensity, many if not most animal communication signals vary in their detailed patterns. Bird songs have been studied as thoroughly as any animal signals; and in many, but not all species their acoustic properties show surprising ranges of variability.

For example, the most conspicuous and prominent type of acoustic display of most song birds is the territorial song of an adult male in breeding condition. It serves several functions, including the attraction of females early in the breeding season and the warning to other males of the species that they are likely to be attacked if they spend much time within the territory of a particular male who is singing vigorously. In some species many hundreds of song types have been identified, while in others only a handful can be distinguished. As far as we know the basic message conveyed by all these songs is simply that the singer is a mature territory holding, breeding male of a particular species. It is therefore appropriate to ask what function is served by the multiple song types. Kroodsma (1976) has shown that female canaries are more strongly stimulated and do more nest building and egg laying when exposed to tape recordings of highly varied canary songs than to tape recordings having less variety. Another function that is probably important in some cases is individual recognition. Neighboring males react differently to the songs of other males, reacting more strongly to those of strangers than to those of familiar neighbors. Even a familiar neighbor's song elicits a stronger reaction, however, if it comes from some place other than the neighbor's customary territory.

It is customary to discuss the varying degrees of variability observed in territorial songs without interpreting their variety as evidence that more is being conveyed than a single relatively simple message. On the other hand the same type of caution is indicated as that suggested earlier. A comparable approach to the sounds emitted by people when threatening each other might lump them all into a single category of threat signal even though there actually is an enormous range of detailed messages conveyed by human language even when it is used for such a simple and emotional purpose as threat. One can threaten to do various things to someone, and yet to an observing ethologist no distinctions other than intensity of threat might be discernible.

Great variability has also been described in the communicative sounds of birds and mammals used in situations other than threat or courtship. Primates have particularly rich repertoires, and as pointed out by Marler (1977) monkey and ape calls vary almost continuously in many properties such as frequency, amplitude modulation pattern, harmonic content, and intensity—so much so that it is very difficult to classify them into discreet categories as can usually be done with bird songs (Gautier & Gautier, 1977; Green, 1975; Marler, 1977). Green has shown that at least some vocalizations of Japanese macaques, which serve as signals of affection and reassurance, convey slightly different messages according to their acoustical properties.

Virtually all ethological evidence concerning the information conveyed by animal communication signals is necessarily limited to observing their effects on other animals. The reactions, however, vary considerably according to the conditions and context, especially the social situation. These in turn clearly influence the communication signals that are generated by a particular animal in a series of social feedback loops. Rather than any clear-cut correlation with a simply describable physiological condition, the communication signals of many animals are attuned in complicated ways to the entire network of social relationships.

Examples of such complications and subtleties could be multiplied almost indefinitely, as one can see from reading the several papers in the recent book on animal communication edited by Sebeok (1977). But those concerned with the analysis of human language will remain unimpressed by most of these instances, because they appear to indicate only the exchange of rather generalized messages conveying information about the physiological or emotional state of the animal concerned. Conspicuously absent, except in a very few cases, is anything one can call communication about something other than the communicator itself. The bee dances are one of these exceptions, since they clearly convey information about something the dancer has encountered at a distance in time and space.

In addition to the gestural communication of honeybees discussed earlier, which obviously has the property of displacement to a high degree, one example from the primates is suggestive and deserves both careful consideration and efforts to gather more definitive data. Struhsaker (1967) in a thorough study of the ethology of vervet monkeys under natural conditions described three distinct types of alarm calls emitted when a monkey sees one of three types of approaching predator: an eagle flying overhead, a venomous snake, or a mammalian predator such as a leopard. As discussed by Marler (1977) it is possible, though somewhat difficult, to interpret these alarm calls as merely reflecting different degrees of fear or arousal. As alarm calls they are obviously accompanied by an emotional arousal, but the differences in sound pattern strongly suggest that they serve a naming function. Yet Montagna (1976) reflects a widely held viewpoint when he dismisses evidence of this sort in the following terms: "With one cry, the monkeys take to the ground; with another, they climb trees; but in neither case do they know what predator they are escaping from." There is a danger here of negative dogmatism. Recently Sefarth et al. (1980) have confirmed experimentally that these alarm calls do designate different kinds of dangers, or perhaps serve as injunctions to perform different types of escape behavior.

As discussed elsewhere (Griffin, 1976, 1978) the progress of ethology in the last few decades has opened our eyes to the reality of many complex patterns of sensory discrimination and communicative behavior that had previously seemed ridiculously unlikely. Of course this does not mean that all speculations concerning possible thinking by animals will prove to be correct; but open minded inquiries are called for, and cautious agnosticism is appropriate pending thorough and imaginative investigation of the possibilities that animal thinking and awareness may be real and significant. Such investigations are likely to be difficult, and we can scarcely hope for a rapid and unequivocal resolution. Neither it is likely that tidy all-or-nothing answers will emerge. To the extent that animal thinking and awareness occur at all, they probably vary along many dimensions, being present under some circumstances in certain species or individuals but not in others. But even partial and tentative evidence permitting a better estimation of the likelihood that awareness and thinking do occur in animals would clearly be important. Such evidence could have profound significance for our full understanding of animals and their behavior, and also for our proper appreciation of the universe of which we form an important part.

REFERENCES

Frisch, K. von 1967. *The dance language and orientation of bees*. Cambridge: Harvard University Press.
Gautier, J.-P., & Gautier, A. 1977. Communication in old world monkeys. In *How animals communicate*, ed. T. A. Sebeok. Bloomington: Indiana University Press.
Green, S. 1975. Variation in vocal pattern with social situation in the Japanese monkey (*Macaca fuscata*): a field study. In *Primate-behavior: developments in field and laboratory research,* ed. A. Rosenblum, vol. 6. New York: Academic Press.
Green, S. 1977. Comparative aspects of vocal signals including speech. In *Recognition of complex acoustic signals,* ed. T. H. Bullock. Berlin: Dahlem Konferenzen.
Griffin, D. R. 1976. *The question of animal awareness*. New York: Rockefeller University Press.
Griffin, D. R. 1977. Expanding horizons in animal communication behavior. In *How animals communicate,* ed. T. A. Sebeok. Bloomington: Indiana University Press.
Griffin, 1978. Prospects for a cognitive ethology. *The Behavioral and Brain Sciences* 1: 527–538.
Krebs, J. 1977. Review of D. R. Griffin's *The question of animal awareness*. *Nature* 266:792.
Kroodsma, D. E. 1976. Reproductive development in a female songbird: differential stimulation by the quality of male song. *Science* 192:574–75.
Liberman, A. M., & Pisoni, D. B. 1977. Evidence for a special speech-perceiving subsystem in the human. In *Recognition of complex acoustic signals,* ed. T. H. Bullock. Berlin: Dahlem Konferenzen.
Limber, J. 1977. Language in child and chimp? *American Psychologist* 32:280–95.
Lindauer, M. 1955. Schwarmbienen auf Wohnungssuch. *Zeitschrift für vergleichende Physiologie* 37:263–324.
Lindauer, M. 1971. *Communication among social bees*. Cambridge: Harvard University Press.
Marler, P. 1977. The evolution of communication. In *How animals communicate.* ed. T. A. Sebeok. Bloomington: Indiana University Press.
Montagna, W. 1976. *Nonhuman primates in biomedical research*. Minneapolis: University of Minnesota Press.
Popper, K. R., & Eccles, J. C. 1977. *The self and its brain*. New York: Springer.
Sebeok, T. A., ed. 1977. *How animals communicate*. Bloomington: Indiana University Press.
Seyfarth, R. M., Cheney, D. L., & Marler, P. 1980. Monkey responses to three different alarm calls: Evidence of predator classification and semantic communicaton. *Science* 210: 801–803.

Smith, W. J. 1977. *The behavior of communicating, an ethological approach.* Cambridge: Harvard University Press.

Struhsaker, T. 1967. Auditory communication among vervet monekys (*Cercopithecus aethops*). In *Social communication among primates,* ed. S. A. Altmann. Chicago: University of Chicago Press.

17 Philosophy of Science and Recent Research on Language, Mind, and Brain

Richard S. Rudner
Washington University
St. Louis

Editor's Note

Professor Rudner's tragic illness and untimely death between the occasion of the Symposium in Gainesville in April 1978 and the time this volume went to press have prevented the inclusion here of the paper he had planned to provide. It was to have been a much longer piece, only a modest fragment of which served as the basis for what he actually delivered at the Symposium. Sadly, he was precluded from completing the manuscript, and the rough lecture notes that he did leave behind were insufficient for the retrieval of anything beyond something more or less approximating his symposium presentation. We are, however, fortunate enough to be able to include a précis, written by Professor Rudner's son, David.

In the paper, "Philosophy of Science and Recent Research on Language, Mind, and Brain," read at the Symposium, Professor Rudner focused mainly on problems of translational indeterminacy and their consequences for analyses of alien languages and cultures.

It seems to us that publication of the rough notes would do disservice to Rudner's work. Nevertheless, they are clear enough so that they suggest a partial remedy for this unhappy situation. In any case, it is at least possible to indicate the kind of concerns that Rudner had planned to address. The underlying theme of the paper was to have focused on a related set of problems concerning the character of uses of symbol systems. These uses include not only the linguistic behavior discussed in the paper fragment presented at the conference, but extend to nonlinguistic symbolic behavior as well; they encompass modes of symbolic representation in the arts and varieties of theory construction in the sciences. Two main aspects of these problems had been a continuing focus of Rudner's research and were, in fact, occupying his attention at the time of his death: first, the analysis and systematization of concepts central to clarifying just what is the character of this nexus of problems and, second, the problem of whether and how the phenomenon of symbolic activity thus construed can be a subject of rigorous or objective or scientific investigation.

Rudner construed 'symbolic behavior' as applying to uses of *symbol systems* in the very general sense in which Nelson Goodman employs that term (e.g., in *Languages of Art*). Also influential were W. V. O. Quine's *Word and Object,* David Lewis' *Convention,* Peter Winch's *The Idea of a Social Science,* and Israel Scheffler's *Science and Subjectivity.* Such books, as well as many more recent journal articles that have been conditioned by the seminal works of these and other authors, helped to set constraints on the specific ways in which Rudner approached the problems he attacked. In his view, an adequate scientific account of symbolic behavior, linguistic or otherwise, was to be construed as dealing with the problem of how adequate "translation of" or adequate "understanding of" symbol systems may be accomplished by exogamous inquiries—by "alien" inquirers—by inquirers who may not be members of the linguistic and cultural community (the "meaning" community) being studied.

In the paper fragment presented at the conference, Rudner addressed this problem in the light of Quine's treatment of theories of inference and meaning, and Winch's negative treatment of prospects for *any* scientific study of linguistic behavior. The fragment was taken largely from Rudner's earlier paper "An Essay at Objectivity" (*Phil. Exchange,* Vol. 1, No. 4, Summer 1973). In its final version, however, the arguments and lessons from that paper were to have been embedded in a discussion of much broader scope concerning "commensurability" relations among both discursive and non-discursive symbol systems. Following the section directed at Quinean and Winchean treatments of linguistic indeterminacy of translation, Rudner had planned to provide a detailed examination of the character of anthropological field manuals of translation and anthropological field notes and field data of various sorts. His primary focus would have been some of the "problems of incommensurability" that attend representing the world or some aspect of it by means of radically different symbol systems. Thus, for example, claims for the way the world is can be made by *telling* how it is—as in an anecdote, a history, or an ethnography—or, by *showing* how it is—as when the world is pictured in photographs or ethnographic films. Rudner had hoped to explore some comparisons between the way an anthropologist's field notes are related to his completed published account and the way in which the raw footage of the anthropological filmmaker—an ethnocinematographer—is related to his finished and edited ethno-cinemagraph. Finally, Rudner had planned to compare both of these examples of ways of representing an alien culture with the way a linguistic anthropologist's field manual of translation is related to something that might be called his *theory* of the relevant translation. A major question to have been raised in this part (the intended second half) of the paper is how we may compare in terms of compatability or incompatability two different accounts of something which are not merely different accounts in the same language or even different accounts in different languages in the same mode of symbolism but two different accounts in two quite different modes of symbolism—say language and pictures—one of which purports to tell and one of which purports to show what is the case.

Unfortunately, it is this part of Rudner's paper that is most sketchily outlined in the remaining notes. Clearly the section would have built upon the important results published in his two papers "On Seeing What We Shall See" (in *Logic and Art*, R. Rudner & I. Scheffler (eds.) New York: Bobbs-Merrill, 1972) and "Show or Tell: Incoherence Among Symbol Systems" (*Erkenntnis*, Vol. 12, No. 1, Jan. 1978). But it is impossible to recover an adequate account of Rudner's further work on symbolic "commensurability" or to judge the precise application of his results to anthropological inquiry. Professor Rudner's position on indeterminacy of linguistic translation is quite clear, however, and his paper, "An Essay at Objectivity" develops in richer detail the arguments presented by him on the occasion of the conference on *Language, Mind and Brain*.

David Rudner

Author Index

Numbers in *italics* denote pages with complete bibliographic information.

A

Abelson, R., *63*
Abelson, R. P., 122, *127*, 134, 137, *142, 143*
Ackerman, N. 165, *176*
Adams, N., 126, *128*
Ahumada, A., 219, *223*
Akmajian, A., 83, *86*
Albrecht, D. G., 217, *224*
Allen, J., *63*
Amarel, S., 233, *239*
Anderson, R. M., 220, *224*
Anderson, S. R., 85, *86*
Antinucci, F., 77, *87*
Apostel, L., 1, *10*
Arbib, M. A., 217, *224*
Austin, J. L., 43, *43*
Avakian-Whitaker, H., 169, *176*

B

Bar-Hillel, Y., 2, *10*
Bartlett, R., 119, *127*
Becher, E., 158, *176*
Becker, J., 149, *155*
Bekesy, G. von, 216, 217, *222*

Bellugi, U. 214, *222*
Bennett, J., 133, *142*
Benson, D. F., 206, *209*
Berger, G., 1, *10*
Berndt, R. S., 167, *176*
Bernstein, L., 214, 221, *222*
Bever, T. G., 158, *176*, 183, 186, *187*, 189, *209*
Black, J. B., 126, *127*
Boden, M. A., 135, *142*
Bogen, J. E., 202, *210*
Bolinger, D., 149, *155*
Borges, J. L., 193, *210*
Bornstein, M. H., 195, *210*
Bower, G. H., 126, *127*
Bradshaw, J. L., 206, *210*
Briggs, A., 1, *10*
Brillouin, L., 219, *222*
Broadbent, D. E., 190, *210*
Brown, G., 60, 61, *62, 63*
Bruce, B., 62, *63*
Brumfield, S., 159, 175, *177*
Bruner, J. S., 228, 234, 236, 238, *239*
Brunner, J. S., 207, *210*
Buckingham, H. W., Jr., 165, 169, *176*
Burt, M. K., 160, *176*

255

Subject Index